My Life's Buffet!

BY JERRY PAYNE

The Incredible Choices From Life's Glorious Buffet!

Contents

Prologue	1
A Foreword	3
Acknowledgments	4
My Greatest Buffet Surprise	5
Dreams of a Little Fella!	9
My Friends - A Stage Full of One-Act Plays	19
I Loved Being at the High School	27
Home Sweet Home, and the Cooking Was Good, Too	33
New Home - More than Just a House	41
Traveling With the Windows Down	55
The Neighborhood	61
High School - Too Busy Having Fun	67
High School has a Dark Side	77
Senior Year 1960 - Drum Spectacular!	83
The ClassCutters Rock n' Roll History	93
College – We've Got to Study!	103
A New Way of Life in Mansfield	111

Back in Bossier City - Life Speeds Up	117
Scopena Plantation and the Big Table	123
Jim Leslie Murdered	131
Buddy Runs for Congress	137
Well, Hello! Birmingham, Alabama	145
Amarillo was Like Applying the Brakes on Life	153
Forty Years Together - Todd, The Joy of our Life	165
"Good Luck, I Hope That is Your Grandmother"	175
Politics - It's Time for a Wake Up Call	181
Jack Binion and Horseshoe Casino "I Gotcha"	189
The Death Penalty and The Louisiana Supreme Court	205
My Life Begins to Change	227
My Record Collection - Just Me and Scatman!	235
The Best Buffet, Yet	243
The Wedding Planning	251
The Republican and the Democrat	253

My Toast to Madonna	257
Our Story Presented in the Wedding Program	259
The Wedding - Roses, Champagne and a Wedding License	261
The Honeymoon - "Look Over There"	273
My Favorites - Recalling the Best	289
50th High School Reunion – It Felt So Good	297
Cancer - "Jerry, There is Nothing I Can Do for You" - BE STILL!	303
Amazing Creations and Precious People - God is Smiling With Us	313
Who Knew? The Payne Ancestry and Genealogy from 1350 A.D.	319

Prologue

As World War II comes to an end, a boy's life unfolds, growing up in a small Louisiana town. He lives in an almost mythical world as the United States turns a War nation into the most successful civilization in history.

America flourishes and a boy's dreams grow into unimaginable challenges and opportunities. A group of small town neighborhood kids plays a leading role in America's history. As a high school boy, certainly on top of the world, the darkness his life held could have ended in a self-inflicted tragedy.

Jerry Payne takes on unusual tasks and turns them into smiles for a lifetime. He would conquer music, politics, and business. A drummer by choice, he played with some of the greatest rock n' roll musicians. As a political consultant, he won 90% of over 200 campaigns. One of his best friends became Governor. His business career included remarkable successes in the brand new data processing field, and then advertising. He was selected as one of the Three Outstanding Young Men of Louisiana.

The intrigue of murder, casinos, death threats, and a Louisiana Supreme Court death penalty appeal that rewrote the law twists and turns through his phenomenal adult life.

A series of family passings morbidly sends him into a depressive spiral. At this point, skin cancer threatens his life. Just when he thought the end of his productive life was near he finds out that it is not. His life's buffet had a new choice, a love beyond belief.

As often happens, they were good friends during high school. They lost track and allowed over 42 years to pass without seeing each other.

God handed them a precious gift of love, and they married in a storybook wedding. Then lung cancer struck. Was this going to be an untimely ending?

God leads us to the very places that touch our hearts and soul. He leads us to the precious people that are more valuable than gold. No one should have to live alone as we grow old, and not have someone there to share the grandeur of life.

A Foreword

Everyone has a story to tell! After much contemplation of what best describes my own personal life I concluded it is not so much what I did, but the actions of the myriad of people in my life that actually made my story.

Never gave much thought to how those people happened to come into my life. My memories of life are certainly enhanced because somehow these folks did come into my life at the times they did. I have always marveled at people's antics and motives. We all have stories and chapters in our lives that others find interesting or curious.

I began to notice people's reaction to my stories around the age of thirty. I was never shy about talking about my friends or escapades.

Several friends encouraged me to write a book, especially about my political involvement. I thought, if I am going to the trouble to write a book, maybe I should tell the whole story. The people in my life, the ones that offered me the choices of nearly every activity and memory, should be included.

At the age of 65, I began to think my life had about run its course. My wife of 40 years had passed away, my son was successful, and on his own. I thought my life had enough experiences to write my story, but I still lacked a real theme. Then my future wife came back into my life. The way we became reacquainted and how we were united after 42 years of losing track of each other since our days at Bossier High School, left no doubt. Madonna finally gave me the excitement, and burning desire to write this book.

It was by God's bountiful grace that He provided to my life a real angel - Madonna! She would be the greatest surprise of all in *My Life's Buffet*!

Acknowledgments

I hope you all enjoy this effort to honor those that have made contributions to my story, and for the special people that have laughed and toiled with me, and reached out and touched my life.

I am dedicating this to my son, Todd, for giving my journey through life a reason to yearn and laugh, and to expect our next treasure of memories. To my brother, Ron, for leading and guiding me in life's varied paths, and for always being there when I needed you. To Dennis, Monica and Mark for accepting me with unconditional love, and granting me my wonderful grandchildren and great-grandchildren.

Especially to Madonna. Our love was so unexpected, so timely, and so amazing. Never has my life experienced such a thrill of sweetness, excitement and fun. I can never say "thank you" enough for the hard work and personal care you have contributed to this effort, and particularly our marriage.

You will never know the love I felt as we treaded through my illness. Your inspiration and guidance has led me closer to God.

MY GREATEST BUFFET SURPRISE!

Buffets are a large, lavishly prepared, spread of food garnished with decorative, artistically designed, and succulently tasting art pieces, and by themselves, are temptations of the eye. The aromas presented by the delectable dishes are so very appealing. Sometimes you are so tempted you suddenly believe you can carry more than a waitress at the local diner. Only later, realizing it was not as appealing, or that the choices were false compared at least to your eye and your ability to consume all that you wished. Sometimes, I guess, you just didn't think the buffet was all you ever dreamed it was, but then sometimes it is.

I never really considered life as a buffet of very critical choices. Oh, the choices from the spread of life! The choices we make from the very appealing temptations, God's art, those things we choose that we cannot handle, make all the difference in our daily lives. At this buffet, we do not always approach cautiously, and, if not careful, we many times make the wrong choice.

We do not set or prepare the buffet of life; that is God's hands at work. It just so happens, I was unsuspectingly standing in a real buffet line one Saturday morning when the greatest buffet surprise of my life occurred. The food became of little concern, but my life changed forever.

Several old adages were staring me right in the face, i.e.: "Sometimes, the best comes when you are not looking for it, or when you least expect it; Doors are sometimes obstacles, but sometimes they open to the newness of life; God always provides us with what we need, not necessarily what we expect or what we want."

All of those thoughts have crossed my mind as I reflect back on that amazing moment. That buffet offered me those things and more.

There are times when we see things that are not really there, and feel the need to do something different.

Other times, we don't know if we are making the right decision, but then the right occasion is provided, and we trust God, and we believe with all our heart that we are making the right choice. I was sure of this choice.

This was a life-changing opportunity. It came late in my years, but it was with such enormity and vibrancy that my life's path was unquestionably prepared for me. All of a sudden, I went from trudging down my life's path to skipping merrily along with a special excitement.

Happiness was something that I had managed to find a way to make happen with much regularity. However, this time happiness was not made up, or invented. No, this time my life was full of complete satisfaction and joy. God had given me an understanding of amazing love. Now I saw every little creature, mountain top and gently rolling stream, with a sense of serenity. Now, but for the love I shared breath by breath, touch by touch, and glance by glance, my life would have never known the heights of God's intended love. God had put an angel in my life to show me what I could do in this world, this life, and this door-opening opportunity. My angel was named Madonna, a heavenly name, and she showered me with an angelic love to share. My Madonna touched my life in ways that I had never known or understood. She is gentle, with a tender heart, a kind, soft-spoken disposition, her smile is genuine, and her sweetness is constant, just the way real love should be shared. Her vibrancy brought a new spirit to me; she is thoughtful, irresistible, always encouraging, very creative and talented; she is perpetual excitement.

My life is now so full of—well, life!

DREAMS OF A LITTLE FELLA!

Families are supposed to have, by definition, an inseparable closeness with undeniable love, a you-can-count-on-me assurance. My mother, Ora Laverne Parnell Payne Thie, had lost her husband only three months after my birth. My father was killed in World War II while on a search mission in the Gulf of Mexico. It seems a surprise to many that German U-boats had made their way into American waters.

Although I have never read the official record of this war story, and although it certainly changed our lives forever, it never changed our family's deep love and allegiance for each other. If anything, it made our bond stronger.

So there I was, having just been born three months earlier in Bangor, Maine, at the Air Corp Base Hospital, now without a father. During the war, I wouldn't be the only fatherless child. Before he died in action, and after I was born, he was transferred to New Orleans.

My mother, with me and my brother, Ronnie, packed up and headed to New Orleans, Louisiana. My diminutive mother, my 5-year old brother, along with me, so I am told, drove in a 1940 Packard from Maine to New Orleans.

Just a reminder of the added hardships, everything was being rationed - gasoline, milk, tires, food, and if that wasn't enough, money was scarce.

Mother told of stopping along the way at some total stranger's house, on whatever highway we were traveling, to warm my baby bottle. It was not unusual to be given a warm meal just as a courtesy. America was in this war together, and times were different.

Ronnie recalls the day our father, Guy Cullen Payne, was reported as missing. Only five and a half years old, he remembers going out to the base to pick up our father upon his scheduled arrival time. He recalls arriving at the base and being told the plane and crew were late, and that they would notify us upon his arrival.

Ronnie remembers that the house we lived in was a typical New Orleans house with a few steps leading up to the front porch and door. Sometime later that night they came and officially notified mother that our father and the whole crew had died. After that, with my mother's sheer determination, she began to put our life back together.

Another angelic person appeared in my life, my grandmother "Mamaw", Virda Simmons Parnell. She didn't miraculously come into my life like the angel Madonna did later in life, but nonetheless there was no mistake she was my angel. Ronnie always said that I was her favorite. All angels must be very similar in gentleness, tenderness, kindness and sweetness, and with such a constant, always there, kind of love.

My earliest recollections are few, but what I do remember is cherished. Being a boy, my interests were likely the same or nearly the same as my families, especially my brother, Ronnie. Wherever he went I wanted to go, whatever he did I wanted to do. That continued all the way through my schooling. He was a great role model for a younger brother.

My mother remarried when I was 4 years old to Paul Cedric Thie, an airman, and a good man. He was very meticulous, with a dry, but special sense of humor. A native of Fort Dodge, Iowa, he loved to hunt squirrels and would have loved for Ronnie and me to follow suit.

I personally saw no good reason to get up at 4 am and go into the woods, sit perfectly still in icy conditions, and wait until he decided the squirrels weren't out that morning. We would walk back to the car, eat a baloney sandwich, and call it a successful hunt. My personal interest were baseball, football, basketball, going to the movies, or whatever Ronnie did was right for me.

We lived in Bossier City, La., at the Barksdale Homes, a project for military and military dependents. Our first friends were from among some of the most interesting and good families, and they were the Ryans, Prines, Fullertons, Heflins, Bryants, Waggoners, Wilsons, Nattins, Hollensheads, and one of my first friends, Packey Foster. I never knew what happened in his life until I reconnected with Packey through the marvels of the computer.

Our favorite treats were the same then as they are today, watermelon, ice cream cones, a roast on Sunday with mashed potatoes and gravy, pan-fried chicken, and the best apple pie I ever tasted (thank you, mamaw).

My first recollections of going to church are vivid to me. Mother and mamaw made sure we were at church and that we participated. I made lasting friendships at a small neighborhood church, Curtis Park Methodist Church, located by the nearby Curtis Park Drugstore, Hamner's Cleaners, Kickapoo restaurant, Kickapoo Motel, Jitney Jungle grocery store, and Graham's Hardware Store.

Dr. Payne (no kin) owned the drugstore, and also had a son named Ronnie, who was the same age as my Ronnie. At high school, this confused everyone, so Dr. Payne's boy changed his name to Billy. This was all at the intersection of Benton Road and East Texas St., known famously as the Kickapoo, a local landmark.

My memories of Christmas in the Barksdale Homes are among the most special. We were kept warm by the old roaring floor furnace. Every Christmas it always seemed to be cold, and the Christmas trees were scarce of limbs, the lights big and bright, and the ornaments were the latest fashion that very little money could buy. Of course, we had lots of those aluminum icicles.

One Christmas, Ronnie got up before the rest of us, discovered Santa Claus had already been to the house, and left his present. Under the tree was a blue and yellow replica of a Michigan football helmet. He put the helmet on, waited a while, and when nobody got up he went back to bed -- with the helmet still on his head. I remember Ronnie's used bicycle, my football and uniform, real fruitcakes, fudge, and divinity.

At Curtis Park Methodist Church, Rev. H.C. Norsworthy had mesh bags for the kids of nuts, apples, and oranges. Maybe that wasn't a new computer game or anything expensive, but I was proud of every almond, walnut, pecan, apple and orange. Life was simple, and we were grateful for everything we had.

During those early years there was a Christmas evening I remember most of all. Supper was finished, and Christmas music was playing on the radio. Hot chocolate was steaming, and mother was curled up on the couch. Mamaw had a blanket covering her usually cold frail body, Paul was reading, most likely a "Sports and Field" magazine, and Ronnie and I, and our dog, were stretched out on the floor in front of the radio. I will never forget, mother gazed across the room at each of us and said so lovingly, "I love Christmas, isn't this cozy?" The windows had frosted over, it was cold outside, but this family felt great warmth that Christmas, even on such a frigid night.

I guess it was just the thought of the whole family snuggling together to fight off the winter chill, but even more meaningful, we were simply sharing togetherness in that small living room. Except for the lone reading lamp, the lights were low from the glow of Christmas tree lights, and that was enough to warm our hearts. That moment provided me with a lesson for the rest of my life - Christmas is for family.

We impatiently awaited Christmas day, and the excitement of the surprises that Christmas morning would hold. Ronnie and I usually hid at least one of the alarm clock, and set it for 4:30 am. I guarantee we never wanted to get up that early any other time.

Christmas wasn't the only special time of the year. My young years are tattered with things unforgettable. Many things stayed with me the rest of my life, like learning to play baseball, how to throw and kick a football, loving my first dog, Spunk, and, probably more importantly, having Spunk love me. We played games like hide-and-seek, but Spunk made me the easiest of all to find. I could hide, but everyone knew where I was because Spunk would always hide with me. His wagging tail could be seen or heard no matter where I hid.

Spunk learned the sound of Mr. Posey's old school bus, and would greet me every day as I climbed off the bus. Together we would run to our front door with him licking me all the way.

There was the time all the neighborhood kids went crawfishing in the ditch along Shed Road. That road was more famous for being a covered road for the cotton pickers to get the cotton to the river than it was for crawfish. But, in my life, that cotton stuff didn't measure up to my fishing story. No, I didn't catch the largest crawfish ever caught. However, my story does go in the annals of my life when mom gave me two pieces of bacon for bait so I could go fishing with all the big kids in the neighborhood - like my brother.

After patiently fishing in the roadside ditch for about thirty minutes, which seemed like hours, I returned home with a somewhat dejected look on my face. Mom asked, "Did you catch any?" I told her no.

She asked, "Did the crawfish take your bait?" I told her that after I had fished awhile, and didn't catch any crawfish, I ate the bait.

Cub Scouts became a big part of my young life, Pack 20, Den 2, and Indian dances, crafts, and refreshments. This was my first industrious encounter with friends. We learned to work as a team with a purpose for starting and completing projects, always with encouragement from our Den leaders.

My first baseball team played at Fort Smith Park, which became Bossier Recreation Center. Now, appropriately, as we have aged, it is currently the Bossier Council of Aging. I guess that is the way life goes. Mr. Adams coached my first team, and his son, Harold, along with Henry Brown, Frank Campisi, Kenny Young, and Cecil Upshaw were my 5-year-old teammates.

Mother worked at the Barksdale Base Exchange, and Ronnie was working at the Jitney Jungle Grocery Store. Once, when mamaw was in the hospital, mother took a chance and left me home during the daytime by myself. She came up with all kinds of things for me to do with my time. Included was the daunting task of shelling a grocery sack full of purple hull peas. Now this was a new experience for me.

One afternoon I tackled this homely job of shelling peas. After a while, about half way through the bag, I thought the pot of peas was full enough to make her think I had completed the task. I carefully folded the remaining half of the grocery bag of unshelled peas, and hid them way back in the darkest corner in one of the closets. It was just not far enough back to conceal the stench of the rotten peas about two weeks later.

What I would give for today's kids to live as I lived and I didn't even realize what an education I was getting. Later in life, David Montgomery, one of my first grade classmates, put it best. He said, "Both of us only had two pair of pants and two or three shirts. Our moms would wash one pair of pants while we wore the other pair. We didn't have a pot to pee in, but we didn't know we didn't have anything."

I only remember a few things about elementary school, but a few happenings stand out. I remember vividly my first grade teacher, Mrs. Whittington, on my first day after school, taking me out and making sure I got on the right bus. I think I remembered it more because she was walking with me, and she was so beautiful.

In the second grade, I got crushed when my teacher, Mrs. Fullilove, informed me that I was the only kid in class that didn't have a part in the Thanksgiving play to be performed in front of the whole school. She gave every kid in class a part in the play, but when she got to me, she said, "Oh, we don't have any more parts." In what seemed like an eternity, as she tried to make amends to a devastated, almost sobbing, little boy saying, "Why don't you tell some jokes?"

So here, I am in the second grade - a stand-up comedian. It never crossed my mind at that moment that I would be standing in front of what would look like thousands in that auditorium full of people. So I was off to tell my parents about my new profession.

My dad, in his stoic humor, tutored me in the art of joke telling. A poem, "A Pelican, a Pelican; I don't know how in the hell-he-can." My mother never saw the humor in that. I do remember my debut and my first line, "Fuzzy Wuzzy was a Bear; Fuzzy Wuzzy had no hair; Fuzzy Wuzzy wasn't so fuzzy wuz He?" I had them in the palm of my hands. My stage presence was cast, and I have loved the stage and an audience ever since.

My days of loving life had begun. There was church and my friends there: Bob and Holly Hollenshead, Tim Crawford, Dan Halbert, Jeanette Bryant, Gary Ricketts, Judy Wyatt; at school, Frank Campisi, David Montgomery, Hayes McGraw, Sid Shelton, Jimmy Starks, Vernon Lawrence, Ruby Dell Brooks, Glynna Manis, Anne Lowrey, Tommy Rachel, Sandra Whittington, Sandra Grant, Tommy Mitchell, Dana Long, Rebecca Adair, and so many more. Why wouldn't you love living with friends like that to share a lifetime with?

With friends, and especially family, always there for us, we never knew what we were missing. I had the love and security to be able to live in a dream world, my dream world. I was going to be a Major League Baseball player like Pee Wee Reese, and the other things going on in the world didn't seem to matter. I was learning, laughing, living, and loving my dog, Spunk. I believed I could do anything and be anything. My brother was my leader. My life was all wrapped up in my mother, my stepfather, mamaw, Ronnie and Spunk. I had all the love and security a child needed.

18

MY FRIENDS - A STAGE FULL OF ONE-ACT PLAYS

Later in life there is a peacefulness about sitting with, talking to, or hugging the lasting friends from those days gone by, each really special in my heart. I have often said that the fastest way to travel is in our memories. In the blink of an eye we can go anywhere in the world. More importantly, we can recall our friends and be in their presence instantaneously. The events that reassured us of our faith in and respect for each other are there for the pleasures of life, forever.

School and church shaped me, not just the education, but also the social activities. From the beginning, my most likely memories are not the events, but the people in my life that I remember most.

I really liked being with my friends, and it became important to me to make and keep friends. They were important to me at school, recess, church, and in the sports, I played. Uncommonly, the bonds of friendship made from my school days, even from the first grade, have lasted to this day. How wonderful it is to have so many truly lifelong friends still in my life.

As I begin this writing, it seems strange that one of my first thoughts is of one of the first friends I lost. He was my buddy at Bossier Elementary, J.C. Mondello. He was Frank Campisi's cousin, my lifelong friend. We were inseparable. He was a small little guy with an infectious smile, and the catcher for our baseball team. He was killed in a horse riding accident. I have never forgotten the moment when Frank told me that J.C. had died. I was sitting out by the yet-to-open, newly built school gym. That was my first experience with death, and my heart ached.

There were not many idle moments that I remember while growing up, leaving little time for boredom. I was involved in all sports at school and in the summer, led by some of the greatest coaches of fundamentals ever, like C.W. Almond and Buddy Maxwell, and later John McConathy.

They were even stronger on sportsmanship, honesty, and personal relations skills, things that every young man should have available to them as they grow up. Losing wasn't very familiar to these giants of youth sports. C.W. Almond's baseball teams probably won more games than any coach did ever. We went three years without losing a summer game in one stretch. He had many teams through the years and they rarely lost.

Coach Buddy Maxwell coached all sports at Bossier Elementary, and I only remember losing one basketball game from the 5th grade through the 7th grade. We opened every basketball practice with passing drills. He literally taught us how to grip the ball, how to step and push with our hands and arms, and how to catch the ball with our fingers. After we got that right, we would run passing/lay up drills, then run-the-weave drill, and we took great pride in making good passes. Nothing was more important than having him encourage us with his unforgettable words, "All right now, that's the way to do it!" We would swell with pride.

We were a team in every sense of the word. Our group started playing together in the 5th grade, and went on to win the only State Basketball Championship in Bossier High School history for the next fifty-one years. We never had an indoor gym to practice in until we got to high school. If you think we were good on a hardwood floor, you should have seen us dribbling through mud puddles out in back of the elementary school.

My friends from my elementary school days were growing with me, and powerful relationships began to develop. I have never given much credence when people say real friends are few. Baloney, that is just not true in my life. I don't know what the cause, or how we were led, but so many of those friends are my real friends, even today. It seems as though we would rather be with each other more today than yesterday.

The treasures of my life are not plaques, honors, or

accolades. Those tarnish and are soon forgotten. There is no warmth in those treasures. My treasures breathe, smile, encourage, help, or stand with me. They always seem to be there when I need them the most, willing to place a hand on my shoulder. Sometimes, it's merely a pat on the back, but always with a look in their eyes that they are there to assure me, and to comfort me.

Not naming those names would be to leave a huge hole in my life's story, and so I shall. It is not as hard to start naming names as I thought it would be. The order may be a little skewed, but the memories are not fictional, and they are the lights in my life, bright and real, and for sure, loved. Each one of my friends has been burned into my mind with a great sense of gratitude. I have a lifetime of lasting appreciation for the time my friends have devoted to my days on this earth.

The roles my friends have played with me have given me a stage full of one-act plays. A litany of what could not be believed would make several novels. These stories, events and friendships are, however, true and real. Some of them are hard to believe, and I assure you, not too many are exaggerated.

Many have gone on before me far too soon, so as for those stories about them, you will have to take my word. For those still here, I count on my ability to tell a story far more convincingly than their ability to tell a story. Besides, they have their own stories from which to draw.

It is my suggestion that everyone should stop and recount with detailed thought and reflection the buffet of life that they have experienced.

Looking back at my little world, I can surmise, without qualm, that our hometown was a village of ordinarily common folks. The streets were filled with frivolity and unencumbered happiness - at least for my neighborhood of young children. While we didn't know, what the real world was like because we were living under a shield of protection, that protection came with a price.

It seems my parents and my friends' parents never let us know from the determination on their faces, or their willingness to produce a nickel or dime when we asked, that this life was not real. We never knew what they were going through to produce a normal childhood for us. I now know there were no rich kids around to make us think we were lacking of anything. We all dressed alike, our jeans had no creases - either pair. It was normal for a button or two to be missing, or to have a slight tear somewhere on our shirt.

School! Suddenly our world had expanded to include new friends, challenges, and a social realm we had never encountered until our elementary school days. We greeted each other every day at school with a full expectancy that we were there to learn and to learn about each other.

Little boys with freckles and little girls with pigtails, we were an experiment in American hometown life. Some were from nice homes, some probably weren't. I never saw the houses where some of them lived. Memories of my friends' homes weren't the house itself, but the reception given by their parents. The relief when Frank Campisi or David Montgomery's mother or dad would give me a sincere greeting as I entered their house.

I learned later in life that some childhood homes weren't always a pleasant place. I am sure that is why a few of my friends seemed withdrawn and not so playful. Some families were farmers and some were military families. They came from all sides of town. It was not important where they lived or what their home life was about. All that seemed to matter was our interaction with each other while we were in school. That was our job and we were totally consumed by our new activities.

I knew one thing - I liked having new people around me. It didn't take long to make new friends. Just like later in life, the people you gravitate towards are the ones that gravitate towards you.

My first school buddies were Frank Campisi (the one with freckles) and David Montgomery (the one that couldn't keep from twirling his hair), Tommy Mitchell (a friend from the first day I met him), Donald Lewis (his mother always had a biscuit for me), Bob and Holly Hollenshead, Gary Ricketts, Dan Halbert and Tim Crawford (my friends from my neighborhood and church); Hayes McGraw, Jimmy Starks, Tommy Rachel, Max Nix, Barry Box, Sid Shelton, Gary Strong and Vernon Lawrence (my school hanging-out buddies).

My first girl friends were Sandra Whittington (always cute as a bug, cheerful and the best smile), Anne Lowrey (the long blond hair), Sandra Grant (a special friend with a very special attraction), Rebecca Adair (her smile embraced you as surely as her arms could), Glynna Manis (the long haired brunette with a beautiful dimpled smile), Ruby Dell Brooks (quiet and gentle), Dana Long (thought she could outrun me, and a real leading lady in my life), and Jeanette Bryant (my first love - we were serious from the 1st grade through the 7th grade).

Jeanette and I grew very fond of each other; we spent countless hours holding hands at the Davis Theater. As I recall, she was the most beautiful girl I knew, and the sweetest. It just so happened that her house was between the Bossier Elementary School and my house, so I got to walk her home many afternoons. Her mom got used to me being around. She treated me as if I belonged at her house, and we were close from the start.

There were other boys that liked Jeanette. Ole Frank Campisi, with his cute little freckles and Italian ways, thought he was cool enough to horn in on my girl. He never was able to make much headway. He just wasn't as good-looking, or as debonair as I was. (I told you this is my story, and he can write his own book).

Let's see, I barely recall that in the 3rd grade, I think, Frank approached me and tried to make me an offer I couldn't refuse. We were at recess, I think. Yeah, that's right. He sided up to me and said, "Because, I'm not as good looking as you, and don't have the moves you do, I will give you a dime if you will sell me your girlfriend."

Now that was a big money offer. I could buy a coke and still have a nickel left. I reflected for a few moments, and I asked him, "Do you think you can handle that babe?" I took the deal. I never knew the effect I must have had on women, even in the 3rd grade. I guess Frank tried to convince her that I had, in fact, sold her to him. She was violently angry and repulsed that Frank thought he could buy her affection.

I guess she was a little angry with me, too. At lunch, out by the coke machines, after I had already spent a nickel of that dime and was holding my coke, she accosted me, but I danced and swayed, and smiled and winked. I was at last back in Jeanette's heart, she was still my girl, and I never gave Frank his money back. That scoundrel!

Sarah Page McCranie became my next girlfriend sometime in the 7th grade. She was so polite and thoughtful, and very cute. A popular girl, we became a twosome that lasted for a few years. The really nice thing about this relationship was that she wasn't taller than I was. I began seeing her at the Davis Theater on Saturday afternoons. We continued this relationship until the 9th grade, I think. All during high school, we had a great friendship. I never thought Sarah Page really knew how much I cared for her at that time. I am grateful to have had her as one of my lifelong friends to this day.

Leaving out the people who meant so much to me just would not be possible. These people have been in my heart since the 1st grade: Sharon Cathey, Martha Sue

Hunter, Elizabeth Connella, Donette McAllister, Janis Ray Tibbits, Susan White, Lou Ann Wilson, and Linda West. All of these would have been in my harem if I could have had one. Betty Jean Carter always stood out in my mind. She was the quiet one, and what a great friend.

My boyhood "Little Rascal" like friends, teammates and confidants were: George "Little George" Brandon, Charles "Brother" Brown, Jerry Butler, Joe Jimes, Dennis Kile, Milton Nix, Ray Nix, Cecil Upshaw, Ted Posey, George Rogers, Lonnie Willis, Lawrence Wood, and Kenneth Young. These people were my world. I was young, and they were the very people in my life that were molding my legacy.

I know many more classmates made an undeniable impression on my life, and I apologize for not naming them.

I LOVED BEING AT THE HIGH SCHOOL

It was a big day in my life when I finally went to the high school. My hero brother had led the way for me at Bossier High School. Teachers like Ms. Charlotte Jaynes, Ms. Kate Gamble, and Frank Lampkin, greeted and encouraged Ronnie Payne's little brother. Outside of my family, I never had three people that influenced my life any more than those teachers did.

Being in high school with the people I loved the most, and the teachers that could get me to try anything, was my first unrealized encounter with life's buffet. Every opportunity was offered to me to make something out of myself, and there were so many choices.

While I was in high school, I put my all into being involved in as much as I could. New friends came into my life, friends that would lead me into the future.

There was much more than school. I worked at several jobs when I got the chance, from selling donuts door-to-door, being a short order cook and carhop at Norman Reese's Lee's Drive Inn (at the location that eventually became the famous KoKoMo), and working at the Barksdale AFB BX, the Big Chain Grocery Store, and the Southland Cottonseed Oil Mill. I immersed myself in sports, plays, stage work, Key Club, Hi-Y, the National Thespians, and even school politics. I began to try to make things happen with my circle of friends.

I loved being in the halls of Bossier High School. I had been there many times watching Ronnie in sports, plays, and his graduation. The halls of BHS held no surprises for me. I was comfortable in those surroundings and I had my friends and some of Ronnie's friends.

Certainly, one of the new additions to my circle of friends was Mary McDowell, Ronnie's girlfriend. She had just graduated the year before I got to high school, and had left an impeccable reputation and many friends. The teachers loved both Ronnie and Mary, and now I had to live up to two legacies.

Now at the high school, in our 8th grade school year, the biggest adjustment we faced was the combining of Bossier Elementary students with Waller Elementary students. We knew very little of each other, only that we had played some of them in sports, or that many of our paths had crossed either at church or our parents working together. With a population of 5,000, Bossier City wasn't big enough to get too lost in the crowd.

Once again, my life would be expanded with another set of new friends as we easily meshed together with a whole new group of lasting friendships.

The "Waller Elementary" group of students became a part of my life forever. Joining our scruffy little guys would be another set of scruffy little guys, Johnny Glass, Richard Johnson, Robbie Hucklebridge, Richard Enis, Bobby Joe Pastiro, Scotty Teague, Archie Ray Wilson, Pat Vaughn, and others.

Not to be excluded would be Waller's Jimmy Tharp, Thomas Buford, and Hal Edwards. They joined with Bossier's Doug Durham, Tommy Mitchell, and me, all better known as "The Chain Gang." We were the guys that ran and operated the Big Chain Grocery Store.

The special and beautiful "Girls of Waller" were an extraordinary addition to those from the Bossier side of town. Oh, what enduring memories and unwavering friendships. Among others, were Cookie Demler, Ann Scott Teague, Jackie Dyer, Ann Galloway, Annie Hamley, Carolyn Lee, Edith Seyburn, Kay Tharp, Paula Spencer, and the Murphy sisters, Martha and Margaret.

One of the first things we had to do as eighth graders was to elect class officers. Charles "Butch" Buddy Roemer, and I began our political careers together that year. Charles was from Waller and I was from Bossier. He ran for the 8th grade class President. I helped him with his campaign, and our lives were locked together forever. During my years at the high school, that friendship became monumental in my life. Buddy went on to graduate from Harvard University, become a U.S. Representative for the 4th Congressional District of Louisiana, and Governor of Louisiana. Nobody was prouder of Buddy than I was.

Television came to town in the early 1950's and everyone's lives were altered forever. During the summer of 1956, television changed me when the Democratic and Republican conventions were televised. I was glued to the TV.

The fascination with the secrecy, and the wheeling and dealing of those proceedings intrigued me as the drama unfolded about how politics made things happen. The oratory and the back room dealings were mesmerizing. There was Estes Kefauver, Adlai Stevenson, and a newcomer during the 1956 convention named John F. Kennedy. Kennedy lost in his bid to become Vice President to Estes Kefauver on the third ballot, even against his father's wishes.

When our freshman year of school started that next fall, Buddy Roemer and I talked about those conventions, and I think that is when we earnestly began to follow politics. It was a subject never far from our minds, especially school student body elections, and even club elections in the Hi-Y or the Key Club, and this became an organized effort for us.

We both learned early, whether it was the sports we played, or our natural desire, that we didn't like to lose. We both came from competitive families that played lots of games. Aren't you supposed to win when you play?

Earlier, at the age of nine, came my first personal introduction to politics. Mr. Hamner, our clothes cleanerman who picked up and delivered to our home, came to our door one morning, but this time he was running for a local office. I answered the door, and as I was by myself, he actually asked for my vote. Something captivated me about his running for office. I never thought of him as someone to lead our community. My God, he was our dry cleaners-man! I wondered why he would do that? He was one of those common people that were so common in our town. I never forgot that day. That day would be very helpful to many others, and to me, later in my life.

As my involvement with politics grew, I kept coming back to the time Mr. Hamner asked me for my vote. He treated me with dignity, and I never forgot the respect he showed me that day. He could have just belittled me and said, "Hey little fellow, tell your mom and dad I came by." He never did, and that was a lesson in the psychology of politics. Respect every person, particularly every voter! A lifelong lesson came out of that little story. If you want to be respected, respect the person you are talking or visiting with, and they may remember that kindness forever.

All of these occurrences made me bolder, and I began to trust my abilities. The opportunities during that first couple of years at the high school gave me the confidence to never be afraid to offer my opinions. I was not big enough to force my opinions on people. I was just a scrawny skinny kid, a new kid at the big school, and a lowly freshman, so I had to be a little more tactful and work my way through by trying to make everyone my friend.

It turns out I gained more from the new friends that I made than I did trying to put my opinions in place. Another of life's valuable lessons was that making friends was the best way for me to get things done, and at the same time my life was so much happier. Much more importantly, liking people and having people like me was a good thing. The Golden Rule, "Do unto others as you would have them do unto you," a tenant I learned at Curtis Park Methodist Church, has served me well throughout my life.

All of these reflections came to me early in my life, and I am grateful for that. Getting along was fun. Making friends meant engaging in new activities. A lot of those activities in some cases were new to me, but not to them. It was the realization my friends had neat ideas and the activities that went along with them.

HOME SWEET HOME, AND THE COOKING WAS GOOD, TOO

Up until this point I think we all lived in our own small world, sometimes of make believe. The most powerful make believe tool, the one that created vivid imaginations, was the radio. Make believe characters lived within our minds with true realness. Only the sounds and words were real, but the pictures, scenes and actions had to be visualized by our own thoughts.

This was a family way of life, and the whole family sat there and heard the same words, but we all had different pictures in our mind. Our console Philco radio, a mahogany beauty, was the center of our entertainment.

As my brother and I lay on the floor as close as we could get to the radio, my dad, mom and mamaw, with, of course, my dog Spunk, were right there. All spellbound, we were laughing, or holding our breath until the outcome was safe, but mostly being together.

The voices boomed as only the readers of our fate and the entertainers delivered. The most distinctive voice was that of newsman/commentator, Edward R. Murrow. America trusted every word he spoke. We had our favorite shows, and the voices had no faces for the most part, except for the faces in our own minds:

Comedy: Lum & Abner, Fiber McGee & Molly, Burns & Allen, Edgar Bergen & Charlie McCarthy, Abbott & Costello, Jack Benny, Red Skelton, Amos & Andy;

Situation: Our Miss Brooks, Sky King, The Aldrich Family, Baby Snooks, Ozzie and Harriett;

Mystery and Sci-fi: The Adventures of Sam Spade, The Shadow, The Fat Man, Green Hornet, The Creaking Door, Lux Radio Theater, Dick Tracey, Inner Sanctum, Batman, Buck Rogers, Flash Gordon, Richard Diamond, The Avenger;

Westerns: Gene Autry and the Melody Ranch, Lash LaRue, Roy Rogers, The Red Ryder, The Lone Ranger, Sgt. Preston of the Yukon, Zane Grey – King of the Royal Mounties;

Variety: Arthur Godfrey & the Talent Scouts, Bob Hope, Danny Kaye, Tennessee Ernie Ford;

Games: Truth or Consequences, Double or Nothing, You Bet your Life;

News Commentators: Edward R. Murrow, H. V. Kaltenborn, Gabriel Heatter, Fulton Lewis, Jr., Drew Pearson.

This may seem like all we did was listen to the radio, but as most shows were only 30 minutes in length, you could listen to the radio and do your chores, sew, cook, clean, study or play games at the same time.

Radio was happening in nearly every home in America. Americans enjoyed the innocence of good family entertainment. We kept that Philco radio until the mid 1960's, and it was sold to a local airman for $50. I remember the sadness I felt as they took that radio away. It was working as good as ever and the tones were still beautiful. Don't know what it cost to buy that radio, but that was probably the best investment our family ever made.

It seems like even the new music, rock and roll, sounded better on that radio than any high-powered music systems I have ever owned. Every morning was ushered in listening to either Joe Monroe, Buddy Blake on KJOE, or Al Hart on KEEL. Local DJ George Carlin also worked at KJOE (the comedian-to-be, became the Hippy Dippy Weatherman). I learned recently that George Carlin was the first DJ to play Elvis Presley's All Shook Up on the radio right here in Shreveport. It seems that

Stan Lewis, of Stan's Record Shop, received a shipment of records from RCA records in 1957, and included in the package was a song that had no promotional material or information - "All Shook Up." Stan carried it to Joe Monroe, the owner of KJOE, and he had George Carlin play it on the air for the first time.

Our life's buffet was made up of good and easy choices in those days. The food was prepared by two of the best cooks two boys could have - our mom and mamaw. The taste of that fried chicken, black-eyed peas; cornbread and turnip greens are still in my mouth to this day. Black-eyed peas, cornbread and turnip greens continue to be my favorite meal. While those dishes later in life don't have the same seasoning of love stirred into them, I still crave that home cooking. More on those special dishes, and the seasonings of love, will come back into my life later.

Until you had a piece of mamaw's apple pie or apricot fried pies you don't know how good an angel can cook. There was roast beef and mashed potatoes, with English peas, and real homemade yeast rolls nearly every Sunday. Just as good was the fried chicken with rice and gravy, chicken and dumplings, skillet-fried hamburgers, no buns in the early days - just two pieces of white bread. Later, we had real hamburger buns; they were slightly rubbed with hamburger grease and then toasted on the stove grill.

Our mother's rolls were things of legend. You had to be careful not to bite into one of those rolls before you tasted anything else on the table. Once you had savored a bite of those light, hot, buttery, melt-in-your-mouth heavenly-tasting rolls you just may not eat anything else. I never remember not having those rolls at any family occasion dinner. She baked at least two dozen rolls every time we ate. Counting all the Sunday dinners, Christmas, Thanksgiving, birthdays and dinners for special guests coming to town, she, by my best estimate, baked nearly

100,000 rolls. On one occasion, when the whole family was there, we witnessed the never-before phenomenon of burned rolls. Stunned to disbelief, we all in unison gasped, until there was hardly any oxygen left in the room. It was such a big deal we took pictures of the charred rolls, and made a much bigger deal than we should have. Now we had seen our sweet mother lose her cool before, but this was a crisis of biblical proportions. She had been upset because somebody was late to a meal, but NEVER because we had criticized her cooking. This was new ground, and she was really offended by us laughing and making fun of the burned rolls. By the way, we ate them anyway out of self-defense.

Other cooks appeared with the bread of life - cornbread. Dorothy Ward, our neighbor across the street, cooked the best cornbread muffins, ever. They were crunchy and had a sweet taste, and no doubt that they were made from scratch. I know because I watched her make them and began begging for them before they come out of the oven. As soon as I got home from school I would head over to Dorothy's, drawn by the cornbread smell that was beckoning me to "come on over." At least once, I ate all of the muffins she had made. She almost gleefully said, "That's all right, I'll just make some more." Even my mamaw admitted that Dorothy's cornbread was the best. Dorothy was a sweet, caring lady with a heart of gold.

Not many years ago, she had moved back to Bossier City and called me to come see her, and have some coffee. I was anxious to see her again as it had been so long. She was so important to me in my young life. Guess what she had with the coffee – CORNBREAD! What a delightful afternoon we had. I love that lady.

Donald Lewis's mother made biscuits every morning, and by the time I walked home from school with Donnie those extra leftover biscuits were calling my name. I have never tasted biscuits that good since. Years later, Donnie was visiting his mother at her house on Riverside Dr. In fact, they were moving her to Tennessee to be near her son, Jimmy. Donnie called for me to come over for a visit. As I always did, I sauntered up to the kitchen screen door, and without knocking, called out, "Hey, you got any biscuits?" And with all her thoughtfulness, always gracious, she came to the door and said, "I sure do." I thought, this lady loves me, too.

In high school, I never weighed more that 120 pounds. I never knew exactly why. With food like that, and I ate like a horse, except at supper. Some night's supper looked so good, but there just wasn't enough room left to eat much more. One night I didn't eat my supper, mother got angry, and sent me to bed without eating. She said, "You're not going to eat any snacks or anything else, because you did not eat your supper." When Ronnie and I got in bed that night Ronnie said, "It smells like a pickle factory in here," and sure enough, mamaw had put two pickles under my pillow so I wouldn't go to bed hungry. My love of pickles is legendary. I told you she was an angel.

Mary's mother, Pauline "Mac" McDowell, knew the way to my heart - food. She had the magic, and one of my most coveted Christmas gifts that I ever received came from "Mac". It was a jar of pickles.

That lady could cook as well as anybody I ever knew. She could cook any home cooking "Diner" under the table. Until you have been in her house and eaten a lunch prepared by her, you just haven't had lunch. She always had a pie or a cake. Later in life, Mac McDowell became the only person I have ever heard of in the whole world that baked her cakes on an outdoor barbeque grill.

You see there was a little secret I kept from mother. On the way home from school, before I got to Mrs. Lewis's house for a biscuit, and before I got to Dorothy's cornbread, I would stop by Cobb's Barbeque.

Well, it was right on the way! The chopped beef sandwiches were only 20 cents each, or five for a $1.00. Usually that was after practice. I always had some kind of practice football, basketball or baseball, so I was always hungry.

On a really good day, when I finally got to the house, mamaw would have one of those heavenly apple pies hot out of the oven. She would have some extra crust waiting for me. She taught me to put mustard on the crust, and that was second best to the pie itself. She held out, but finally gave in and always said, "That ought to hold you till supper," but she loved me too, and I was able to get a piece of that hot apple pie anyway. Then, I would go over to Dorothy's.

You see why I believe that God always has a buffet for us to choose from, but come on; this one was laid out right there in front of me.

A NEW HOME - MORE THAN JUST A HOUSE

In 1952, we moved from the Barksdale Homes to 210 S. Youree St., in Bossier City. It was a modest house with three bedrooms, one bath and a large living room totaling 800 square feet. No, the whole house had 800 square feet. There were five of us to divide among the spacious home. It was in a new subdivision and the only tree in the whole subdivision was the huge cottonwood in our yard.

My first memory was that it had no grass, so our first duty was to "dig in the yard". On March 19, 1952, we bought 100 lbs. of fertilizer ($2.30), and on April 4, 1952, we bought another 100 lbs. of fertilizer (another $2.30). We dug in the yard until we had every square inch tilled (dug) and leveled. It wasn't long until we had grass, which led to mowing the grass. A total of $20.08 was spent improving the new house for all of 1952.

Not long after the yard was prepared and looking good we had to dig it up again so Paul could build a garage. On August 25, 1953, Paul got 5 yards of fill dirt for $4.00, and paid $1.32 for bolts for the garage foundation, $8.65 for reinforcing rods for the foundation, because on August 31, 1953, Braswell Supply poured 5 ¾ yards of concrete costing $85.63.

If you want to know what he paid for nails for that damn garage, I could tell you that, too. In fact, I could tell you what was paid for everything, who he paid it to, and on what date. He kept the detailed records of all expenditures for that garage and everything else he did. The total cost of the garage was $739.01, exactly.

No labor cost was figured in because we were cheap labor, when he could catch us. It was a double garage with a single garage door opening, with no door necessary. As an avid squirrel hunter, he was able kill and skin enough squirrels to hang enough squirrel tails to have the only fur-lined garage door in town, and maybe in America.

There was never a more organized person. His

penmanship was immaculate, and his writing skills were expert. He had been a member of the high school swim team, and was the very first Eagle Scout in the State of Iowa. He attended the first Boy Scout Jamboree in Washington D.C. He was a good student; I have seen his report cards.

His military duty during World War II was served in India. He kept a detailed diary account of everyday life in the war. I only knew the diary existed after mother died when we went through her things. The man could really write seemingly effortlessly. The diary was many pages long, and not one strikeover or scratch out; every word was perfect, and no misspellings.

He was a master at wood crafting, and completed many airplane models. Both were hobbies he spent hours patiently working masterfully at until his project was perfect. His other hobby was squirrel hunting, a hobby neither Ronnie nor I took up. Sleeping seemed like a better and more productive thing to do.

Paul Cedric literally lived to get up and go out into the woods and hunt squirrels. He spent weeks preparing for the hunting season, cleaning his guns, and sighting in the shotgun patterns. I think he even pressed his hunting clothes.

He kept detailed records of every squirrel hunt he went on, including where he went, what he had for breakfast, the weather, the temperature, and the kind of squirrels he killed. His hunting statistical pages looked like major league baseball stats. It wasn't hits, runs and errors, but kills, misses, and excuses.

All of this was going on while he worked as a Civil Service airplane mechanic at Barksdale after being discharged from the Army Air Corp. His work was hot in the summer and cold in the winter. I am sure he was as meticulous at his work as he was at home.

My mother was a gentle, a fun person to be with;

she was patient, and always encouraging. She always worked and did very well in the business world. She worked at the Base Exchange at Barksdale, beginning as a sales clerk and becoming the Head of Personnel for her Region of the Army Air Force Exchange Service (AAFES).

She worked under many Exchange Officers, some fair and some not so fair. One of the disappointing responsibilities of her job was dealing with some of the wives of Base Commanders, and other Generals that graced Barksdale AFB. If any one of the Exchange employees didn't meet the expectations or wishes of those Commander's wives, the trouble came to my mother's desk.

My mother made many friends from the Base Exchange. She was good to them and they were good to her. She was a faithful employee, and at the same time, she was a great and respected mother. We never lacked for anything, from cookies for an elementary room party, which she also attended, to taking us to baseball games, which she knew nothing about.

Mother told a story of taking Ronnie to a Shreveport Sports baseball game. After nearly five innings, she asked him what the score was. Embarrassed, he leaned over and whispered so as not to be heard, "Mother, don't you see the scoreboard out in center field?" Mother said it must have been thirty yards wide and thirty feet tall.

Our mother's dedication was exemplified when I told her I had volunteered her to make her fabulous spaghetti for our Sunday School Class. I just didn't explain that our class was sponsoring a fund-raiser, and the whole church would be invited. We expected around 300 people. She looked at me with disbelief and said okay. That was my mom.

Her humor and desire to surprise seemed to come out best at Christmas. Keeping the gifts she gave a secret at Christmas was a big thing for our mom. We never knew what we were getting. She never labeled the gifts so we wouldn't know whose package was whose. Paul especially didn't know, but that didn't keep us from asking, guessing, shaking or peeking.

She wised up, and would put fake gifts under the tree. She loved to wrap and put a decorated box within a decorated box, within a decorated box and, so on. It would sometimes take several minutes to finally get to the last box. She was laughing the whole time.

She got excited when we put up the tree and cooked the Christmas goodies. My mother glowed at Christmas time, and she cried when she heard "Silent Night" because it reminded her of her sister. No one could have wished for more in a mother than we had. I know we are better because of her. People who knew her still tell me today that she was a saint. Yeah, I know.

When I was thirteen or fourteen, I got a brand new red three-speed English bicycle with a speedometer. It was loaded. As usual, Ronnie and I got up before everybody else, and I found my new bike by the tree. At last, we got the whole group up and I could wait no longer. Still in my pajamas and no shoes, I had to quickly take it out for a spin.

The problems were as follows: it was thirty degrees, 5 am in the morning, asphalt street, and front and rear wheel brakes. That baby would fly. The speedometer got up to 30 mph, incidentally, and that made the wind chill factor approximately zero degrees. As I got directly in front of the house I clamped down on both brakes at once, thinking it would slide like my old rear wheeled brake bicycle did. I quickly realized that only the front brakes worked, and the rear brakes did not. Meaning the front of the bike stopped instantly; however, the rear of the bike did not, and neither did I. Over the handlebars I went, sailing through the air onto the asphalt street, sliding on the end of my nose, hands, chest, and knees. The bike did not slide, I did. Every Christmas was always a memorable event, but the South Youree Street asphalt tattooed this one on me.

Ronnie and I both had been married and gone from home when we gave Paul a Christmas gift that he never expected, and it moved him like we had never seen him moved before. Ronnie and I legally adopted him to be our father. Keeping in mother's tradition of Christmas surprises, Frank Harlow, our neighbor for years and now a lawyer, prepared the papers for us, and was there when we gave them to him at mother's annual Christmas party. The whole neighborhood knew about this, except Paul.

Mamaw, my grandmother, is forever part of my heart. A lady with a very funny humor and a golden heart, she was true to her God and faithful to her friends.

I think she was her most intriguing when she was at Mrs. Parilee's farm in Evergreen near Minden, Louisiana. Minden is where mamaw and mother grew up. Mother graduated from Minden High School in 1935. Mrs. Parilee was mamaw's best friend. She lived with Mrs. Parilee for a short period in her life. To watch the two of them together was to go back in time -- their time.

These two ladies were a dictionary description of how life was lived in their days. The history of the 1920's through the 1940's was on the tip of there tongues. Oh, how I wish I could go back and listen to them tell how to solve the world's problems. Bear in mind their world only included mostly the hills and hollers around Minden. The humor between those two could keep you laughing for a lifetime.

To me, this farm was so far from the modern conveniences of the modern era. The walls weren't painted, no central air or heat, no indoor plumbing, a real icebox, a butter churn, but the only thing that I noticed being especially different about these two ladies from the rest of the world was neither one drove a car.

This was a working farm with cows, chickens, pigs, horses, mules, a smoke house, real water well for drawing water, outhouse, fig trees, pear and peach trees, and a wood burning oven. From that farm kitchen came the best fried chicken (after wringing their necks), just-picked peas, corn, and every other vegetable you could think of, huge yeast rolls, fresh eggs, biscuits, bacon, cakes, pies, all from that wood burning stove, and real Coca Colas (small ones) from a real ice box.

I am convinced that Julia Childs must have learned how to cook at the hands of mamaw and Mrs. Parilee. Mrs. Parilee even sounded a little like Julia Childs. Then at night, you would get in a real feather bed. She even had a real pot to pee in for the cold winter nights. That was living!

They had conversations about their friends from around the countryside. In this case, the countryside covered probably 20 square miles. Never realizing the historic value of what I was hearing how, I wish I could remember those talks, stories and tales. Those two ladies, and I mean ladies, knew so much about life and how to use what they had to make life so pleasurable.

Mamaw played checkers and cards with us, cared for us, cooked for us, and she was there while mother worked. She had so many health problems, everything from getting her arm caught in the ringer washer, bruising her arm, and trying to heal it by wrapping it with vinegar soaked paper towels. She was hospitalized for gall bladder problems and pneumonia a couple of times. Later in age, vertigo was a continuous problem for her, and she fell a couple of times and hurt her hip.

She never stopped doing things for us. She was a faithful member of the Curtis Park Methodist Church. When the new church building was to be built, she turned the first spade of dirt. On Mother's Day, the Church always honored the oldest mother in attendance.

Although mamaw was there every Sunday, on

Mother's Day Mrs. Enis would show up. She was a few months older than mamaw, and therefore got the honor. Every year mamaw would grumble for a week.

When I was around 7 years old (1949), mamaw and I traveled by train from Shreveport to Kansas City, and then by bus to Vernal, Utah. R.B. and Charlotte Hatcher picked us up, and we drove to their house in Bonanza, Utah. It was my first train trip, and it was so exciting to hear the conductor yell, "all aboard." I felt the thrill of the train start rolling, and then the clickity clack sounds. I was sleeping in a sleeper car at night, and lying in mamaw's lap during the day. When we arrived by bus in Vernal, Utah, I remember getting off of the bus that night and it being cold and windy, and being greeted by R.B. and Charlotte.

They were my Aunt and Uncle, and some of mamaw's other favorite persons. She loved being with R.B. and Charlotte, but then who wouldn't. They were two of my favorite people in this world. Here were four people that absolutely loved each other.

What a visit!

It was hot in the day because it was in the desert, but their house basement was cool, and the cokes were kept down there. R.B had a jeep, and one night we went looking for jackrabbits, which were huge.

I remember driving back into Vernal to go grocery shopping and R.B. asking me how far the mountains were from the road. I was astonished to learn they were 50 miles in the distance. I had never seen real mountains, desert, or been in a mining camp. That is what Bonanza was - a mining camp. I don't remember how we came home, I don't even remember coming home, but I remember everything else about that trip.

Mamaw, Ronnie and I would ride the city bus from Bossier to Shreveport to go shopping. Even that was a big event in that time. There are so many good memories of my mamaw, and I cherish them all.

My brother, Ronnie, was a tough act to follow. Being five years younger I had the advantage to learn from him, about well, just about everything. Whatever he did was all right with me, as long as he wasn't beating me in any kind of game.

I watched him play sports for some of the same coaches that would later coach me. Because Ronnie played for him, I would have been devastated if I was not on Mr. Almond's baseball team. I played football, basketball and baseball, because he played those sports, and he taught me all of those games.

Ronnie always encouraged me to do better. When I got to high school, I had to be involved with stage and plays, because Ronnie was in plays. I loved my teachers, Mrs. Gamble and Ms. Jaynes, because Ronnie did. Ronnie used to sneak up behind Mrs. Gamble and take her earrings off. She loved it, so I did it too.

Ronnie and I played together hard. Mother would get us to paste wax our hardwood floors. We made them slick and shiny, and we then used the floors to practice our baseball slide in the living room, further shining them by sliding over them with our long pants on.

We listened to many Shreveport Sports baseball games on the radio at night while we were supposed to be sleeping. I Z for 5 D translated into IZ-Irv Ziedman, the announcer, and 5D for a CitiService Oil product, the sponsor for all the ballgames. We hurried to get to the breakfast table to see who could get the sports page first. Sports were a major part of our life.

In 1951, we went on the family trip of a lifetime, traveling all the way to Utah. I was nine, and Ronnie was 14. It was in the dead of summer. A lot of cars on the highways had canvas bags of water hanging on the front grills in case their car engine got too hot. I guess when you put two brothers in a car without air conditioning for more than a couple of weeks things get testy.

As we arrived in Salt Lake City I guess, we had argued just about everything. Mother bought a game at Sears and Roebuck that was intended to keep the tensions down. Mother thought this All-Star baseball game was the perfect activity for us, both hating to lose, so things were okay for a while. The game consisted of spinning a needle and landing on a space for a single, double, triple, homerun, strikeout, fly out, etc. The rub came when the needle stopped spinning on the line or barely inside the allotted little space designated as a hit or an out. I thought the game was going to get thrown out of the car.

We kept that game and played it for years. Christmas 2006, I gave Ronnie a brand new replica of that game from the Baseball Hall of Fame in Cooperstown, New York.

We set up a basketball goal in our bedroom – yes, in our bedroom. The room was not much more than 10x10 and had a dresser and two single beds. We scaled down the game by hanging a box by the lid that an Old Spice cologne bottle came in over the top of the closet door, and used a ping-pong ball.

Do you know how hard it is to shoot a ping-pong ball into an Old Spice box? There was no dunking; in fact, we had never heard of dunking a basketball back then. It was never boring in our house.

Then there was the summer that our lifelong friend, John Jones, came from Greenville, Mississippi, to play summer ball on Mr. Almond's team with me. Robert and Henrietta Jones were mother's best friends from Bangor, Maine, where I was born.

Robert was in the same Air Corp unit as my dad, and John was their only child. For years, we had continued the family friendship, visiting back and forth from their house and ours. I had gone over to Mississippi to play Little League baseball with John the summer before, and he was visiting us to experience baseball in Bossier City.

We won the championship, which was normal for Mr. Almond's teams, but the real memories were the miseries we dealt Ronnie. You see, here John and I were with all day long to find something to get into. Ronnie was working, and even worse, he was in love and dating Mary. At night, he wanted to spend time with her. Well, that just wasn't right in our eyes as we had things we wanted to do, and he had a car.

John and I were left at home during the day as mother, Paul and Ronnie were working. Oh, the time on our hands was too much to bear. I have to admit when John and I began planning it was like a volcano preparing to blow the top off of the mountain.

Mamaw must have been out of town, or stayed out of the way, or we were devious enough to not let her know of the plans for the night. Nearly every night when Ronnie finally did come home we had some concocted scheme to make his life a little more miserable.

There was the short sheeting of the bed, salt in the bed, the alarm clock set for the middle of the night - you know, whatever it took. To set the stage for a very special night -- it was hot, and all we had was the attic fan, meaning the windows would be open. This was going to be the best yet. What a plan!

We strung a cord out of Ronnie's bedroom window and along the back of the house into our bedroom window. The cord was hidden so no visible evidence could be found, as that would foil our plans. Several empty tin cans were tied to the end of the cord, which went under his bed.

Of course, it was dark when he got home, and we lay in waiting, laughing and giggling until he finally arrived and prepared for bed. When he did come in the house that night, the excitement began building until both

John and I were shaking uncontrollably. We faked as if we were sleeping like babies, because Ronnie, in self-defense, usually came into our bedroom to make d--- sure, we were asleep. He had finally figured out that something lay in store for him nearly every night. That was the hardest we ever bit our lips to keep from laughing when he checked on us.

The night finally settled into a silent quietness. Everybody was fast asleep, mother, Paul, Ronnie, and, supposedly, John and I. When the moment was right, and that would be when Ronnie was asleep, we yanked the cord from our window, tugging it through his window to the cans underneath his bed. All hell broke loose. From under Ronnie's, bed the sounds of empty cans clanging loudly and continuously. Remember the windows were open, as well as every other window in the neighborhood, and, you could hear him screaming all over the neighborhood. Mother and Paul jumped up to see what was happening.

It never occurred to John or me that Paul might grab a gun, or that Ronnie wanted to. Ronnie, after turning on the lights and finding the cans under the bed, with the cord going out the window, began figuring out that it might be trouble striking - again. He headed straight for us. I had never seen so much commotion and confusion in the hall of our house as mother, Paul and Ronnie all going different directions in that little ten foot long hallway.

But the two little angels - that would be John and me, lay still, as if we were the only people in the whole neighborhood that never heard anything, and faking sleep. The dead give away was that we were shaking so hard from laughing our beds were bouncing.

That may be the only time mother let Ronnie beat the tar out of John and me. All I can remember about the beating was John yelling and laughing at the same time, "Ora, Ora, help me!"

We forged through our younger years, and I can say that Ronnie and I had so many special times together. When the time came for living without him, I was real upset. Not that Ronnie was getting married, but that he was not going to be home any more.

However, Mary was an amazing girl, and she was a great addition to our family and particularly to me. She has always treated me with nothing but love. As far as I am concerned, Ronnie could not have done any better.

TRAVELING WITH THE WINDOWS DOWN

My parents taught me the experience of adventure through the travels we took. It may have been going to visit friends in Monroe, La., or Vicksburg, Miss., or going into Arkansas, or the trip experienced through the wide eyes of a young boy going from home, west to Colorado, and Utah.

The American roads opened a whole new world to me. The automobile was the best method of travel if you wanted to really get to know your family and your country. We all sat within three feet of each other for hours at a time, watching as America passed by. Automobiles with air conditioning was not an option in the 1940' and 50's. Besides, what better way to travel than with the windows down, feeling the wind blowing your hair and under your shirt, and not just seeing America, but smelling it too, or was that my brother?

In my early years during the 1940-50's on the open roads, there was plenty of time at the 50 mph to pay attention the scenery, the way other towns looked and just how the rest of America lived.

I discovered real rivers, open plains, crops other than cotton, different architecture, funny talking people, eating different food, reading a map, and majestic mountains. What better way to experience the world around us?

Occasionally, we took the wrong road. Our wrong turn from hell occurred while we were vacationing in the Ozark Mountains. Dad wanted to get out of our rented cabin. He loved to ride in the car, and it was always exciting to get in the car and go somewhere. We had no idea where we were going; we were just looking around.

We all had this strange sensation that dad did not know where he was going, especially when he made a right turn onto a road with no directional signs. The armrest squeeze now invoked; it was only a few hundred yards until a guttural fear overcame each of us. My dad gripped the steering wheel so tightly that his knuckles were turning white, and he sat forward in his seat. That meant he was horrified. The road narrowed to a path with bushes scraping in the open windows, and of course, we ducked. Then came a small creek, it was either drive through it or back up over a mile. There was no place for turning around. We must have gone at least 5 miles into the back woods of Arkansas. This had to be Arkansas's most undesignated scenic hillbilly road. Not a word was spoken since mother's tirade right after the fateful turn.

At last, there was an opening in the woods! No, it was the end of the trail. On the right was the best definition of real original hillbilly we had ever seen. Sitting in the opening was a quintessential, sure fire, original dogtrot house, complete with a coon dog with long ears, howling. His howl must have echoed through dem hills and hollers all the way back to civilization.

From around the side of the house came a real live hillbilly right out of the history books. We feared for our lives as he approached and said, "Golly, there ain't been no car over that there road in nigh ten years." Dad, speaking in his best hillbilly slang, said, "We're lost, how'd u git out of here?" Ronnie and I thought, silently, "Lost, no kidding."

Traveling was the excitement of sharing those experiences with your family. This was about the education of learning about this world and the memories of all of us seeing a scenic attraction for the first time together. This was different from our radio experiences where we all had a different word picture of what we had just heard. We may have put a different description on what we just saw or experienced, but there was no imagination necessary about what we had seen. We had pictures in our mind to prove it.

These adventures left us with knowledge of real things. Yeah, we took hundreds of photos, but those old Kodak moments turn yellow with time. Our minds were equipped with moments that we could recall in an instant. All we have to do is close our eyes and drift off into life's amazing moments, and in the blink of an eye, we can travel miles and miles, and memories and memories.

Nothing excites me like planning for a new trip adventure, except actually taking that trip. America is a beautiful and diverse country in every way. Its people are warm and inviting; for the most part, they want to help make your travels enjoyable. They are proud of where they live. The landscapes are magnificent in so many ways. The cuisine is as varied as the turns in the roads.

I finally learned to eat more than hamburgers. I have even planned trips around the restaurants I want to try. Thanks to my parents, traveling had given me a yearning to learn, and see and seek new things. I used to consider that first trip out west, when I was nine years old, the perfect trip, but it was only the first perfect trip.

Going west and its wide open spaces and unique land formations fascinates me, and is probably my favorite direction, but the northeast, Florida, mid-America, Alaska, and especially Europe, holds extraordinary memories and intrigues me with alluring history, cultures and architecture.

The time we spent in Jackson, Wyoming, with total strangers over a hearty breakfast on a cool, crisp morning with air so clean you can't wait for your next breath. We were talking with them as if we had known them forever. We shared eloquent dinners with cruise shipmates nightly for two weeks from Germany, Scotland, Minnesota, and Tyler, Texas. It becomes all too apparent that all people can find commonality even with the stress of world affairs.

I learned about a life cycle that staggered my imagination. Beginning with the desert up high rocky cliffs where trees cling to the most uninhabitable rocks. Then dramatically the sheer rock cliffs drop waterfalls to a peaceful stream spilling water into a lush green meadow, and finally becoming glass smooth blue lakes that reflect the white clouds and heaven itself.

High above the symphony of grandeur that lies below can be seen a horizon in the distance that is wide enough to accommodate even the most impossible dreams. Over the entire sweet spectacular scene is a refreshing gentle wind blowing across the world. Below the steep sided rocky valleys adorned with precious tan, green and blue hues, gentle streams become roaring rivers; so much water, all going to some place else.

THE NEIGHBORHOOD

What would a home be without the neighborhood families, friends that would be forever burned in our memories? It wasn't just my school age friends; it was also their parents and their added experiences to our everyday life.

From the first days of moving into our new home, it wasn't long before this neighborhood came to life. The families and friends started with the next-door neighbors, the Dunns on one side, and the Adams on the other. Across the street were the Wards, down the street one direction were the Honeycutts, Allens, Pooles, Perdues, Humphreys; the other way was the Sewards, Mowdys, Streeters, and the Martins.

We had no parks; the houses had no fences, so the backyards made up the football fields, basketball courts and the playgrounds. Our gathering places were our houses, front or backyards. The backyard of one of the neighbors had a large tree in the ravine that went along the back of the west side of the subdivision. They owned a furniture store, had no children, and were never at home until late. We were very careful to never mess with their things and always cleaned up when we left for the day. This would be known as the VT (Vine Tree) and a large limbed sprawling tree with some vines hanging from the upper limbs. It was easily climbed, and a perfect place to lie on the limbs and wile away the day.

Many of our dreams resulted from our time lollygagging around in that tree, both boys and girls. Most of our playtime happened at the VT, or at the Poole's, where Frank and Joe Harlow lived with their mother and stepfather, Jack Poole.

After several years of using the VT, we upgraded to the Poole's house. They had an enclosed patio on the back of their house which became our place of choice during the hot summer days because it was air-conditioned. Now we had our own "Valley Girls" with their short shorts, and much time was spent at their houses, also. The hotties of the neighborhood were Marion Streeter, George Ann Allen, Judy Martin, Jill and Jean Mowdy, and over on the street behind us was Jean Jones and some girl named Velma. Wow!

The South Youree Street gang consisted of Bruce Humphrey, Diane and Edwin, Rand, and William Perdue, Frank and Joe Harlow, Jerry Stringer, William Allen, Richard and Randolph Seward, Freddy Green, George Anne Allen, Marion Streeter, Judy Martin, Larry Felts, Jill and Jane Mowdy, and Jimmy Taft - common names and common families.

At the other end of South Youree Street was another large tree, which we appropriately named the BT (Big Tree). It had no redeeming social value other than it was a landmark for us. Two basketball courts were available to us -- well, backyards with goals. First was Jerry Stringer's house, to be replaced when he moved by the goal in Frank Harlow's backyard. I think I was the first to score at least 20,000 points on that goal. We played all the time, even after coming home from basketball practice at school.

We always had something going on in the way of activities, from the normal birthday parties, to swimming at the Recreation Center, going to the Davis Theater, swinging on a long rope out over the Red River, to Shock Night parties with scary movies. Those parties didn't start until midnight because the scary movies came on TV at midnight, and parties were happening all over town. Our moms supplied the refreshments and lasted until... Kick the Can, Annie Over, to playing poker with Jack Poole's poker chips. We had our share of parties, and we included lots of kids from our school. I never knew what the parties were in celebration of, or if they really had a reason.

Back in the 1950's and 60's our neighborhoods were small, which was so common in Bossier City. We shared that with neighborhoods all over town, and we shared the same values.

I recall that our neighborhood was bound together by lock step friendships, with recollections that we all attended church, and not necessarily the same churches. Most of us worked at jobs, we played games, experienced the newness of television together, played basketball, football, and baseball, all in our own neighborhood stadiums - usually someone's backyard.

We played games of "war", crawling among the hedges, digging foxholes and play shooting each other with a "I gotcha"-- only missing, when the person being shot at loudly disagreed with a, "No you didn't!" We all wondered what we would be when we grew up, and where our trail would take us. Not that we dwelled on those high ponderous decisions, we just thought things would be okay. Those early years, and the values we lived with, propelled one of those neighborhood buddies to soar to unimaginable heights and achieve greatness never conceived by us. Freddy Green has moved on from those innocent days of laughter, endless energy, but not from our family of friends.

United States Air Force, Colonel Freddy Green flew 384 combat missions in Vietnam. He was responsible for the management and testing of the upgrades and modifications to the B-52 and KC-135 fleets, keeping the B-52's in operation and up-to-date. This was the single most important reason Barksdale Air Force Base remained open and viable.

He became the Director of the Air Launch Cruise Missile Test Operations at Edwards AFB. Assigned to the Pentagon, he was the Program Manager for the development of the B-2 Bomber. He was among the founding group of seven officers, and served as the Program Manager of "The Stealth Technology Weapons Systems", a $44 billion program. Freddy was an Air Base Wing Commander, and completed his Air Force career as the Director for special test programs at the Air Force

Operational Test and Evaluation Center.

Our neighborhood was about being good buddies, friends forever, lessons learned, the smell of great cooking wafting all over the neighborhood at suppertime every night, and most of all the sounds of laughter forever in our memories.

HIGH SCHOOL - TOO BUSY HAVING FUN

Bossier High School, here I was, surrounded by the friends I knew best and knew me best. The special part of every school day was before the bell rang, being in the halls between classes, and after the bell rang. To say I was anxious to go to class would not be stating the truth.

My confidence level was highest when I could be myself with the student friends. I didn't have to prove anything at those times. In the classroom, I was usually so unsure of myself, and I tried to hide from the teachers because I didn't want them to ask me questions.

There were some exceptions, and Speech class was one of them. I loved the challenge of delivering a speech in front of the students. Beginning in my freshman year, Ms. Jaynes taught me to have confidence and encouraged me to do things most students hated to do.

She made me feel as if she depended on me. I think she understood my lack of classroom confidence. She made sure I was on the stage or at a podium as much as possible. I did not realize her encouragement was her way of making me come out of my shell. I had no idea what she was doing with me until our senior year.

During the Senior Class play dress rehearsal, she brought the rehearsal to a screeching halt. The cast was not prepared, and the play looked as though it was doomed to failure. She called out almost every cast member and stagehand out individually, including me, and I had never had her speak to me like that. She demanded we do whatever it took that night, even if it meant staying up all night, to be ready the next night – the opening night. We had never heard her talk to students in that raised tone of voice.

After almost the whole cast had left, and I had turned the auditorium lights out, she approached me and said, "Jerry, I want you to find the time tomorrow to encourage everybody in this play that they can be good on that stage tomorrow night. I am counting on you."

It took me a couple of years to understand what happened that evening. She thought I had connect-ability with my cast member friends to give them the confidence that would bring that play together successfully. All I did was assure them, as much as I could, that they could deliver on that stage. Out of fear of Ms. Jaynes, or out of fear of failure, they took to that stage and performed beyond all expectations.

We were all beaming at how things had gone. Ms. Jaynes was happy, and that mattered. Again, the lights were turned out, and I was walking out of the auditorium toward the front door of the school. There she was, standing at the door waiting. We were the last to leave. I was smiling and she was too. When I said, "that went real good," all she did was give me an "A" by simply winking at me, and saying, "It sure did."

One of my most memorable moments in the Senior Class play (Onions in the Stew) was my part as the boss Mr. Curtis, a dapper slick dressed plumber wearing a silky suit appeared just ahead of my wife on stage, Mrs. Curtis (Pat Almond Hill). She came bounding on the stage in her work overalls and a huge toolbox. I was short, she was tall, and it drew huge laughs. For the rest of my life I loved telling people that Pat was my first wife. Of course, Pat had to be there when I told that story to get the full effect. She and her husband Kenneth Hill are two of my favorite friends.

I have spoken to crowds of thousands and groups of hundreds and never had a fear. I have had to speak without any prior notification to groups of civic clubs, and to students, for as long as 30-45 minutes. The trick Ms. Jaynes taught me was to know your subject, and not try to talk about an unfamiliar subject. She taught me that if you get in a bind, change the subject to something you know about, preferably something you have done.

One day, years later, I was visiting The Bank of Reform, Alabama, and the bank president ask me to go to a Lion's Club luncheon with him. The meeting started in about 15 minutes. He said, "Why don't you be our guest speaker, you can speak on banking." I was trying to sell the guy our data processing services, so what was I going to do? I had gobs of speech notes on banking back in Birmingham, but none with me. I thought of Ms. Jaynes, and agreed to speak. I sold the bank our data processing services.

Never being comfortable in classrooms, or studying, and my grades showed that, but I was excelling in most other activities of school. I always did pretty well in sports, not great, but okay. The civics part of the activities is where I wanted to be. I guess I did nearly everything from making signs for cheerleaders, to operating the auditorium with Joe Averitt. Joe and I knew every nook and cranny in that auditorium. Only he and I could operate the stage lights and baffles, one of us always had to be there every time the stage was used.

The organizations, plus sports, put me in contact with many others in school, and nearly all of my friends from the elementary school were there. Before I knew it I was loaded with extra-curricular happenings, and studies took a back seat. My friends and I knew how to make "fun work". There seemed to be plenty of what I now know were distractions.

An upperclassman, and a neighbor from the earlier years, George Nattin, and his family, shared our maid, Johnnie. Johnnie kept George apprised of what was going on at my home, including my grades. He made sure I knew, that he knew if I had not done good on an assignment or test. Mother always said, "Johnnie had a butt as big as a pot of gold, and a heart even bigger." Johnnie only wanted what was best for me, and she thought George could encourage me.

Jimmy Griffin's family owned the little store next to the Davis Theater, and he coached our ball team one summer. He later moved next door to our house. We loaded up in his car one day, and left school to go see the New York Giants play the Cleveland Indians over at the Shreveport Sports Park, and Hall of Famer Dizzy Dean announced the game.

Bossier High School had plenty of beautiful girls. Beverly Norman, Miss Bossier City, became Miss Louisiana, but the runner-up to Miss Bossier City that same year was Eurlyne Howell. All Eurlyne did was to go on and became Miss USA, and runner-up to Miss World. I am not so sure they were even the prettiest girls in school. There were lots of distractions.

The class of 1959, one year ahead of my class, had a lot of great students and fun people. Doug McGowen was probably the most creative person I have ever known. We sold magazines one summer, which didn't last very long, but we put together some of the biggest shenanigans ever at BHS.

We created a political party for the high school elections, the "DixieKat Party", and won the student body elections four years in a row. The last two years of those elections, I was in college not even in high school.

Doug and I attended the Hi-Y convention in Vicksburg, Mississippi, along with a busload of BHS Hi-Y members. We decided we would run Henry Brown for President of the Tri-State area. Henry was busy and knew nothing about his candidacy.

Between Doug and I, we got Henry elected. He slept in and didn't attend the Sunday morning election meeting. We told him he was the new President on the bus on the way back home.

Henry would later in life become the Bossier Parish District Attorney. The television show "60 Minutes" called him the "Deadliest DA in America." He had the most death penalty executions in the United States, and later became a Senior Judge for the Louisiana Circuit Court of Appeal. I ran that election campaign for him, also. This time he knew about the election.

At the beginning of my sophomore year, I was among eleven boys from my grade to be selected for Key Club membership. There were eleven boys from each grade and those thirty-three were all movers and shakers in the school. Being among that group was almost invigorating, and gave me even more excuses to ignore my studies.

In my own mind, I was too busy having fun for schoolwork, and that was exactly my attitude. There were plays, club meetings, sports, church, working at the Big Chain, Dixie-Y Phylanx, a outside social group, and hanging out with my friends. I was busy having fun. My life was involved in those things, and the people that went along with them.

The National Thespian Club brought me even closer with some of my closest friends. Gary Ricketts went back to the first grade and my church days early in life. Gary was one of the finest actors we had. He went on to star at the Shreveport Little Theater, and later went into broadcasting. He now lives in New York City, having retired from CBS TV.

Dana Long holds a special place in my life, and made a real impact on me as a person. She was very active in the Thespian group. Dana went to church with me, and we have been very close friends since our early elementary school years. Dana always impressed me as we sang hymns at church. You could tell that she really enjoyed singing those hymns. She never knew I was listening to her more than I was listening to anybody in the church. We tried dating, and had really good times. The first pizza I ever tried was at her encouragement at the Piccadilly Restaurant in Shreveport. We went to the Homecoming Dance our Senior Year. My band played for the dance and while we were on a 15-minute break, I remember dancing to "The Theme from A Summer Place." That may have been the only dance we had together that night.

That always made dating a problem, me sitting up on the stage playing the drums, and my date dancing with everybody else. Dana and I fell in and out of love a few times, at least. I felt so comfortable being with her, no matter when or where. She was always, in a good way, pushing me to do more, and to have more confidence in myself. She was good at that; she probably wishes she hadn't done such a good job on the self-confidence part.

There are only a couple of other friends in my life that wanted me to succeed any more than Dana. I always appreciated that Dana thought I did too much for other friends, instead of putting myself out front. I shall be forever grateful for her respect and concern, and for looking out for me.

Dana and I were both strong-willed types, and we clashed a lot, but we both knew we only wanted what was best for the other. I have often wondered if she really got as mad at me as she acted. She could give me the same kind of look that my mother could give me when the time was right. Dana was one of the first to accuse me of being hard headed, a trait she will attest to, even today, I am sure. Her mother and father were, from among all of my friends' parents, rated as my parental favorites.

Lasting bonds of friendship were forged with my church friends. We spent as much time as we could together - not just at The First Presbyterian Church in Bossier, but it seems we were inseparable. Dana Long, Sandra Grant, Cookie Demler, Tommy Mitchell, David Montgomery, Doug Durham, and Hal Edwards were all in the same grade; the other member of that group was Julia Ann Hoyer, who was only a year behind us. Julia Ann might as well have been in our grade, because she was with us as much as her own classmates were. These were the girls that were in my life, and if I dated anyone else, they always thought they had to approve. I never asked for that approval, but that didn't seem to matter; they told me their opinion anyway.

Cookie Demler was always the quiet one, but had a great laugh and always a pleasant demeanor. Cookie always had a kind word for me, and she was a friend I could count on. I never dated her, mainly because she was going with my friend, Buddy Roemer. They later married; we have shared many happy times together.

We once went on a trip to Houston with them, and the Campisi's, and had a memorable trip to the zoo. I watched a monkey sucker Frank and Buddy over to his cage, and he proceeded to spit water all over them. Then we all went to a Houston Astros vs. Atlanta Braves game that was the lowest attended game in Astros's history. Cecil Upshaw was pitching for Atlanta, but the reason for the low attendance was a hurricane was headed straight for the Astrodome, but that didn't stop us.

Buddy and Cookie became my first experience with my friends divorcing. This was very hard for me, as their kids and my son were childhood friends, like we had been.

Julia Ann Hoyer will always be one of my very best friends. I thought she was cute as a pixie doll, rosy cheeks, little turned up nose, pretty eyes, vivacious, and my friend. There was a time when I felt like I was in love with Julia Ann. We dated some, and I remember going to the Strand Theater with her to see "Lawrence of Arabia." We must have had four large cokes apiece going back and forth through the desert. That movie was so long her mother thought we had run away together. I remember our date on her graduation night, and the parties leading up to that day. We stayed up all night sitting on her front porch looking at the stars and talking. Donna Singleton and her date from Benton were with us.

From the first time I met Sandra Grant in the first grade I knew we would be friends forever. I have only a few friends that I would trust in any situation, and Sandra is one of them. So many times in my life I have needed her help and, to this day, she has never failed me. I have probably laughed more with Sandra than anyone else I know. I got more credit than I deserved for different projects that we undertook, and turned out to be successful. The truth is, Sandra always seemed to be right there with me making my thoughts turn out to be good ideas. She could make a piece of cardboard look like a twinkling star. Through church, even church camps at Camp Alabama, our school days, and our days as parents, our lives have been enriched by each other's presence. We have spent a lot of our life together, and I loved every minute of those times. To me, Sandra was "Short Fat Fannie", "My Destiny", and I loved the times we have spent together. When Sandra hurt, I hurt, and likewise.

Her husband, and my close friend, Doug McGowen, died in a plane crash while serving his summer tour with the Air National Guard. That happened after serving and flying in Viet Nam. I miss Doug, and I hurt for Sandra through all of that. I thought maybe someday we would be together, but that was never to be. Either I was dating Jeanette Bryant, from the 1st grade, or she was ignoring my passes at her from the 7th grade on. I guess I would have had to date Sandra some before we could have been serious. Then Doug McGowen came in and knocked me out of the picture, and I loved them both.

HIGH SCHOOL HAS A DARK SIDE

I had begun to have conflicts within my own mind as I tried to sort all of these relationships, and the avalanche of activities. I think I tried to withdraw to a safe haven.

My problem was that I did not know how to do that without letting down my friends. I tried to keep all the balls juggling at the same time, and that was putting a lot of pressure on me. A darkness of conflict was beginning to tear at me. The results of my schoolwork were really beginning to wear on me, and the girlfriend thing was bothering me a lot more than it should have. That only added to my hidden misery.

The urge, and almost the necessity, to make things happen, and the pressure of all my responsibilities, were trapping me. I was depressed, and I was searching for relief. I didn't even know what depression was.

I knew of schizophrenia. My stepfather's brother, Stanley, had been institutionalized in Iowa for years, and I had overheard my parents talking about it. I began to wonder if I had that kind of problem, but I really didn't know what the problem was. The only thing I knew about psychology was what I had learned from the movie, "The Three Faces of Eve." Was that my problem? I never told anyone of this, especially my parents, because I thought everybody had their own problems, and I didn't want anyone to think I was having any difficulties or that I couldn't handle my own situation. I was scared of letting anyone know what I was going through.

I had no idea of what was going on in my mind. It stayed inside of me until I finally did away with some of the activities, or I matured enough to handle my responsibilities. It finally went away later in life.

Almost every Sunday night following Pioneers (the Presbyterian youth group) during our Junior and Senior year in high school the guys would go play pool at "The Spot Club", or to some place with pinball machines on Milam Street. I do not remember the name of that place. Thank goodness, we never got caught in a police raid at either of those places. We had heard that gambling went on in these places, and these were places good church-going kids would not want to be found. We all had cars, which made us agile and mobile.

During most of our high school years our church sponsored a basketball team in the YMCA sponsored Church League. We usually had a pretty good team. We added a few walk-ons and made up a full squad. We played, my brother Ronnie coached, and the girls hardly ever missed a game. There was fun and companionship. We all went out to eat after those games and the laughs kept coming.

My life was very involved - sports, school activities, church activities, dating, and the Classcutters band, eventually added to my life. I was beginning to pay way too much attention to the girls at the same time all the other things were happening. Seemed there were always events to attend, and I didn't want to be the only one there without a date.

I could never settle on just one girl. I dated Dana Long, Edith Seyburn, Jean Westbrook, Sarah Page McCranie, Betty Jean Carter, and Cathy Lowe. Sarah Page and I dated during those early days of high school, the 8th through the 9th grades; nothing dramatic, but there were lots of happy times.

I realized Betty Jean Carter, someone I had known since my early elementary school days, really didn't seem to care or be impressed with all of the stuff I had going on. She seemed proud of me, but did not act as impressed as some. She was more interested in just being friends, but she had a very soft manner that calmed me down. I definitely know she never realized the affect she had on me at the time, and probably not even today.

During my sophomore year, we had started a much more friendly relationship than we ever had before. I was, at least in my mind, falling for her. We talked a lot on the phone, and we had the occasion to be together some, but the school year ended too soon.

In the summer following our sophomore year, we continued to see each other and talk on the phone. I even caught her driving her dad's pickup truck by my house one day, and in my mind that meant she cared, because you didn't just drive into my neighborhood. There was only one way in and one way out. She was going with the Bossier High School Band to New York City, and that meant I wouldn't be able to see her, or even talk to her. My neighbor and friend, Bruce Humphrey, also a band member, knew how much I was seriously enamored with her. He was to keep an eye on her on this trip, and sent me post cards, giving me almost daily reports on her activities. Like the band usually did, they won the World Championship, and at last, they were triumphantly heading home.

A big welcome home celebration was held at the high school. A huge crowd, complete with dignitaries, was on hand to greet the band members. It was always a proud scene when the band came back to town, led by scores of police escorts. There had been several of these victory celebrations because this band was the best in the world. I was so excited by the fact that Bossier City had done it again.

I would be lying if I told you that was what made me so excited. Betty Jean was coming home! I greeted her with much more enthusiasm than she greeted me. She didn't know how much I missed her.

We finally got back to school for our junior year. Not long after the year started, the Classcutters Band came into existence, but Betty Jean was still the apple of my eye. We had some dates, and things seemed better with me, but the pressures of my junior year activities were only compounded by the emergence of the band. People seemed to expect more of me, I thought, and I loved the new attention that came from being in the band.

My old feelings began to creep back into my mind as my grades were plummeting. I always had an excuse not to study.

I loved the activities, but I was afraid of being a failure. I couldn't seem to help myself, and I hid my despair in basketball, and somewhat in the band. When I played basketball, I could totally concentrate on nothing but the game, the passing, dribbling, shooting; it was as if I could run away from my troubles. When the game or practice ended, the problems were still there.

During my junior year, I struggled through, appearing to be on top of the world. My smile was there, and my ability to please my friends, literally got me through that year. I don't think anyone noticed my fears. Towards the end of that year, things looked and seemed so good for me.

The outward me was moving at a fast pace, and I squeaked by in my classes. My friends, and my activities, probably kept me from having a real problem. I even contemplated some very horrible things, and at times, I wanted to just end it all. I had so much to live for, if only I could just make my grades. Here I was living two lives, the person everybody saw, laughed, and seemed to enjoy being with, and the withdrawn dark person that nobody ever saw. I can tell you when I was alone I was not thinking about anything but the dark side. I was miserable, and felt so much gloom.

It is really hard to understand that person as I write this. What could I possibly be missing in life? So many good things were happening for me. Why did I have this feeling? I had to make it work. I fought through all this, knowing that I could not fail in schoolwork, while being so successful at school. So many were expecting me to do well, and thought I was doing well. These pressures were self-imposed, because there was not one person that ever hindered my progress. Did I ever hurt outwardly? Probably. I hurt especially when some girl spurned me, or broke up with me. There were some of those disappointments, and I took them seriously. However, I ended the junior year on a high. Betty Jean Carter absolutely made me the proudest guy in school when she said she would go to the Junior-Senior Prom with me.

I remember the morning of that Prom, because it is one of those moments where everything finally went right. I met her in the front of the school, walked her to her locker, and then to her first period class. I don't think my feet ever touched the floor all the way down the hall. It did not matter one bit that she had her hair in rollers and covered with a scarf, and was embarrassed by that fact. She wasn't the only girl like that. The whole school was getting ready for the Prom.

My summer was filled with the usual baseball, swimming, and now music. Joe Averitt, Richard Berlitz and I spent a lot of time on Lake Bistineau completing the largest barge ever built on the lake. We burned up Mr. Averitt's boat motor and lost a propeller slowly towing the barge to its final resting place. It is probably still right where we parked it in 1959. That barge was too big to steal or move. It was the perfect launch place for fun and skiing.

My senior year finally arrived, and the Classcutters had become much better known and more regional. We were no longer just a Shreveport/Bossier City band. Everything was on more of a grand scale. I was Treasurer of the Senior Class, Student Council member, President of the Key Club. This was the year we were going to win the State Basketball Championship; I was in the Senior Play, and on the Tennis Team.

SENIOR YEAR 1960 - DRUM SPECTACULAR!

The whirlwind had really taken hold. My school grades were being neglected, and that feeling of pressure was always front and center on my mind. As well as things seemed to be going, not all was good.

The year began with me having a good feeling about Betty Jean, and she went with me to several functions. Probably the most memorable night is one that she could tell about more accurately than I can. I was having one of those dates, with me on the stage playing the drums, while Betty Jean was dancing with the guys.

When the band took our fifteen-minute breaks, I had her go in the kitchen to heat a pot of water so I could soak my hands. The drumming was causing my hands and arms to tighten up and cramp, and hot water was a relief. It was really nice just watching her taking care of me. She was so concerned; I was faking it just a little.

This is where things took a turn, never to be forgotten. I usually did a drum solo each night. Well, this night was going to be a "Drum Spectacular." Starting with some show-stopping rudiments that went from rhythmic to as fast as I could play, then with an extra drumstick sideways in my mouth in case I dropped or broke one, I got up from my drum set and worked my way out onto the Recreation Center dance floor. Keeping the rhythm going by tapping on chairs, the walls, the floor, and the jukebox, anything I could reach. Finally moved halfway to the back of the room, and turned and sprinted back toward the stage.

Let me pause to tell you what was supposed to happen, compared to what actually happened. The stage was up to my waist in height, and I had practiced all afternoon in rubber-soled shoes. I was to sprint at the correct speed toward the stage, and leap as if to fly up on the stage, land and slide on my stomach to the rear of the stage, right up to the front of my base drum.

Now my base drum had a blinking light inside,

and that was my target. I would slide to a stop just in time, and at the precise location, and while lying on my stomach, restart my drum solo on the front of the base drum. Spectacular - Right?

Seems like every friend I ever knew was there that night. I was going to put on a show they would never forget. It was one of those moments in time that everybody can say, "I was there, and I will never forget that." Now this was definitely one of the best showoff moments of my life.

Okay, it went as planned and practiced, except now the dance floor was full, and as I made my way to the center of the dance floor, people scattered to get out of my way. I remember up to this point the crowd was really into my antics.

Only a couple of things had changed from the afternoon. Number one, I now had on leather-soled shoes, and, number two, there was coca cola spilled at the exact spot I pushed off to make my leap onto the stage. I began my ascent up into the air, and everything went wrong from that moment. My foot slipped and I never made it off the ground, even though I had attained the correct foot speed. In an instant, my waist hit the front of the stage, belt high and my face went down squarely onto to the top of the stage floor, nose first. Or was it teeth first?

The crowd was still watching in excited anticipation, so I'm told. The next thing I remember, after bouncing straight up and standing there in a daze. I saw my base drum light blinking on, off as it floated up, and to my right out of my sight.

Somehow, I made it up to the stage, climbed on my drum seat, and started to finish my solo. My fellow band members stopped me, and all I remember them saying was, "Oh my God, you are bleeding!", as they came rushing over to help me.

The crowd gasped, and immediately lost their

enthusiasm for the climatic ending to my drum solo. Needless to say, that ended the dance while they stopped the bleeding, and removed the drumstick I was still clinching. If not for the drumstick between my teeth, I would have lost more than my two upper front teeth.

The worst part of the whole story is that while Betty Jean was feeling sorry for me, and she was the perfect nurse that night, but she didn't want to kiss a guy with teeth hanging out of his puffed up and bruised lips. As I said, as good as things seemed to be going, not all was well.

Not long after that excitement, during the fall of that year, our band was going to play for one of the dances after a high school football game at the same Bossier Recreation Center. We were setting up our instruments, and I was working on my drum set on the stage, and a couple of members of the Pep Squad were there decorating. I finished, and they needed some help, so I helped. Cathy Lowe was the girl asking for help. I had known Cathy for a long while, because her mother worked with my mother.

She never went to the game that night. She went home, got dressed for the dance, and came right back. We were going to go to the KoKoMo after the dance. I took her home that night, and we started seeing each other in earnest. She was cute, fun, and we had a great time. That would be a relationship that got more serious as time went by. She was my first steady girl friend. I really liked her friends, and things went smoothly for a while. We were off and on throughout my senior year.

We went to my Senior Prom together, and I was to read the senior will, which was several minutes long. I picked Cathy up at her house, told her we needed to hurry because I was part of the program. She threw a fit, saying, "You always have to do stuff like that." I was taken aback, and her mother got onto her about not supporting me, and told her she should be proud. That turned out to be a lovely evening.

I'll say one thing for Cathy. If she hadn't been friends with Madonna Bigelow, my life probably would not have turned out so special.

A major blow came just days after basketball practice started. Coach McConathy called me to his office and told me that I had been ruled ineligible to play high school basketball because I had played in a sanctioned basketball league. Someone had turned me in to the State High Athletic Association, because I had played in The YMCA Church league. I would not be able to play on the team that I had worked so hard for since the 5th grade, and had such high hopes for, after all. I knew we were going to win the State Championship because we decided we were going to do that by the time we got into the 7th grade.

That was devastating, and now I couldn't follow in my brother's footsteps. He had played in the State semi-finals in his senior year at BHS, and I was being denied one of my dreams of a lifetime. We did win the State Basketball Championship just as we had planned, but without me. In a very satisfying moment as my teammates handed me the championship trophy to carry off of the court that night.

My senior year was still a very special year in my life, even with my personal concerns. Being President of the Key Club was a real leadership challenge, and the Senior Play, as it turned out, became a major event for me.

The Student Council slipped several changes by the faculty sponsor Ms. Montgomery that weren't approved or sanctioned by her. While Ms. Montgomery was out of the room, we voted to move the annual Senior Sunday to the First Presbyterian Church from the First Baptist Church where it had always been held. You should have seen the look on her face when we told her.

The Classcutters really took off, and that provided long career opportunities for some of the band members. I was selected the "Best Citizen" of Bossier High School, and received the annual "School Service Award."

The annual He-Male Beauty Contest saw its last performance in the history of Bossier High School. Our homeroom, led by Sandra Grant, and a couple of others that shall remain nameless, dressed Bill McClung, one of our classmates and football players, as a Stripper, "Candy Bar McClung." The stage crew was in on it, and when Bill came gliding complete with jiggles down the winding staircase, the spotlight focused on him/her with stripper music. He was throwing clothes everywhere.

The applause was thunderous. The reaction by the students was wild, but the teachers, (one actually fainted), took a slightly different view. Mr. Rupert Madden, Assistant Principal, immediately bolted down the aisle, closed the curtains, and very sternly announced, "The show is over - go back to your homerooms." That was the last ever He-Male Beauty Contest, which had been an annual affair for years at the school.

Tommy Mitchell was a classmate and almost inseparable friend from the 1st grade. At one time or other we went to school, played on the same football, basketball, and baseball teams, went to the same church, even worked together at the Big Chain Grocery Store. We even tried smoking cigars together. I am glad that was a bad experience. Tommy, Hal Edwards, and I were in Doug Durham's Volkswagen bug. It was very cold that night, and we all lit up cigars in that tiny little car, at the same time. The windows were up and shut tight, and we came to a stop at a red light on Fern Avenue in Shreveport. We were right in front of the El Chico Restaurant. A car pulled up beside us, and I know there was no way to see what was going on in our car, because we couldn't even see out. We didn't know if the red glare on the front windshield was the car in front us, a red stop light, or a police car.

Somebody in the back seat got sick, which made all four of us sick. It wasn't easy getting out of the back seat of a Volkswagen Bug when things were normal. The doors flew open, and smoke billowed out in heavy waves, as we all piled out into the street. I am sure the car that had pulled up beside us, at first, thought our car was on fire until they saw our natural fire extinguishers spewing all over the street. Oh well, we never recognized them, and I guess they didn't recognize us because our parents never said anything about somebody calling them to report our smoking habits.

That was a Saturday night, and we all looked pretty pale when we got to Sunday school the next morning. We had to be there because Doug's mother taught our class. I am sure we failed to actively participate in that Sunday school lesson, but that wasn't unusual. That was for the girls and Joel Anderson.

David Montgomery and I were also friends from the 1st grade. David, Frank Campisi, Hays McGraw, and I were real close buddies. The only difference was David and I also went to church together. We played ball and did just about everything together.

My 1st grade teacher, Mrs. Whittington, was his aunt, and that made him special right off the bat. I remember David as a little boy like me. His laugh was memorable, and his constant twirling of his hair in the very front of his head permanently put a little twist right in the front. It's funny what a person remembers.

David had an excitement about him that made you want to get up and do something. I never knew what, but we had to do something! His mother was always volunteering as a room mother, and she and my mother became friends also. She was petite and so full of fun. Mr. and Mrs. Montgomery were another of my all-time parental favorites. I had the privilege of going to the

Presbyterian Church with the Montgomery family, and I always felt that I could call them family, too.

David's brother, Mark, was with us whenever we would let him. Mark is also a very close and dear friend. I survived riding in a car driven by either David or his cousin, Monty Rhodes. I never knew anyone that drove as they did and survived. Their term, "Cuz" still holds a special place in my heart today.

I am mentioning the Jaycee organization for the first time in this writing, and there is no place more appropriate than while I am remembering David. For now, I will let this be a cursory mention of the Jaycees, but I just couldn't think of the David, and not think of the Jaycees. He ran for Louisiana State Jaycee President. He didn't win because we got out politicked, and I vowed no Jaycee would be treated like that again, particularly if they came from Bossier City. I spent the next thirteen years making sure we never lost again, and the Baton Rogue Jaycees never won again. They didn't, either.

I would have never learned as much about politics, or had the desire for politics without David's run for the presidency. That put a fire in me that continues today. It was a lesson in losing elections, a lesson I did not like.

We ended the year with our Senior Party at Caney Lake. That is a day that will live in infamy. Susan Allen, our girl with the hourglass figure, and I mean spectacular figure, ask me to spread suntan lotion on her. Here was the opportunity of a lifetime. I don't know how long it took me to complete the job, but I used two and a half bottles of suntan lotion. She had so much suntan lotion on her body that when she jumped in the lake she kept sliding out of the water.

The final act of horseplay came at our graduation ceremony. Cecil Upshaw, our Class President, had to give a speech. Now public speaking for Cecil was not something he relished; in fact, he was scared to death. We helped him write his speech, and he nervously practiced right up until the time we started marching in for the ceremony. As we helped him get the papers together, we deliberately put the pages out of order. Poor Cecil, if you have ever seen a gangly 6'6" shy guy sweat bullets, stammer and stutter, only then would you know the horror of what we had done.

The adults said, "Buddy Roemer delivered the best graduation speech ever given at Bossier High School." Parents and faculty remembered his speech for years.

I passed my classes, and that made graduation a perfect ending to my Bossier school years. I was left with special friends, memories, and mind pictures that I travel back to by closing my eyes and thinking back to those special days of my life.

THE CLASSCUTTERS ROCK N' ROLL HISTORY

During my freshman and sophomore years the Hi-Y club, and sports, kept me busy. Hi-Y was a big thing at school, and I was beginning to find my way among the activities at school. The Key Club and Student Council always had events scheduled that kept us all busy.

When sports practice wasn't going on, I spent countless hours after school helping Pat Seabaugh, Judy Nichols, and other girls, paint signs for various games or activities. During my junior and senior years things began to blossom in my life.

My junior year I had Mr. Kenneth Green for homeroom period and that would become one of the most important class periods I would have in high school. The class was in the Band Hall, and Mr. Green was the Band Director for the world famous BHS band.

What did that mean to me? One of the practice rooms in that building had a full set of drums just waiting for me. Now, if only Mr. Green saw the burning desire that I felt, and would let me play on those drums, wouldn't that be the best of all worlds? I asked, and he said, "Sure, just don't damage them."

I had never used homeroom for what it was intended -- to study. But this year I used it for learning to play a set of drums, and it changed my life. No drum lessons, I just worked my way through my own different rudiments. Drumming came naturally for me, and I was fascinated with the sounds of the different drums, especially the floor tom-tom. I loved that deep bass sound.

That would have been 1958, and I had begun paying attention to music more and more. I really began to feel that I had some rhythm. I had tried to learn to dance before, and that was finally slowly coming around. The furniture at home was beginning to show signs of wear and tear from the constant beating with pencils to the music on the radio. One of my Christmas presents was a set of bongo drums, purchased to save the furniture.

A guy named Jerry Beach, a new student whose parents were military, moved to our school that same year, and he played the guitar. Somehow, we got together and decided we would play in the Junior Variety Show at the school.

I don't know how scared he was, but I could hardly breathe. Ms. Jaynes had not prepared me for this, and I didn't know if I was ready for this. There was no material to learn for this; it would be all feel and rhythm. I was about to get in front of the whole school - not to speak, but to play music. The question was - was I really ready? And was the other Jerry ready?

During that Junior Variety Show I took a step that changed my life. I daringly performed musically for the first time. Not trained in music, I had never played the drums publicly, and Jerry Beach had not played the guitar in public, either. We didn't tell anybody we were going to perform, in case we chickened-out. There I am, in the center of that stage, we were introduced, "Jerry Beach and Jerry Payne are going to play Duane Eddy's Ramrod," and their was no applause - only silence.

I know my friends thought, what in the world was I doing on that stage behind a set of drums? I could almost hear everybody in that audience thinking, yeah right, what is this.

Out in that audience, I was looking at everybody I had grown up with, and they were looking at me. I had never felt that kind of pressure! The stage darkened and the spotlight came on us - there was no stopping us now.

Amazingly, we actually ended the song at the same time. The crowd applauded, politely. But, my life was about to get real interesting.

The band (the two of us) started a driving beat with a slight wavering tremblo effect, a driving beat and sound that would become our trademark. We didn't need an echo chamber since the High School auditorium gave us the perfect echo sound chamber.

The crowd was stirred as this bluesy sound began. The audience was getting into our "sound." Then our singer, George Horton, after only one rehearsal, came ambling onto the stage, in his best roadhouse swagger, and we played a Chuck Berry song, "No Money Down", about an ole broken down, muffler popping, Ford.

He had his hat on backwards, and was in black face (a surprise to us). He grabbed the microphone, and put on a show as he sang this song about an old broken down Ford. You'd have thought he was a gospel singer with years of experience the way he wrestled with that microphone.

It was on that stage, that day that I learned to relish, and not fear, being in front of an audience. I loved the spotlight, and I won't lie, the adoration that came with that performance became habit forming. And as the "Rock and Roll" story goes - the crowd went wild that day, and for several years to follow!

Now this was 1958, and none of those kinds of theater antics would be possible today. The band didn't even have a name yet. The three of us were in a zone we had never experienced before. If you think this surprised us, how do you think my closest friends felt? They knew nothing about me being musically inclined either.

We liked this music stuff, and we added another student, guitar player, Jerry Horton. Jerry, Jerry, Jerry and George. It might have sounded confusing, and sometimes it was. Since I was in charge of the auditorium, and knew how to operate the stage equipment, and since we liked the natural echo sound in the auditorium, that is where we practiced.

Out in the hallway one of the teachers asked George what we were doing in there and he told him we were practicing. The teacher asked him, "What is the name of the band?" George said, "We don't have a name." The teacher said, "It sounds like you are cutting class." George, always quick on his feet, answered, "The Classcutters". George was the best in front of a crowd. I figured he could have been a perfect car salesman, and in fact, he did become one later on.

Now, my extracurricular activities really got in the way of studies. This band thing was getting serious. One of the first dances we played was at the Ra Lu Lane Roller Skating Rink on Benton Road, sponsored by KEEL radio. Mack Sanders, the hottest local disk jockey at the time, was the host.

We weren't even close to being ready for dances. We had only tried to play maybe twenty songs. In order to make him think we were good, we made sure our close friends (lots of them) were there, and screamed after each song. Thank God for friends. After a few songs our future manager, Mack Sanders, got the feeling we were a big hit with the crowd. I wonder why?

We worked hard at this music thing. Butch Toland, a lanky classmate from BHS, began hanging around and wanted to sing with us. Butch loved Jimmy Reed songs and he could play the part. Butch was a natural entertainer.

He danced as if he had no spine, which is probably where his nickname "Bones" came from, and which was perfect for working out front of the band with George. Jerry Beach and I had perfected Bo Diddley songs, and we would need a maraca player for those songs. Butch played maracas and danced. What a showman!

Bo Diddley had a distinct sound and beat, and Jerry Beach and I worked especially hard on those Diddley beats. As we played for a few more dances, we had to add to our song list. The songs of the day were not really hard to learn because they were really pretty simple. If you could play one Chuck Berry song, you could play nearly all of them. The same for Fats Domino, The Coasters, The Everly Brothers, Jerry Lee Lewis, Dale Hawkins, Ricky Nelson, Little Richard, Carl Perkins, Larry Williams, The Champs, Buddy Holly, and many others.

We eventually added another guitar player, also a graduate from BHS, Van Weaver. He was one year older than we were, and had been playing around town for three or four years. Between Jerry and Van, we had two really excellent lead guitar players.

It was fun to watch those two battle back and forth playing almost off of each other, but making us sound like real pros. Jerry Horton was probably the heart of rhythm section, and was a solid guitarist. George and Butch made us a show band with a real tight sound.

One of the most talented singers of the area, and a BHS student, was Norma Dee Murphy, a small girl with a powerful voice. She first sang with us during another event in the BHS auditorium. She amazed the crowd with her powerful and tonal, yet sweet voice as she sang, "In the Still of the Night". He backup singers included Loree Johnson, Cathy Lowe, and Madonna Bigelow.

Norma Dee Murphy went on to sing professionally for several years all over America. She later honed her artistic talents into Renaissance oil painting, and teaches art to this day. She is one of Bossier City's greatest talents.

The Classcutters were becoming the rage in the Ark-La-Tex. Mack Sanders of KEEL radio was making a fortune off of us. This was during the times of radio payola, and he got caught up in that scandal. He concocted the KEEL Sock Hops, and was advertising them constantly over KEEL radio. KEEL was the hottest radio station, in an area with one of the most colorful radio histories in the radio world.

The Sock Hops were usually held at the largest

venues available. We went anywhere he and we could draw a crowd. We were the headliner band for these Sock Hops.

Some of the largest events were held at skating rinks, and nearly all the smaller towns had a skating rink. Skating rinks were big enough to hold the big crowds these events drew, and inexpensive to rent.

At the height of these shows the two largest crowds I remember drawing were, unbelievably, in Plain Dealing and Vivian, Louisiana. More than once the crowds reached over 2,000 kids. I doubt there have been that many people in either town since. Plain Dealing only had 600 living in the whole town.

We played at VFW, American Legion, 40 & 8 clubs, high school dances, college dances, military bases, parties; we even played for a high school pancake supper.

In one day, we played for an 8 am rummage sale at Tuxedo Junction, (a black neighborhood), 1 pm at the Big Chain grocery store in Bossier City, and that night at the Officer's Club at Barksdale Air Force Base. Even though we were underage, we played at probably every nightclub on the Bossier Strip, and clubs all over Shreveport.

The Classcutters had become a real show band. The summer following our senior year, we played nearly every night, and sometimes twice a night. We went all over the place, and played with some of the Rock n' Roll greatest legends.

Our music became our second and most fluent language. It seemed we knew every note the others were playing, or going to play. We communicated with an understanding as if this music was written, scored and directed - which it was not. The greatest satisfaction came from the smiles of each band member during and at the end of the song. We had musically communicated what we felt, and as if, our heartbeats were perfectly in the same tempo.

Jerry Beach and I had a remarkable feel for what was about to be played by each other. We loved to try the unusual. "Caravan" was a song that intrigued us even though it wasn't a rock and roll song.

Jerry would lay his guitar flat while holding it up so I could tap the strings with my drumsticks. He would play the fret board and I would play the strumming area of the guitar with my sticks. It was a very strong version of "Caravan" that really pleased the older crowds. However, all ages of the crowds seemed to appreciate the amazing sound of that combination.

Nearly every night we ended up at The Amber Inn Restaurant. Either owners Buddy or Charlie Lombardino would be there whenever we arrived. The food was great home cooking, and you could get a half of fried chicken for a $1.50. The fried shrimp was the biggest and best I ever ate. My order was always the shrimp and lemon pie. Amber Inn was a staple of the restaurants in the local area. It was clean, but late at night it had its share of seedy characters.

One night we met a singer named Johnny C. (Sea), and he could sing just like the real Johnny Cash. His guitar player was Jerry Magee, and he was one of the two best guitar players I ever knew.

The other was Shreveport's James Burton. Burton played with Dale Hawkins, Ricky Nelson, Elvis Presley, and many others, but probably what made these guys great were the unique sounds that James Burton and Jerry Magee produced on their guitars. We played many gigs with these guys.

Now Johnny C. was a very unusual guy. He had a Model "A" Ford that he could choke down to sound just like the Johnny Cash sound, chick-a-boom, chick-a-boom. One night we were both playing a Sock Hop at the VFW in Arcadia, Louisiana, and they had played the set before us.

We played and took a break and went outside to visit with Johnny and Jerry. We went over to Jerry Magee, but didn't see Johnny; we were standing by the flagpole in the front of the building. All of a sudden, the chain that went up the pole started pounding violently against the pole. Johnny had climbed up the pole to the top. It was swaying so much we thought it would break. Johnny began to laugh and hoot and holler and I thought he had a nervous breakdown. That was just Johnny, and we just never knew what was next.

Later, while I was at Northwestern State College, I kept playing in bands. The Classcutters had kind of broken up because we all went in different directions.

One particular place we played on the weekends only was the very popular Danny's Lounge in Shreveport. We had played there for a few months, and Jerry Magee played with us. After many weeks, Jerry Magee told me he was going to have to quit because he was moving to Los Angeles to play with some guy named Bobby Darin.

After Jerry left us, we continued to play at Danny's Lounge. We had been leaving our instruments at the lounge during the week. All that ended one night when, fortunately, I had decided to take my drums home to do some maintenance on them.

My brother called early the next morning (he knew where we were playing) to tell me that Danny's Lounge had burned to the ground. The significance of that is my mother did not know I was playing in nightclubs. In fact, I don't believe she ever knew I had been playing nightclubs all over town, and was underage at the time. I know she would not have approved.

Jerry Magee, all by himself, was a colorful chapter in my life. He had played with The Ventures of "Walk Don't Run" fame, and was later featured on albums with Bobby Darrin, Rita Coolidge, blues great John Mayall, and many others. He became a studio musician in Los

Angeles giving him the opportunity to record with many famous artists. The Los Angeles recording studios were as prolific at producing recorded music as anywhere in the world. During the summer days of 1960, he spent most of his time at our house and we would piddle the time away, or we practiced together. He was a guitar player of so many genres, everything from Rock and Roll to Classical.

Jerry Magee loved the cooking at our house, especially mother's spaghetti and her red velvet cake. It has been years since I have seen Jerry, but I know to this day that he remembers my mother's red velvet cake.

The Classcutters didn't play together again for over forty years, until a very special occasion. We played a few songs at the wedding reception for Madonna and me. We still had the sound, and we still loved playing music together

COLLEGE - WE'VE GOT TO STUDY!

Before heading to college I was still playing baseball, the band was really busy, and I had some loose ends to tie up. My friends, Freddy and Raymond Shewmake, and I spent most of our days together talking or playing baseball as we had each summer. Those were our lazy days of summer, and we made the most of every minute.

Freddy Shewmake, Burgess McCranie, and I, coached a group of 13-14 year old local boys' baseball team. We entered them into the local American Legion League with an age limit of 18 years old. We were prepping them for the World VFW-Teener Tournament in Hershey, Pennsylvania. Mr. Almond's teams had been to Hershey the two previous years, and behind Cecil Upshaw's pitching, had won the World Championship Tournament.

We picked up the team, and won our way into the area tournament with teams from seven states. We went to Hershey the two years following Mr. Almond's teams. Freddy and Burgess were 19 years old and I was 18 years old when we went the first of the two years. The second year we lost in the finals of the World Tournament. Being World Runner-up wasn't so bad.

That same three month stretch of summer our band played every night but one. I broke up with Cathy for good, and looked forward to College.

My roommate was Frank Campisi, and our whole world changed. The very first night there was a knock on our South Hall dorm room door. It was Jimmy and Ronnie Smith, former classmates at Bossier. College was going to be different from the knock on that door and forward. They said, "Let's go get a beer." Frank said, "We can't, we've _got_ to study." That was probably the last time either one of us ever uttered those words again - at least with that much emphasis.

Oh, by the way, we did go get that beer.

Northwestern State College was an education, believe me. In the room next door was a guy named John F. Kennedy (not that one), down the hall was Butch Toland, from our band, and he roomed with Jack Eversull, other dorm residents included Gary Piper, Toby Cooper and a host of other memorable characters. Here we were with our heads shaved, and about 3,000 girls. Now you know why we went to this school and not Louisiana Tech. NSC had more girls than boys.

A lot of Bossier students went to Louisiana Tech, and they became our bitter rival. Everybody from my church group went to La. Tech, except me, and the fun began.

My studies were not as bad in college as I had done in high school. I didn't have all the distractions for one thing, and this new world focused me a little more. I actually liked being in class at college. I was on my own, and if I wanted to eat, get up on time, get my clothes cleaned, it was all on me. My memories of class go straight to my accounting classes. I think I had an 8 am accounting class every semester I was in college, and another one at 1 pm.

Natchitoches was a small college town, and the oldest settlement in the entire Louisiana Purchase. History was all around. The town is located on the Cain River that flows through town and the campus. The rolling hills and tree lined campus streets, offers a beauty not found on many college campuses anywhere. La. Tech on the other hand was full of pine trees and famous for a couple of peach trees, and not really that pretty.

The Northwestern State buildings were mostly old and architecturally unique. The various educational specialty buildings were scattered across the campus. That meant you better be in good physical shape because it was a challenge to get to your next class on time.

Sports were still a big part of my life, and now it was tennis. I played my way onto the NSC tennis team, and that meant practicing or playing matches nearly four hours every day. That went on all four years, and I was a four-year letterman at NSC.

The campus literally cleared out for the weekends. Mother's home cooking was never very far from my mind. I guess the same was true for all of us, away from home for the first time in our lives.

We left for home as fast as we could on the weekends, either Friday afternoon or Saturday morning, depending on class schedules. My car was always full - Patsy King, Susan Allen, Frank Campisi, Jim Coleman, and others.

The dreaded return trip had the same riders. Patsy reminded me of the night we were going back to the campus, and during the trip she discovered she had a button on her blouse come off. She put on a jacket to cover up so we promptly turned on the car heater full blast. She sat there and steamed.

College life was mixed with new friends, a lot of fun, mostly not so important stuff. Late one night Frank and I bet each other to a 100-yard challenge race on the track over in the football stadium. I never remember him ever beating me in a footrace, but this was a first class track, even with starting blocks.

We marched ourselves across the street to the stadium, and lined up to start the race. This argument had gotten loud and a few of our dorm buddies came to see this spectacle. It was around 10 pm, and dark. The spectators couldn't see any better than we could. I won the race, and as I remember, Frank ran full speed into a hurdle about 50 yards down the track. I beat him by at least 50 yards.

We had new friends, but our high school friends were still on our minds. Frank and I wrote to let them know what a great education we were both receiving, and the mistake they made by going to La. Tech, or in Buddy

Roemers's case, Harvard. These were classic literary writings, bound for somebody's archive somewhere.

Sometimes these letters contained visual aid items, like the time we included several dead bugs in a letter to Dana, Sandra, and Cookie. The letter was memorable because they opened the envelope at the La. Tech cafeteria in front of a whole group of their new friends.

We sometimes assisted Buddy with his studies by doing research for him, all the way from Natchitoches. Harvard had never seen such fluent prose. Buddy even posted some of our works on his dorm bulletin board. No telling how we may have influenced the future leaders of our nation.

My best memories of college, other than the people, was gathering at the student union building to pick up our mail, eating at the Town and Country Restaurant for hamburger steak, going to the A&W Root Beer stand after tennis, and Maggio's Liquor Store.

My music continued at college, thanks to Toby Cooper of Coushatta. Toby was an accomplished saxophone player, but really excelled at the clarinet. He also roomed in South Hall dormitory down the hall next to Butch Toland and Jack Eversull.

We had met before college when his band and our band were booked for the same dance on the same night. They played Dixieland and we combined the bands for the night with some Rockin' Dixieland music.

Toby was a protégé of Pete Fountain, and could play and sound just like him. I loved Pete Fountain music. He was also a member of the Demonaire Dance Band, a 22-piece big band sound. This orchestra was part of the college music program. All of the participants were on scholarship, and, more importantly, could all read music.

The band's drummer had graduated and they needed another drummer. Toby asked me to play with them. I loved big band music and played along with Glen Miller, Tommy Dorsey, and all the other famous big bands, but only with their record albums. I told Toby that I couldn't read music and had never played with an orchestra. That didn't deter him, and I joined the band and received a half music scholarship for the next four years.

Because I was on a music scholarship, I had to play with the concert band and the symphony orchestra. I faked reading music, and played by ear for the next four years.

The head of the Music department, Dr. Carlucci, announced during my senior year that all scholarship recipients had to join the marching band. Not only could I not read music, but also I had never marched in a band, either. I went to his office and announced I could not march with the band, and that I could not read music, either. He laughed and said, "I knew you couldn't read music, but I could play by ear as well as anyone he had known." I asked how he had figured it out, and he said, "One day in concert band we were playing a calypso-Latin song and the beat you were using wasn't the rhythm written for the song, but I liked what you were playing better."

Toby and I, and others, were messing around one night in a music building practice room with the windows open, and we tore into Dave Brubeck's song, "Take Five." It is a complicated, long jazz song, but was very popular. We had never attempted it before. When we finished a loud round of applause came from outside the building as a group of students had gathered to listen.

Toby was always getting us into different musical situations. He informed me we were playing for a Minstrel Show. Now that is a completely different style of music and should require practicing with the Interloper (Master of Ceremonies). We never practiced and it went off like a charm. We even recorded a couple of songs with

NSU student Jim Hawthorne, who later became the Voice of the LSU Tigers.

In June of 1964, I joined the U. S. Air Force and went to Lackland, AFB for basic training. Six local boys signed up and were inducted on the same day, including Ronnie Mercer, who became my good friend. Our AF serial numbers are only one digit apart.

Upon arrival for Basic Training, we were greeted pleasantly, and that would be the last pleasant greeting we would have for the next nine weeks. A tornado had just come through the San Antonio base the night before we arrived and the place was in shambles. We were processed in by flashlight, adding to the ambiance of horror we were experiencing. Basic training is as bad as you have heard, not so much physically, but mentally.

Our drill instructor was in our heads every minute of the day and night. We did push-ups in sticker patches, marched in 100 plus temperatures, pulled KP, and when we did get a break, I went to the canteen and ate four hamburgers (they weren't on our regular diet). It was an eye-opening experience, and all young men should have to go to military basic training.

A NEW WAY OF LIFE IN MANSFIELD

I met Cheryl Holt after our band had played for a Teen Town Revue at Barksdale Air Force Base. She came up on the stage after the show with a friend, and we went to a party at the Officers Club for the participants of the Revue. We dated for over a year before we got married in January 1965. Cherry was a 1963 graduate of Bossier High School.

In December 1964, I was hired by Central Louisiana Electric Company in Mansfield, Louisiana. We lived in a small house on 214 North St, in Mansfield. I made $1.70 per hour. My high school friend and college roommate, Jack Eversull, helped me get my job. He and his wife, Brenda, were the only people we knew in Mansfield.

Not being full-blooded Mansfield life-long residents, we quickly found out how cliquish that town could be. However, the employees at CLECO were a close knit and good group of cohorts.

Some of the younger people of Mansfield were acquaintances that had attended Northwestern State. They were not as above the peasants as were their parents. Mansfield, the site of a major battle in the Civil War, did not like change, and that war was still a big part of their life.

I became the Division Storekeeper for Central Louisiana Electric Company. I was the youngest to ever earn that title in the company. That entailed purchasing all of the equipment and electrical parts for distributing and transmitting electrical power for much of central Louisiana.

We also supplied the natural gas to the area, and had a gas production unit. The storeroom handled more than 250,000 separate items, and I was responsible for keeping those items in stock and accounting for it all. I appreciated the opportunity to work six years with some of the best people while at CLECO.

Jack and I had intended to change the world, but Mansfield's powers-to-be did not think change was necessary. Nothing was going to deter us from making this place and the world better. Mansfield, a small town had next to nothing to do in the way of social, or entertainment opportunities. Most weekends we headed to Bossier City to be with our families.

Because of my brother, I had been in the Jaycee organization in Bossier City, and the Mansfield Jaycee Chapter was one of the richest Jaycee groups in America. They sponsored sports car races at the Mansfield Airport during the 1950's and 60's., and were still racing there.

Thousands of sports car fans came from near and far to watch these races. Some of the world's greatest racecar drivers showed their racing skills in Mansfield, Louisiana. Drivers such as Dan Gurney, A.J. Foyt, Carroll Shelby, Jim Hall, Roger Penske, and Bossier City native, Harry Washburn. Washburn and his family were members of the Bossier City Presbyterian Church where our family were members. He won the 24-hour Sebring International race during that time period.

After joining the Mansfield Jaycees, I became very involved. In the beginning, the most important thing about the Mansfield Jaycees was the home cooked meals prepared by Mrs. Brown. That lady made some of the best home cooked meals I ever ate, and her rolls were worth fighting over. That was the only Jaycee Chapter I ever heard of that had nearly 100% attendance every week. We always had other Jaycee Chapters coming to visit; it was no doubt the food.

The more this young group of men began to try to make changes in Mansfield the more active we became. The senior fathers of the town would just have to relax; we wanted this to be a better place. I was elected President in 1969, and we pushed for a bond issue to improve the sewage and water systems of Mansfield.

One morning I went on the local radio station owned by one of the Jaycees. I was asked, "What is it going to take to get this bond issue passed?" I thought, and replied "four big funerals", meaning the four largest and most powerful families who were all against the bond issue would have to just go away.

By the time I got to my office (about 30 minutes after that statement) I passed by the Division Manager's office door, and he called my name to come in and close the door. The city patriarchs had already called and complained to him. John Clements, the boss, asked me, "Did you have to say it that way? I know you are right." I told him I could probably have worded that another way, but it was so frustrating trying to get anything done in this town, and that we needed these improvements. He smiled and said, "Go get'em!" For the first time in the history of Mansfield a bond issue passed.

Together, Jack Eversull, my friend and fellow worker, became involved in Louisiana Jaycee programs and took on the unimaginable. This little town Jaycee Chapter ran Jack for State President.

It is almost unheard of for a small chapter to win a statewide election against the larger city chapters. We traveled to nearly 120 Louisiana towns, bayous, and cities. We ate their crawfish, drank their beer, and talked as if we were Cajuns, or rednecks, whatever it took to win their votes. Jack was elected and then we spent our time going back to those same places for the next year.

We fed off of the excitement and humor of the young men all over Louisiana. It was amazing the accomplishments and improvements these young men from 21-36 years of age were making in communities all over Louisiana and the nation for that matter. That was one of the greatest experiences I have ever had.

The education I received from the people, places, and cultures of those Louisiana young men built another family of friends that has lasted to this day. I learned how to sell, convince, and plan. I learned about politics and dealing with all kinds of people.

That lesson in politics provided me with knowledge to eventually make a living in political campaigns. The friends I made opened many paths in my future. The stories are too many to tell here. That is a subject for another epistle. However, some of the things we did must be mentioned.

It all started at a State Convention in Monroe, Louisiana. My childhood friend, David Montgomery from Bossier City, was running for State President. We traveled all over the state with David helping him win votes. We traveled in a car and his opponent, Tommy James, of the powerful T.L. James contracting family, traveled via private airplane, which he piloted.

It was the classical little against big, poor against rich, small against large. David out-worked Tommy, but in a power play during the roll call vote Tommy cut a deal with the largest chapter in Louisiana, the Baton Rouge Jaycees, to help them host the next State Convention. David lost. We were devastated and angry with the Baton Rouge power brokers, but I had learned a lesson in power politics.

I pledged more to myself and to those in the car on the trip home that Baton Rouge would never host another State Convention. I really got involved, and after managing the successful election campaigns of 12 of the next 13 state Presidents, I made damn sure Baton Rouge never hosted another State Convention. To the day, I became an Exhausted Rooster (every Jaycee has to terminate his membership at the age of 36); the Baton Rouge Jaycees never hosted another state meeting of any kind, and lost three state presidential campaigns to my candidates.

BACK IN BOSSIER - LIFE SPEEDS UP

Soon after moving back to Bossier City along came a politician named Congressman Edwin Edwards, whose aide was a fellow named John Breaux. John and I had become friends while playing college tennis against each other, and John had become active in the Jaycees while Jack Eversull was state president.

We had moved back to Bossier City in 1971, in order to work with Buddy Roemer and the Roemer family at the newly formed Innovative Data Systems. We lived on the Scopena Plantation in one of the homes. Buddy and I were working together at the time, and were attending a Jaycee state meeting in Monroe.

The Louisiana Governor's race was just beginning, to take shape and John Breaux, also a Jaycee, had brought Candidate-in-waiting, Edwin Edwards, to the meeting to introduce him around. John wanted Buddy and me to meet Edwin, and we met in my motel room. It was the first time Buddy, or I, had met Edwin Edwards.

I didn't realize that would be a historic meeting, but my how things happen. We liked Edwin, and we enlisted in a huge group of Jaycees from all over the state to support him. The group was named "Louisiana Alliance for Good Government." Edwin Edwards became a four-term Governor, John Breaux a powerful U.S. Senator, and Buddy a Congressman. Buddy would then beat Edwin to become Governor of Louisiana.

In 1973, at the encouragement of the Louisiana Jaycees, Governor Edwin Edwards called for the writing of a new State Constitution, and called for elections around the state to elect delegates to the Convention. Buddy decided to seek election to this Constitutional Convention. This was a perfect place to begin his political career. He would have the ear of the media and the citizens of Louisiana.

Thus began his elective career in Louisiana politics, and our planning of a career in politics kicked off in earnest. He won, and quickly became a force at the Convention. His oratorical skills were immediately put on display. Buddy was now on the political stage. His ability to speak forcibly, and his very public disagreements with the Governor, became a big news story during this important time for Louisiana.

The state's constitution had been last re-written in 1920. It had become outdated and unwieldy due to the huge number of amendments added through the years. One year over 90 amendments were put before the voters at one election time. With the full support of the Louisiana Jaycees, the time was right to pass a new Constitution, and it did pass.

The Jaycees were consuming enormous amounts of our time, both locally and statewide. When we were not working on as many as 80 to 100 local projects a year we were also spending time with statewide projects.

The Bossier City Jaycees were determined to be a more productive chapter than Shreveport. That meant being in the news more and outgrowing them in membership size. Shreveport had always been one of the largest chapters in Louisiana. They generally had 200-250 members, so we grew to as large as 420, and we began calling the shots in nearly all of the Louisiana Jaycees' business dealings.

We had taken crap from Shreveport all of our lives and we decided we weren't going to take it anymore, so we began by starting another Jaycee chapter in Shreveport. Well, that split their britches. They called to complain to the State President, Skip Russell, who was, incidentally, one of my candidates. He just laughed at them.

The Bossier Jaycees decided to bid to host the State Convention in Bossier. Bossier City didn't even have a place large enough to host the 1,500 delegates - they thought. Besides, state meetings had been reserved only for large city chapters. We would simply rent a gigantic tent. The Friday night welcome party would be at Louisiana Downs new nationally acclaimed thoroughbred racetrack, never to be rented out for a private party again.

They just laughed at little Bossier City, but we out politicked them, and with Frenchy Villemarette, our resident coonass, delivering our bid presentation in French, we walked away with the bid.

With brilliant chairman and planners like: Ken Hill as convention chairman; Dan Roemer, food; Richard Davis, reservations; Mark Montgomery, parade; Ken Booth, publicity, Bossier hosted the 1976 Bi-Centennial State Jaycee convention, which was hailed as one of the most memorable events in Louisiana Jaycee history.

The largest and longest parade in Bossier City history lasted over 3 hours, and 140 units participated. Those Cajuns just thought they could drink beer. More than 80 kegs of beer were consumed, and a Bossier Jaycee wife won the beer-guzzling contest.

The 1976 Jaycee year was loaded with over 125 projects, and the most important may have been forcing a change in Bossier City's form of government.

The citizens followed our lead and voted to approve an elected City Council form of government, which has served Bossier City well, and continues into the 21st century.

The Bossier Jaycees had become a leader and gained considerable power in Louisiana Jaycee, and Bossier City municipal and parish politics. The early 1970's through 1976 set up the Bossier City Jaycees to continue a long line of powerful and successful accomplishments. Bossier welcomed the first black member into the Jaycees in Louisiana, and in all of America, Glendale Stroud.

As promised, I saw to it that neither Shreveport nor Baton Rouge elected anyone as State President or held another statewide meeting until I retired from the Jaycees.

Robert Adley became first State President from Bossier, and Bossier's Don Jones became the only Louisiana Jaycee to ever be elected as President of the United States Jaycees in 1981-82. On top of that, in that same 1981-82 year, under the leadership of Bossier City Jaycee President Mike Weber the Bossier Jaycees were selected the Top Jaycee Chapter in America. That was the only Louisiana chapter to ever earn that honor. In a banner Jaycee year the Louisiana Jaycees were the Number 1 state in the nation. Take that, all you arrogant big city Jaycee chapters!

I served as Mansfield Jaycee President 1969-70 and Bossier City Jaycee President during the bicentennial year, 1975-76. I was elected as Louisiana State Treasurer, Regional Vice-President, and served as a National Board of Directors of the United States Jaycees. I was honored as one of the Top Ten Jaycees of America 1973-74. I had attended National Conventions in Louisville, Kentucky, San Diego, California, St. Louis, Missouri, and Miami, Florida, and was honored as a Jaycee International Senator.

In 1978, while working at Innovative Data Systems, operating the Valley Voice newspaper, helping to direct Buddy Roemer's campaign for Congress, and taking 9 hours at the new Bossier Parish Community College, I received some appreciated good news.

I was named as Bossier City's, and Bossier Parish's Outstanding Young Man, and in early 1979 was selected as One of Louisiana's Three Outstanding Young Men.

SCOPENA PLANTATION AND THE BIG TABLE

The line was drawn in the sand, and the Constitutional Convention was only the first of many conflicts between Buddy Roemer and Edwin Edwards.

The only thing that kept those two in order was Buddy's father, Charles E. Roemer, II (Budgie). Mr. Roemer was the chief architect for the election of Edwin from the beginning. Because of Gov. Edward's trust in Budgie, he was named as the Commissioner of Administration. He was second only to the power of the Governor himself.

Things eventually became contentious, even between father and son. Buddy wanted to go his own way, and dad only wanted what was best for his son. There was never a loss of respect or love for each other, only two great minds, and with different opinions, clashing about how to make things happen for the state and personally.

Maybe I give myself more importance than I deserve, but I was right in the middle of keeping the lines of communication open between those two strong, opinionated, and sometimes hardheaded people.

Mr. Roemer once told me, "Jerry, you are part of this family if only by osmosis." I was honored to be among a family of more answers than there was, sometimes, questions. Never let it be said that this group of people could never come to a final decision, for when the chips were down there was enough firepower among that family to rival any family. When they agreed, and that was more often than not, they were a powerful force.

If a final controversial decision had to be made it was usually engineered by the family matriarch, Adeline. She could charm the bark off of a tree, and skin the toughest hardnosed man with her grace, her genteel manner, and the intellect of an encyclopedia.

Believe me, when she spoke we all listened. We were living on Scopena Plantation and living a modern plantation life, so to speak. Some cotton farming and cattle were still on the plantation, but computers were new to the farm and to the world. I moved to Scopena in 1971 to be part of Innovative Data System, a computer service company. So there we were in the middle of a way of life many thought was glamorous, but it was hard work - that's what it was! It was a vehicle for Buddy and me to work together as we had envisioned during our school days.

Computer services quickly became only a part of our interest. Politics was our real zeal. First, it was campaign management, then computer polling (one of the first pollsters in Louisiana), and from that we went into newspaper publishing because we didn't like the Shreveport Journal.

The Valley Voice newspaper was a great idea that we didn't know anything about. There was never a dull moment at Scopena. If all described above wasn't enough, there were the midnight phones calls from Randy Lefler, Margaret Roemer's husband, asking me to help him round up some cows that had gotten onto the highway, or put out a fire in a cotton combine in the middle of a cotton patch.

During all that, we also played hard. Tennis was the game of choice on the Scopena Tennis Courts. Everybody played, and it sometimes got very intense. These weren't beginner tennis players. What terrific memories on that court!

When I think of Scopena and those days, my vision of the past goes directly to my thoughts of the big dining table. At "The Big Table", you had to bring your "A" game. Nothing was off limits, and no one ever left his or her opinion unsaid. If you didn't have an opinion, you better make up one because you were expected to have one and express your feelings.

Mr. and Mrs. Roemer sat as the head of the table.

Always present were the well-educated Roemer siblings, Buddy, Danny, Margaret, Melanie, Melinda, and their respective spouses, Pattie Roemer, Judy Roemer, Randy Lefler, Charlton, Lyons and David Melville. The Big Table hosted some of Louisiana's most fascinating political figures: U.S. Senators, Allen Ellender and Bennett Johnston; U.S. Congressmen, Edwin Edwards, Jerry Huckaby, Speedy Long, and Buddy Roemer (yes him, too); and candidates for nearly every statewide office in Louisiana; and countless political wannabes.

Many political good fortunes were tampered with, if not stopped dead in its tracks, at that table. On the other hand, most of the candidates selected by the team of people hunkered around the Big Table were elected.

Saturdays were built around activities at The Big Table. The morning always started with an early meeting. We discussed the business challenges of the past week, and what the plans for the coming week would be. That was followed by the current events discussions, and each one's thoughts and opinions. These talks were thought provoking, at the very least. Usually, guests would arrive and join the group. Many Saturdays were taken up interviewing candidates about upcoming elections. These meetings were very argumentative, intense, and no questions were withheld.

We were the hottest campaigners in North Louisiana, and some said the state as a whole. Having our support was a big step toward getting elected. Joining the family were political notables such as Jim Leslie, Alphonse Jackson, Leon Tarver, Elloitt Stonecipher, Laurence Guidry, Ernie Roberson, and many others that would make their names in Louisiana political history.

As captivating as all that seemed, the highlight of the day was always the fried chicken dinner. Oh, Man! The Big Table was, after all, a dining table. Some of the kids, namely my son, Todd, and the Roemer boys, Franklin Roemer, Chas Roemer, Drew Lefler, Havard and Peter Lyons, learned that Josie or Idella would slip them a couple of pieces of chicken out the back door before dinner was served to the guests.

One of the more significant meetings at The Big Table took place without Buddy or me in attendance. On a Friday afternoon local Congressman Joe Waggonner, announced his retirement in The Shreveport Journal. We generally received the afternoon newspaper about 2 pm, and as surprising as the announcement was, I knew exactly what was about to happen. Margaret Lefler, Buddy's sister, brought me the paper and pointed out the news. I had until 5:30 pm to think about the development.

As soon as Buddy returned from town, he walked in and headed straight for me. My blood pressure must have spiked. I could feel the excitement! Buddy asks, "What do you think?" I never asked, "About what?" I never flinched, and told him I would meet him at 6 am to start calling people about the campaign. It never even entered our minds that perhaps we should consult the family first. We had been preparing for this day since high school.

I was in one office, and the door between us was open. I would call people and hold them on the phone until Buddy could take the next call. Family members walked by on the way to The Big Table Saturday morning meeting, but we were busy. Finally, Mr. Roemer came down to let us know they were waiting on us. Something they never did was wait on anybody. Without giving it a second thought, Buddy said, "We're running for Congress."

A few minutes later, Adeline presented herself, and in her sternest voice, suggested we come and talk to the family at the Big Table, but we were too busy. We didn't stop until late afternoon. When we finally did meet with the family this was the one time that neither Buddy, nor I, had a good answer. About all he would say is, "I'm going to run for this - it is time." With little eye contact, I mostly mumbled. The family let us know, in no uncertain terms, that this was about family, and, if Buddy wanted their support, he better ask for it. Buddy was a good talker, but he was put to the test that time.

    A few years later, while I was living in Amarillo, I received a phone call from Len Sanderson, Buddy's Congressional Administrative Assistant. He said, "Jerry, you need to talk to Buddy. He is going to run for Governor, and he wants to limit contributions to $10 a person." I immediately thought, hell if everyone in Louisiana gave him $10 it wouldn't be enough to run for Governor of Louisiana. The conversation that took place with Buddy was as contentious a one-hour conversation as we ever had. I reminded him that the original plan was for him to run for U.S. Congress, U.S. Senator, and then for President. I told him, "You are a philosopher, not a manager, and you will have to manage over 100,000 employees." I urged him not to run for Governor, but his heart was set on making a difference in Louisiana.

    The campaign started slowly, but caught fire when most of the large daily newspapers picked up on his "Slay the Dragon" slogan (meaning Edwards), and endorsed Buddy. I returned to Scopena as often as I could to help. It was a zoo, but the campaign was making headway.

    On election night, I was in Amarillo, and in constant telephone contact with Scopena, and just about everybody else, I knew in Louisiana. They knew I was still close to the situation and wanted to know what was happening.

    Around 1:00 a.m., the final returns showed Buddy came in a very respectable first and Edwards a more distant second. It was doubtful that Edwards could overcome Buddy in the general election; however, Edwards had never lost an election, and that weighed heavily on his decision to stay in the race, but not for long. My phone quit ringing about 1:30 am, and I finally went to bed an hour later. After a couple of deep breaths I relaxed, trying to go to sleep - dozing off just in time to receive a call from Randy Lefler, Buddy's brother-in-law, telling me that Edwards had withdrawn from the race, and Buddy Roemer was going to be Governor of Louisiana.

The speculation began immediately about the role that Budgie Roemer had played in the Edwards' withdrawal. The school of thought was that Budgie had enough on Edwards' activities to force him to withdraw. Two years later Budgie privately confided in me, saying, "I did not call Edwards to force him out of the race, but I didn't think I had to make THAT phone call." He smiled the way he always smiled when you knew, or somebody knew, they had been checkmated, and stated, "I did discuss with Edwin the difficulty he would have in beating Buddy in a runoff." That must have been enough said, or maybe Edwin saw Budgie smiling over the phone!

The stories that evolved around the Big Table would be important enough, fiery enough, and spellbinding enough to write a book of significant historical value. The title would appropriately be named, "The Big Table."

JIM LESLIE MURDERED

We had become consumed by the mystic of Louisiana politics. The allure and excitement of creating the twists and turns of each campaign was exhilarating. Campaigning was a 24 hour-a-day business, and each decision seemed more important than the last. Winning at politics made our eyes glaze, and that voodoo that you-do made this game entertaining and exuberant. As long as you are winning this was a fun game, but the losers took losing seriously.

The paths and challenges we took were at times monumental. While teaming up with political consultant, Jim Leslie, the big campaigns were constantly at our doorsteps. His team was the best we ever worked with - Joe Callicoatte, the media writer, and Dino Seder, the media producer, had prepared the most powerful ads Louisiana had ever seen, or would see for a long time.

During this period of time, we had handled 34 straight winning statewide campaigns in Louisiana, included in that string was the new Louisiana Right to Work Law. It was the most gut wrenching of all, in my opinion.

It pitted good government against the very large and powerful unions throughout the state. The television ads depicted strong-arm tactics and riots, even killings at shipyards and other union strongholds. The tensions ran about as high as possible, even in a bare-knuckle state with a political history as brazen as Louisiana.

Buddy Roemer, Jim Leslie, and I, stood in the back of the Louisiana Senate Chamber as the crucial final vote was being cast. In the front of the State Capital stood 10,000 plus angry union members. That was one of the eeriest and longest moments of my life. It was as if the clock stopped and the world quit breathing. The tension was incredible.

Once the votes started lighting up the huge voting board behind the President of the Senate's chair slow motion was the order of the day. In the silence, you could actually hear the voting buttons being switched either green or red. The lights seemed to light up one at a time, and it was like minutes before you could even hear a whimper of a sound in the Senate Chamber.

The Right to Work Law Bill had passed, and the low-rumbling sounds of voices in the gallery, and on the floor of that law-making body, began to shout even louder. At last, the people in that stately room started breathing again.

After handshakes and smiles, I turned to Buddy and Jim and announced I was going home right now! Jim suggested I stay for the victory party at the Camelot Club in the Baton Rouge Sheraton, but I had no interest in that. I left immediately out the back door of the State Capital building, escaping the demonstrators and headed straight for Shreveport via the airport.

Back in my bed at home, I was awakened the next morning by a phone call only a few hours after the vote. In fact, it was 4:30 am when my friend, and local KEEL Radio News Director, Ken Booth, said, "Jerry, I am calling to let you know that they killed Jim last night."

Politics in Louisiana had reached the bottom once again. Not since Huey P. Long had been assassinated inside the State Capital had an event of such proportion rocked and tainted Louisiana political history.

The murderer, and triggerman, hid behind a wooden fence at the Prince Muriat Motel in Baton Rouge where Jim Leslie had stayed during this intense campaign. The killer shot Jim Leslie in cold blood with a single magnum load 12-guage shotgun blast from twenty feet away.

Elliott Stonecipher, a close friend and one of our campaign team members, later wrote about his recollections of that horrible night. His statement summed up the thinking of the insiders on the Jim Leslie team, and those that knew of the corruption in local

Shreveport politics. Elliott wrote, "For those of us who knew the real story – the George D'Artois, the Shreveport corruption investigation story – the early conjecture about the killing being somehow related to the right-to-work campaign was foolish and frustrating."

This would become one of the most investigated crimes and 'who-done-its' in Louisiana criminal history. It was easy to immediately look at the Right to Work campaign, or the George D'Artois, Shreveport, Commissioner of Public Safety campaign, also handled by Jim Leslie, as the two likely suspects.

D'Artois had attempted to pay Leslie for his campaign services with public funds. Leslie had returned the first two checks with a warning that if D'Artois tried to pay him again with public funds he would go the local *Shreveport Times* newspaper. Leslie had previously worked for the paper. Still D'Artois handed Jim a sealed envelope at a party, and this would be the third and final time D'Artois tried to pay Jim with public funds.

Jim did as he had said, and the Saturday morning *Times* headline screamed the news of the attempted payoff, and the die was cast. Our world was now changed forever.

After the cold-blooded murder, investigators went in all directions, and left the public to wonder, 'which one?' Five separate men eventually filed sworn affidavits that D'Atrois had tried to hire them to kill Jim Leslie.

The eventual prime suspect, Rusty Griffith, was himself murdered near the Mississippi River during the investigation. D'Artois died suddenly of a heart attack after being arrested for the murder of Leslie, but before a trial could be held. What a disappointment.

Politics got more frightful and ugly all of a sudden. I now realized politics were rough, and not as innocent, as I had glamorized in my mind. My political world had been relatively mild since the memorable day

Mr. Hamner, our cleaning man, came by the house with his guileless and gentle approach. I remember how gentile he was that morning, and he impressed me by asking for my vote.

We had learned how to manipulate the voters and move them to vote for or against issues and candidates. However, these were real people with real families. We were affecting the lives of many families, and some of them had lots of money, and long memories. They would not hesitate to get their way. As somber and sobering as this had become, it did not deter us from doing what we thought was right, and continuing to make a difference.

Neither Buddy, nor I, or all of our Jaycee friends numbering in the thousands, ever forgot the Jaycee slogan that, "Young Men Can Change the World." We moved on, but with a much greater sense of responsibility learned.

BUDDY RUNS FOR CONGRESS

Congressman Joe Waggonner's resignation put Buddy Roemer front and center into politics. The time had come for Buddy to step up to the plate, but it wouldn't be for his favorite team, the New York Yankees. The fact that he ran for Congress was no surprise to almost anyone. He had been preparing for this day most of his life and those of us around him jumped into the fray with him.

Jimmy Wilson of Vivian, Buddy Leach of Leesville, Loy Weaver of Homer, Robert Briggs of Shreveport, and Mickey Prestridge of Bossier City, and three others were in the race with Buddy Roemer, also of Bossier City. Prestridge had been the attorney for Bossier City, and shared some of the same friends with the Roemer team. Without question, many of his 3,363 votes would have gone to Buddy, and vice versa. Buddy missed the 1978 runoff by 1,539 votes. We tried to be genteel with his supporters, because no one in our camp thought Mickey had a chance of getting into the runoff.

Our job was getting into the runoff, knowing that Wilson and Leach would be the real competitors. Everybody on Scopena got involved up to his or her ears. That place became a campaign factory, and the slogan, "One Man Can Make a Difference," became common to the whole Fourth Congressional District. We were doing everything from making signs, telephone banking, polling, and computer generated mailings, meetings, meetings and meetings.

Buddy had only recently married Patti, and she had no idea what was entailed in a campaign, especially one like a Roemer family campaign. To be fair to her, she had never been in anything like this campaign. She quickly got frustrated with Buddy being gone most of the day and into the night. Campaigning became a problem for her. After all, she was new to the family, and they didn't give her the patience she needed in trying to understand all of this. Patti wanted to help, but nobody had the time. Finally, Cherry befriended Patti, and they started going to businesses during the daytime hours and campaigning for Buddy. This was a big plus for the campaign to have the candidate's wife out publicly working hard. It didn't hurt that these two very attractive ladies went into stores, brake repair shops, welding shops, etc., and asked them to vote for Buddy. Now Patti felt like she was contributing.

One funny situation came out of Patti's involvement in the campaign. Not far from the Plantation, there was an oil-drilling rig. North Louisiana, being big in the oil business, we were filming a television ad about the oil business. Of course, it was necessary that Buddy and Patti both be in the ad. Everybody was there early in order to get cameras, et cetera, and set up. It was a hot day, so I brought Patti to the location after everything was ready to start filming. The scene required Buddy and Patti to walk toward the oilrig away from the camera. They both wore jeans, and almost immediately, someone realized that Patti's jeans were tight and her panty line was showing. Cut the filming - she went back to my car, took her panties off, and put her jeans back on. Problem solved. Well, not quite. A couple of weeks later, after all of that had been forgotten, I discovered she had left her panties under the seat of my car. How was I going to explain this to Cherry, or to Buddy, for that matter? So I walked into the office with the panties in my hand and dropped them on Patti's desk, and said, "I think these are yours."

This was far from a totally grassroots campaign. The Buddy Roemer 500 Club was the most workable political organization ever formed in Northwest Louisiana. It was made up of 500 volunteers that worked with zeal and foot power. Groups were subdivided into volunteer teams that challenged each other to grow its membership, and to provide workers that met the needs of the campaign. They organized to knock on doors, attend rallies, provide a show of support at speaking engagements; they made telephone calls, and were there to build excitement for the campaign.

The 500 Club provided much needed, and often missing, answers when campaign workers want to be involved, but so often there is nothing for them to do. There were mini convention-like meetings with the team with the largest attendance winning prizes. The teams sat by team groups, and the team leader would give reports on that teams' activities. Here were 500 members wearing campaign t-shirts, and lapel pins; there were young and old, men and women, fathers/mothers and sons/daughters. In all the campaigns, I have been a part of this organization exceeded by far the volunteer activities and efforts of any other campaign. Many members still have their lapel pins.

This race was going to be close because two candidates were from Bossier City, three from the northern part of the district, one from the southern part, and three minor candidates. Without going into all the details, the election was getting near, and the retiring Congressman had publicly stayed out of the race. Now we knew he was meddling with some of the Shreveport leaders, especially in the donation area, but we had done okay with raising money.

Ten days before the election, Buddy made an off-the-cuff remark about the Red River Navigation Project being a pork barrel project, and it got reported in the *Shreveport Times*. That set Joe Waggonner off, and he made some harsh remarks about Buddy. Waggonner was held in high regard throughout the district, and that hurt our chances. We dropped 10 points in the polls and went into crises mode. The campaign went into high gear, and it was a case of did we have enough time left to repair the damage.

On Election Day, we were doing all the things necessary. I received a phone call at the Scopena offices from Bob Munson, our guy in the Southern part of the district. He was calling from Leesville with an incredible story about money changing hands in an empty lot, under a huge tree. It seems cars were pulling up to the lot and the people arriving were being paid cash. He recognized the drivers as workers for the Leach campaign. We called the FBI and they went to investigate. Leach supporters were paying voters cash for their votes.

The election was tense, but the die was cast, and Buddy Roemer fell just short of getting into the runoff. Leach and Wilson eked out just enough votes to push Buddy to third. He had gone from first to third in ten days. Waggonner, it seemed, had worked his magic, but there was another factor, which caused a lot of hard feelings. With Mickey Prestridge in the race, and vying for some of the same Bossier/Shreveport voters, he probably took just enough votes away from us to keep us out of the runoff in spite of Joe Waggonner. Some of those feelings have never been repaired to this day.

A lot of our Bossier friends later said they had voted for Mickey because they were friends with Buddy and Mickey, and it looked like Buddy was a shoo-in to get into the runoff. I can't tell you how devastated we were.

Thirty-nine people were convicted of a vote-buying scheme, including some elected officials in Vernon Parish. However, Buddy Leach himself was not convicted. Even with that hanging over his head, but with the help of Joe Waggonner, Leach beat Jimmy Wilson in the runoff.

Following that Congressional election, we were charged with handling the campaign of Kelly Nix for Louisiana Commissioner of Education, against the incumbent Louis Michot. It was a huge challenge, and would be a major upset if Michot were defeated. When you are the head of education in Louisiana, you must deal with thousands of teachers, school workers, and school bus drivers, and yes, their families and friends. There were charges of hundreds of workers on the state education payroll that had never been to work, or even worse, not even alive. That campaign turned this state upside down. Thousands were angry, and the general public was outraged at what had been exposed in the state education department.

The television ads we ran made a laughing stock of incumbent, Louis Michot, also the hamburger king of Louisiana, known for his new fast, cheap, nothing-to-them hamburgers. His hamburgers were made like Yankee hamburgers, not the thick juicy, lettuce, tomato, pickles, onions, with mayonnaise and mustard. God forbid that you would put ketchup on a southern hamburger. To the tune of the Blue Danube waltz, Michot's hamburgers floated across the screen as the announcer shamed his ability to make a real hamburger. Now that was not much of an education issue until it was pointed out that if Michot couldn't even make a hamburger, how could he possibly run our state's education system. It was also pointed out that the top three floors of the State Education Building were full of cronies. Kelly Nix beat Louis Michot in a major upset. Team member, Elliott Stonecipher, had done a great job of investigating the Education Department, and played a huge role in the victory. We had done it again!

The Associated Press selected IDS to tabulate the statewide votes on the same election night of the Kelly Nix race. We were involved in other local races. As midnight drew near, it was decided that Cherry and I would make our appearances at the local victory parties. Buddy and Mr. Roemer would stay and finish up the last of the election returns.

We returned around 3 am; all was silent, and the dark night air was heavy and damp. I parked on the street in front of the house at the end of the sidewalk leading up to the house. As we started towards the front door, I heard a low voice calling my name. I looked around, but saw no one. I ask Cherry if she had heard somebody calling my name. She said she had heard it too. Exhausted, we started again toward the door. Then a louder voice called out, and I turned to look toward the main door of the office building across the dimly lit parking lot. I saw a man with a shotgun rounding the corner of the office. I strained for a better look. It was Buddy. Oh God, what was going on? I thought, "What have I done now?"

It never entered my mind that this was about how the victory parties had gone. He quickly told us that soon after we had left for town, three calls were received and in each call, they had threatened to kill us. He let us know that the State Police were all over the plantation grounds, and to let him know if we saw or heard anything. As we walked back toward the house I looked over behind the office and main house, and there must have been 25-30 State Police cars. Remember, Mr. Roemer was the Louisiana Commissioner of Administration, and this was a very serious situation. This all occurred after the murder of Jim Leslie.

Everybody at the plantation had police guards from that September night until the following January. I told you there was never a dull moment at Scopena.

WELL, HELLO! BIRMINGHAM, ALABAMA

Joe Harlow, a next-door neighbor as we grew up, had been calling me off and on for two years to encourage me to move to Birmingham and go to work with him in the bank data processing area. Shortly after that threatening incident at Scopena, I was called once again by Joe. This time I listened more intently, and they flew us over to Birmingham, wined, and dined us.

I thought I had had enough of politics, so in 1979 I accepted the job and left Scopena and the Roemer business. That was a tough decision as I only knew two people in Birmingham, and I knew nearly everybody in Bossier. I was leaving to get away from politics as I had given nine years to constant political campaigning. I was tired and dejected because of Buddy's loss, and the loss of Jim Leslie. No one disagreed with my decision.

We moved and I went to work with Joe Harlow at the Birmingham Trust National Bank as the Director of Marketing and Customer Service. Everything got off to a really good start, as Todd went to a better school system and settled in well. Marsha Harlow, Joe's wife, a real live wire and wonderful lady, helped Cherry stay busy, and she seemed to enjoy her new life. They had a son, Trey, who was Todd's age, and a younger daughter, DeeDe. We spent hours with them loving every minute.

But before I even got moved in; in fact, as we were having the movers place the television in the living room, I said we better make sure the TV works. We plugged it in and the first image that came onto the screen was a close-up of the only other person I knew in Birmingham. Frank Parsons was a Jaycee I had helped in his campaign for National Jaycee President, and a good friend. He was announcing his candidacy for Mayor of Birmingham. I looked at Cherry and told her not to let anyone know we are here! I was determined to be through with politics.

I never found out how he knew I was in town, but within two weeks, he found me and ask me to not just work on his campaign, but manage it. I really did not want to do that, what with a brand new job, but somehow Joe, the President of the Data Processing Company, found out about this and was excited that I had been asked. He called me into his office and wanted to clear the way for me to take this on. Never in a million years did I think the bank would okay something like this. Joe went to Wallace Malone, the owner of the bank, who thought it was a great idea.

Within two weeks of moving out of politics for good, I had moved right back into politics. I did not know one thing about Alabama politics, only what I had heard about Birmingham, i.e., Bull Conner, George Wallace, and bloody race rioting in Alabama.

On the first weekend after we moved to town we went riding around just to look to see what we had gotten ourselves into, and into downtown Birmingham. Well, Hello Birmingham! We were stopped at the main downtown intersection traffic light, and here came KKK members with hoods on and buckets in their hands. They were collecting for the KKK. Our eyes were big as saucers. I didn't give them anything, and I drove off as fast as I could.

All of a sudden, Louisiana didn't sound like such a tough political place. I took on the campaign and against all odds; we went from fifth out of five candidates into the runoff. Here we were a white Frank Parsons, and a black Richard Arrington, pitted against each other. Isn't that the way things happened in Birmingham? Birmingham had never had a black mayor. White flight had changed Birmingham and the city itself now had 55% black registered voters. Needless to say, this was a chance for a black rebellion, and they meant business.

Frank Parsons ended less than 1,000 votes behind Richard Arrington, and Arrington became the first black Mayor of Birmingham. He held that position for 20 years, and I think did a very good job.

Finally, I could get into my new job, and that was a terrific experience. My tutor was Ray Stivers, fondly called, "Mr. Alabama Banker." A most dapper man, always impeccably dressed with a kerchief and a fedora. He had a joke a day and was as nice a gentleman as I ever knew. He knew more about banking than anyone I had ever met, and he was willing to teach me. I was taking his place; it was going to be hard to replace the irreplaceable.

My new data center was on the leading edge of technology, being the first bank ever to install ATM machines; the first to ever transmit checks via the telephone and remotely process the data; and then print the reports via phone lines back into a Marianna, Florida, bank. Ray Stivers had been the mover behind that kind of thinking. They moved fast and into banking history.

We traveled together to nearly every bank in Alabama, Georgia, Northern Florida, and Mississippi, and he knew all of those bank presidents. The man was a wealth of information and always had an opinion so we got along just fine. He had been in banking so long he knew most of the founding fathers of most of the banks we would visit. After spending a little time with a new president of one the banks he had been in many times before he would come out and say, "Jerry, there are a lot more banks than there are bankers." Meaning, the young sons that had inherited the president's job could not match up to their fathers. It frustrated him to no end.

Electronic funds transfers between banks and banking accounts was a new phenomenon, and we were the first to accomplish this technology. My job was to promote the idea all over the south. Joe suggested I write a book on the 'whys and wherefores' of the operational management of electronic funds transfers.

The book entitled, <u>America's Electronic Funds Transfer System</u>, 1979, introduced the idea in terms that bankers could easily understand. It focused on how America's money system handled the movement of money and checks physically and electronically through its clearing houses, and the operational management centers of America's banks. The advantages for the banks and the bank customers far outweighed the old way of physically transferring a mountainous avalanche of paper items, specifically checks. Now it would be instantaneously, or as fast as 2,400-baud rate telecommunications would carry signals. That was the fastest electronic transmission rate available in the early 1980's. It is a snail's pace by 2013 standards. The book was 276 pages long, was written in longhand, and then typed, and printed. Personal Computers had not made a presence at that time.

I was also the driver behind a new in-the-bank data processing computer software system named the Indy (Independent) Banking System. This system included many new features highlighted by the latest idea in banking - Central Information Files (CIF). CIF allowed bank tellers, loan officers, and others, the ability to look at every type of account a customer had with a bank on one computer screen. For the first time the bank could see the whole snapshot of a customer's entire history – checking, certificate of deposits, savings, and loans. I was invited to speak on banking technology, and specifically this new system, all over the state. I spoke to the Alabama Bankers Convention, Alabama Credit Union Association, and was a guest speaker at several universities.

We developed a completely new Demand deposit Accounting System (Checking), and converted over 100 banks to the new system over a three-month period, never encountering any major problems. That may have been the best organizational effort in my life, along with a very competent team of employees. We had only 12 marketing and customer service representatives in the field, and a like number of people in the office, and they flawlessly handled each of the conversions in the banks without error.

The things I recall from my time in Alabama were

the deep-sea fishing trips in the Gulf of Mexico. Our data company made two or three fishing trips with our clients each summer. On one trip, we were fishing 300 feet deep, and I caught a 32 lb. red snapper. It took 30 minutes to finally get that fish in the boat. I was exhausted, and after drinking, a 7-up, without thinking, dropped my line back into the water. Quickly back to the bottom a 29 lb. red snapper hit. I had to have help getting him in the boat, and I was done for the day.

My cohort, Sammy Freeman, our comptroller, went with me to a Goodwill Store one day to look at old record albums. I had been a casual collector of albums through the years, and now I had Sammy hooked also. We spent many lunch hours and Saturdays searching for albums. My collection grew to about 2,500 albums while in Birmingham. Sammy's numbered at least that many.

The best times we had in Birmingham were at sporting events. We went to the Birmingham Barons baseball games at the historic Rickwood Field many times. We learned about ice hockey and loved to watch the Birmingham South-Stars, and became huge fans of the UAB Blazers.

Probably the highlight was watching the Blazers reach the NCAA Final Eight at Birmingham Jefferson Coliseum, losing on a very controversial call near the end of the game to the University of Louisville.

Back in Louisiana, Buddy Leach was finishing his first term in Congress. Buddy Roemer ran again and beat him handily. I had come back to Bossier to help Buddy with his campaign as often and as much as I could. My brother and I were at Buddy's house (just the three of us) watching the first returns come in on election night.

Buddy didn't want to be around anybody until he thought he knew how the race was going to turn out. The polls had Buddy comfortably ahead, but you never know. After the early hours of returns, we thought it safe to go to the victory party being held at the Student Union Building on the campus of LSU Shreveport. We drove over and entered the building triumphantly to an overflow cheering crowd. Congressman Buddy Roemer had taken a major political step.

The next morning we had breakfast on The Big Table at Scopena. What a glorious and proud feeling it was to have accomplished this! When I left, late in the morning, Buddy walked out with me and said I could go to Washington with him if I wanted. I thanked him, but said no, I didn't want to raise Todd in Washington, DC. We talked nearly every other week, and sometimes more often, for the first couple of years. I was so proud to have been a part of Buddy's success.

I continued to throw myself into my job for three more years. Birmingham and SouthTrust Data Systems all came to an end when Joe Harlow was offered the presidency of Western Data Systems in Amarillo, Texas. He told me to give him three months and he would bring me out to Amarillo as Director of Marketing. We had completed some outstanding things for Birmingham Trust, now named SouthTrust Bank, and he intended to do the same for Western Data. Once again, we did not want to leave Birmingham, especially to go to the desert and wide-open spaces. Cherry was working with the Vestavia Hills school system, and Todd was really entrenched in that school. Joe made me an offer I couldn't refuse, and we headed west.

AMARILLO WAS LIKE APPLYING THE BRAKES ON LIFE

Joe Harlow, my boss and lifelong friend, said, "The land is so flat in Amarillo that you could stand on a Coke case and see downtown Dallas." The West Texas skyline is painted with brilliant colors and hues not seen anywhere else. Amarillo only had one really tall building, and no mountains - just miles and miles of beautiful sky.

Culture, four seasons, very friendly laid back people, beautiful sunrises and sunsets, real Tex-Mex, Texas barbeque, all new twists and choices in the buffet of life. Moving to Amarillo was like applying the brakes on life. God had provided a complete change of scenery. All the trees, what trees there were, grew leaning towards the southeast because of the usual and not so gentle breezes.

The prairies were vast with rolling hills, some grassy, but mostly dusty and rocky, dotted with mesquite trees that hardly counted. The skies were huge with gentle to massive clouds of all shapes, the sun's rays sprayed across the earth. When lightning storms did happen, they were spellbinding. The night skies were brilliant with an unimaginable number of stars. Common were groves of trees, usually with a small still pond for watering the cattle. Barbed wire fences were all that stood between you and the horizon. In the distance, a sporadic windmill dotted the old west. Wide riverbeds were normally dried to an occasional trickle, or completely dry from the constant sun and wind.

The first night in Amarillo introduced us to the not-so-gentle breezes of West Texas. Seventy mile-per-hour winds nearly blew the roof off the house. Sand found its way into every tiny crevice, but as I looked over the neighborhood, the next morning all was well. Nobody even mentioned the high winds from the night before.

The weather was different from anywhere I had ever been. Amarillo gets a bad rap about its weather. Now don't get me wrong, it gets cold, and hot, but never for very long. The average snowfall is only 14 inches a year, and rain is rare. Nearly every day it would be 70 degrees at some time. Mom would call all concerned about the weather reports in Amarillo, and I would calmly tell her the news had been wrong again. Amazing how the TV reporters could make things seem so much worse than it was.

However, it is true the wind blew a lot - no, it blew a whole lot, and constantly. This was no place for outdoor badminton. Golf was played with another set of rules - the wind rules. Hitting lofty shots with the wind and you could end up in the next county. Once on a 460-yard, par four hole, hitting into a 50 mph wind, I hit a good driver, a solid 3 iron and a five iron, and was still short of the green. On the other hand, the next hole was with the wind, and I drove over the green. The wind was a great excuse for bad putts.

We really had four seasons of the year - spring, summer, fall and winter. Sometimes they all came in one day. One morning, as I set off for the office, I noticed a beautiful calm, clear, blue sky, with a temperature around the low 70's. However, during the mid-day a blue northern front came through town like a posse of outlaws. Being new to town, my co-workers called me to the office windows and told me what was about to happen.

A huge dark blue wall of clouds lined the northern sky, and the wall was moving like a monstrous solid wall of concrete. The winds blew, a sandstorm came with that, rains followed, and then sleet fell, followed by snow (brown snow). The temperature fell to the 20's, and almost as quickly as the winds blew it in, it was over, by 5 pm it was as if nothing had ever happened. It was back to the 70's and the skies were blue and clear.

That evening we had a beautiful, fiery West Texas sunset. God can do anything, anytime. If I had not seen it with my own eyes, I would not have believed it.

Another morning I woke up, opened the front

door to get the paper, but it was still dark. The glass storm door was covered with snow all the way to within six inches from the top. I looked out the back door and realized it had snowed all night. I walked around the back yard through the empty lot toward the street in front of the house. Snow had drifted from the street to the very top of the house. My house was completely buried. I could not find the street curb, a newspaper, or my mailbox.

I called Kit, my neighbor next door, and asked if he got his paper that morning. He said, "I don't know, I'll go look." I thought to myself, "Kit, wait you see this," I could hear him over the phone as he opened his front door and the same thing had happened to his house. "Holy----!" I heard him scream. Everything was closed for that day except the Safeway grocery store near our house. After taking orders from all the neighbors, we went to the store and we were the only customers. We bought over three buggies worth of junk, chili makings, spaghetti, popcorn, et cetera. All huddled together and laughing we built a fire, cooked, and all ate for a week on all that stuff.

There was a peach tree in the back yard that yielded three bushels one summer. The neighbors loved that tree. Our yard had the most beautiful green grass of any house I ever had. Because we were on the far western side of the time zone daylight lasted until 10 pm, making leisure time longer, and time to socialize with our wonderful neighbors. It was not uncommon to holler over the backyard fence, "We got the vegetables, and some dessert," and to get a return holler, "We've got some pork chops." With that, someone would fire up the grill and before you knew it, we had a neighborhood feast. A little wine - no, a lot of wine, spectacular sunsets, a hearty meal, and that 70-degree temperature would all converge at the same time.

Occasionally our neighbor, Sharla, would call over and say they had the blues. That was code for 'it's time for sipping some blueberry schnapps." Kit and Sharla Jackson, and Jim and Melissa Boiles, our neighbors, spent many hours contemplating. Only the Lord knows, or remembers, all we contemplated. We golfed, or we skied, we drank wine or schnapps, or ate at the drop of a hat. It was only a four hour drive to the New Mexico ski slopes, and it only took a, "Why don't we go skiing in the morning?", and off we went, often with no sleep.

Jim and Melissa had a pre-school aged son, John, who loved to sneak off and come down to our house. John was barely able to climb up on the bench at our front door and ring the doorbell. We would call Melissa to let her know where he was, as if she didn't know, and we would enjoy having a little one around the house. John and I sat on the couch eating Fritos, and talking for hours. Those neighbors were one of life's great priceless treasures.

We had become members of The Polk Street United Methodist Church. This was the very first church of any denomination in the entire Panhandle of Texas. It had 4,500 members, many activities, and one of the best Sunday school classes. The Aldersgate Class was so supportive and loving, and seemed to be part of our family. The church is a model of Methodist Church architecture; it has a 6,000 pipe organ, and a 4-story educational building.

In my third year of membership, I was named Chairman of the Finance Committee. I was told we had to meet the annual budget of $1,000,000, plus another $1,000,000 for educational improvements. The Finance Executive Committee consisted of Tol Ware, the owner of the largest family-owned bank in America, The Amarillo National Bank; T. Boone Pickens, the oil and gas magnet; John Evans, President of the Independent Oil Producers of America, and me. I was scared to death, but I found them all to be genuine and easy to work with. What an experience that was, and we easily made our budgets.

Ira Williams, Jr., was our Pastor, and he made a powerful impact on our spiritual lives. No doubt, he was one of the greatest most spellbinding storytellers I ever heard. He still does to this very day continue to be an important part of our relationship with God. Ira and I became very close, and we continue to stay in touch. Todd has certainly grown in the footsteps of the Lord as a result of being a part of that church.

Ira, as an annual practice, wrote short Christmas stories for his children as Christmas gifts. Those published stories reflected his experiences with the different cultures where he had ministered. They included Native America, China, New Orleans, the old West, Indian villages, Santa Fe, even a story written for the 100th Anniversary of the Polk Street Church. That story was based on the original chapel constructed by Polk Street, a chapel that still exists to this day.

I took the liberty of reading one of his stories at Christmas time to the Midyett Class at the First United Methodist Church of Bossier City. I have now read his stories nearly every year for twenty years. It has become a Christmas tradition for the Midyett Class.

Amarillo is a town rich with, well riches; I mean money, culture and characters. Sybil Harrington, survivor wife of a West Texas oilman, became the largest single donor ever to the New York Metropolitan Opera. Stanley Marsh 3 (not III), an eccentric owner of the largest helium reserve in the world planted the Cadillac Ranch along I-40. "Amarillo Slim" Preston, of Amarillo, had won the World Series of Poker at Jack Binion's Horseshoe Casino. T. Boone Pickens, famous for his corporate raiding and oil and gas fortunes, was a member of our church. I was completely taken aback by the Amarillo Symphony, and the music, theatre, and poetry programs in the city, and especially in the Middle schools and High schools.

Near the end of Todd's first school year there, he

implored us to go the Amarillo High School Graduation ceremony. Not one of my favorite rites of passage unless somebody very close is participating. The ceremony was held in the Amarillo Coliseum with a capacity of 8,000. Remember, we are in the West, sometimes referred to as the Wild West. As usual, people were dressed in all kinds of garb, but the difference I noticed was – a lot of cowboy hats and boots. This completely new setting for me produced the most amazing cultural event I had ever witnessed. This would be a most memorable graduation.

The reason Todd wanted us there was the high school symphony orchestra played Beethoven's Fifth Symphony as a part of the ceremony. He had instructed us to sit at the end opposite of the stage. There was hoopin' and a hollerin', but when the high school symphony started playing that audience settled into complete silence.

The quality of music was superb, then in astonishment, at the appointed time, the music score called for the cannons to be shot, and the coliseum turned into an explosion of sound. Policemen were positioned back in the rear of the team entrance tunnels, out of sight from the unsuspecting listeners. With shotguns, they fired into large barrels and using blank shells, they sounded like howitzers.

Around the top of the coliseum was a walking track hardly noticed by the audience. At the crescendo, as the cannons exploded, another 150 trumpets, trombones, and brass of all kinds stepped to the front of the walkway at the top of the coliseum, and created a moment of sound I shall never forget. I immediately knew this place was culturally above anything I had experienced before.

Even more incredible was the reaction of the cowboys, and even the students, as the whole crowd rose applauding, recognizing this for what it was. It was the cultural side of West Texas appreciating more than dust, cows, and barbed wire. It's not right or fair Amarillo is considered a cow town, because it deserves much more than the credit than America gives it.

Joe Harlow and I continued to transform the data processing products for banks. Western Data Systems was the largest data center in West Texas. Our customers were in Kansas, Oklahoma, New Mexico and the vast area of the Panhandle of Texas. Among the latest services came Asset Based Lending, Personal Computers in Banking, and all the programs and services they provided in banking. Our facilities were first class, and owned by The First National Bank of Amarillo, the first bank in the Panhandle of Texas.

While serving on the IBM Personal Computer Advisory Board, I made trips to Boca Raton, Florida, to plan and implement how the personal computer could be best utilized in business, education and homes. To my dissatisfaction, I could never get the IBM powers to be to focus on what I thought would move these computers into the mainstream of American homes or schools. They were still stuck in the business-mostly mode. They didn't have the flexibility of programs or pricing to meet the needs of small businesses. They were still mired in old marketing models for larger computer systems. Personal Computers were not powerful enough at that time to accomplish their ideals for business. They never thought Personal Computers would amount to much in the computer world.

Eventually, they came up with the PC Junior, a home friendly idea, but not supported with home or educational software applications. After several contentious meetings with the IBM, I gave up. During that time period, the top three PC thinkers from IBM were all killed in a plane crash.

They never got it, and never moved on from the larger mainframe sales strategy. IBM was doomed from the beginning, and never had success with Personal Computers. The Compaq's, Hewlett Packard's, Apple's, and MacIntosh's, blew them out of the Personal Computer world.

We conceived a Western Data Users Conference, inviting nearly every area bank president customer or not. First National Bank had just completed building a powerful audio/visual theatre, and we presented speakers and visual programs to educate the bank presidents about what the banking world was implementing all over the America. The featured speaker was Congressman Buddy Roemer of Louisiana, now on the congressional banking committee. The attendance was enormous, and as expected, Buddy blew the crowd away and made national news with his comments about the Comptroller of the Currency.

Buddy could have been elected to Congress in West Texas. The West Texas bankers loved him and he was still being quoted in the local television stations weeks after he left town. I never had a problem getting in the door any banker's office after Buddy came to town.

First National Bank was in need of some capital to cover a lot of their losses, and Western Data was the best candidate for sale. They sold the data company to Systematic Systems, a Little Rock company. I had to lay off my entire marketing staff in one day. Some had been with the company since its inception.

One of my staff members, Jerry Irwin, and I met with Electronic Data Systems and convinced them we could win contracts with Western Data's customers by out-maneuvering Systematics. We signed every customer bank to a contract, leaving Systematics with only The First National Bank. Jerry and Karen Irwin were two of the finest people I have ever known. What fun to work, and be with them. Jerry and I drank way more coffee than we should, and also solved many of the world's problems in our office. We were a very good team.

I was being encouraged to go to Louisiana to open

a data center in the only state EDS did not have a single customer. I resisted as long as I could.

The banking business was having problems all over America, but especially in Texas. Banks all over the Panhandle were failing. Since we did the data processing for most of the banks, we had the banking records. When a bank was in trouble we knew first, from the reports the FDIC was asking for, which banks were about to fail. We couldn't say anything to anyone about what we knew or when we knew it. It was a dismal time, and some of our good customer friends were devastated.

EDS was encouraging me to move to Louisiana to get a data center opened. Mr. Ross Perot knew I was a friend of the new Governor, Buddy Roemer, and Louisiana was the only state that EDS had no clients. I was going to give it a chance, but from Amarillo.

Mr. Perot always wanted to know all the personal details of potential clients, including their dog's name, if they had one. He asked me what I thought about opening a Louisiana data center. I surprised him by informing him that I knew that EDS once had a client in Bossier City, and that The Bossier Bank and Trust had literally run EDS out of town because of horrible service. I asked him if he remembered Mr. Bubba Gandy from that bank. Surprised, he smiled and said, "You have done your homework."

Bubba Gandy, a colorful character, to say the least, was an old family friend, and the comptroller at the Bossier Bank. He knew the kind of banking work I was in, and he unloaded on Ross Perot's company at Cobb's Barbeque one day. I was on vacation and was in Shreveport/Bossier, and I never forgot the story Bubba told me. Ross Perot never forgot that story either, as this was the only bank EDS was ever asked to leave.

Traveling between Amarillo and Shreveport became a weekly thing calling on potential Louisiana clients. Todd, a student at Texas Tech in Lubbock, was only 120 miles away from us. Leaving Amarillo would mean he would be out there by himself.

I was considering an offer from Governor Roemer to come to Baton Rouge to be his Chief of Staff. We had talked at length about the move. Things were not going well for him, and in my opinion and others, including the Roemer family, his staff was the crux of the problem.

I had informed Governor Roemer I was in a time crunch, and if EDS moved me to Louisiana, I would not forsake EDS. Time went on as Buddy studied his options. Two weeks after EDS moved us to Shreveport, Buddy's mom; Mrs. Roemer called and said that Buddy was ready to make the move. I declined their offer, and had nearly finished the contract negotiations with Bo Campbell at Pioneer Bank and Trust in Shreveport.

After a year and a half of flying back and forth from Amarillo to Shreveport, the Pioneer Bank and Trust signed an agreement with EDS for data processing, and we opened a data center in one of their buildings. We really liked Amarillo, and we struggled with the decision, but we finally gave in and moved to Shreveport.

Working with EDS had great benefits, and the most intense sales training course I have ever attended. Dress codes were strictly enforced, including wing tip shoes, dark suits with white shirt and ties. I was honored for professional achievements with the EDS Pinnacle Award. This is presented to only five employees from the over 110,000 worldwide total workforce.

All went well, and I signed more and more Louisiana banks to data processing contracts. EDS then sold out to General Motors, but all the data operations continued as EDS. Mr. Perot received 2.6 billion dollars, and also was awarded GM stock, and was given a slot on the General Motors Board of Directors. That was a clash of cultures, the practical versus the lavishly impractical.

The Ross Perot and GM romance lasted only two

years. GM bought out Perot's GM stock for another 2.1 billion dollars, just to get the prickly Perot off of the Board.

    This was my chance to get out of corporate politics and to finally do what I really wanted to do in life - politics. Besides, real politics wasn't as cutthroat.

FORTY YEARS TOGETHER
TODD,
THE JOY OF OUR LIFE

Cherry's family were good Christians. Her dad, Truman Holt, had worked in the service station business for years, and was a good-natured man with a happy disposition.

Beulah, her mother, had been a schoolteacher and eventually retired after 42 years of teaching. Most of those years were in the very same classroom at Plantation Park Elementary in Bossier City. They were pillars of the Waller Baptist Church of Bossier.

Sandra (Sandy), her sister, was one year younger than Cherry. She also became a teacher, and a fun person. She tragically died at the hands of her second husband, Bob Manning, who in turn committed suicide. It was an unexplained act of violence. The murder/suicide still puzzles us to this day.

Sandy had a daughter, Kristy. Kristy was spared the trauma of the event, but not the trauma of losing her mother. I'm sure this was a major reason for her decisions and actions later on in her life. Ironically, Kristy's father was named Sandy Sanders, a Bossier High School graduate. Sandy and Sandy had divorced some years before this tragedy, and he had moved to Florida. He has not been heard from in years.

We moved three times during our marriage, all to change jobs. Each move was particularly hard for all of us, except when we left Mansfield. Neither of us liked Mansfield. The moves from Bossier City, Birmingham, and finally Amarillo, were all like the end of the world. We had made so many friends in all of those places.

Moving back to Bossier City from Amarillo was a move we dreaded and fought for a long time. We loved our families, but we loved our freedom to live our lives without getting involved in Kristy's problems.

Kristy had two children and failed to take any responsibility raising those children. James was the first, and Michelle followed soon thereafter. Both were very special children with real talents and good attitudes. Beulah and Truman raised them both with hardly any interaction from Kristy. I never understood why she shirked her children, and she will never know what she gave up and missed out on.

James eventually went to live with his father, Tully, and we kind of lost track of them. James still occasionally talks with Beulah and Michelle, mostly at Christmas.

Michelle has grown into a very industrious, wonderful Christian young lady. She has worked her way through nursing school and made extremely good grades. She has so much to be proud of, and I believe she has found the man for her, Cody Mollenkamp. Cody is very attentive to Michelle and they enjoy their life together. They married in March of 2013, and are looking forward to a long happy life.

On October 5, 1968, God blessed Cherry and me with a son, Stephen Todd. Todd has always been the life of our family, and the center of our lives. I have always been in awe of my son, and he has never let me down. I couldn't have asked for a better buddy, or teammate. He was always a good student, and he seemed to enjoy studying. He became an avid reader, and grades were never a problem for him. Sports have always been a major part of his life.

He and I played, and played. As time went on, he became knowledgeable and proficient in nearly all sports. We taught his mother about sports, something she had to acquire, because she had no interest in sports at all. But when Todd started playing and watching sports on TV, she did too, and became a true sports mom. Cherry became an avid Dallas Cowboy fan and loved the Chicago Cubs. You have to be a real fan to be a die-hard Cubs fan, but we all were die-hard Cubbies.

Todd started playing little league baseball and

football early on, and was really quite good. In baseball, he always had a strong throwing arm and could hit the ball a mile. Since I coached him in football, he was given the toughest job. He was the only kid on the team that could long snap to the punter. I know he hated that.

In baseball, he was the catcher and handled that with the skill of a much older player. He won his share of championships. I have a lot of memories of his games, and I think he was happiest when he was playing ball.

Perhaps the most fun we had playing ball was in Amarillo, playing softball together on the same team. Memories of those games are still fresh in my mind.

Once, while Ronnie and Mary were visiting us in Amarillo, we were supposed to play a game, but the other team didn't have enough players show up. So we split up the players from both teams that did show up, and Todd and I ended up on opposing teams. In my at-bat, I hit a huge fly ball to deep left centerfield, right to the top of the fence. Todd was playing centerfield and he must have run thirty yards and made a spectacular catch. The ball was in the air long enough for me to get almost to second base before he made the catch. I will never forget my brother screaming and cheering for Todd's unbelievable catch. I was too!

Another night we were playing and Todd was playing third base. He fielded a ground ball and had to hurry his throw. When he had to, he had cannon for an arm. He let it fly and it sailed slightly to the right of the first base and hit the runner squarely in the back of the head. I have never been as scared in my life as the guy landed face down and was lifeless for several moments.

We moved from Birmingham to Amarillo in the middle of Todd's sophomore year in high school, he became very active in several things, especially band.

We were very worried about moving him from the Vestavia Hills High School in Birmingham, but he survived the move better than we did. The band was a big reason.

He was immediately accepted into the Amarillo High School and became a big part of that storied band. He was selected as the top brass player in his senior year. The band director, Jimmy Edwards, gets credit for leading Todd into Band Directing, and introduced him to the Texas Tech University Marching Band.

Todd became a leader in the Tech band, and put his heart and soul into all of the band activities. Keith Bearden, the fabled director of the Texas Tech band, gets a lot of credit for Todd's successes. He took Todd under his wing and made sure he took the right steps in his career. Todd became a Graduate Assistant at Texas Tech. Among his many activities, I was most proud of was his directing the Tech Band halftime show at the Sun Bowl one year, and the Cotton Bowl the next year.

He also made most of the arrangements for Texas Tech band when they traveled to Dublin, Ireland, to march in the St. Patrick's Day Parade. Todd loved Ireland and England.

His music career has taken him to Texas schools in Amarillo, Brownwood, Garland, Lubbock, and he has settled into the Garland School District with the North Garland High School band program.

Todd owes only his own perseverance and hard work for the successful life he is living, the home he owns, and the Christian values he is so willing to share. No father could be any prouder than I am of Todd.

We tried to travel as much as we could. I always thought traveling with my parents was an enriching activity, and I wanted Todd to have the same experience of learning from the rest of the country. We went all over - to the Rocky Mountains; the West coast, California; the East coast, Boston; to the Central United States, Kansas, Missouri; Florida; Illinois; Chicago. We marveled, looked and learned together.

Todd and I took a baseball trip over a two-week period all the way to Cooperstown, NY, to Yankee Stadium, and ate our way through the East coast. On another trip, we went in search of the best barbeque in Texas, and ate our way through Texas. Those trips left us with some wonderful memories and an appetite for more of America's best food. I hope more travel trips are in our future.

Cherry was a good wife and mother. She was always supportive in whatever Todd or I wanted. A mother could not love a son more than Cherry loved Todd. Cherry rarely missed Todd's participation in any school, athletic, or music event. She was amazingly tolerant when Todd practiced his trumpet. She was, however, thankful that he didn't follow in his father's footsteps and play the drums. She always welcomed and encouraged Todd's friends, and made them feel at home.

Much to the scorn of Todd and me, she became a huge Dallas Cowboy fan, so much so that Thanksgiving Day dinner was planned around the starting time of the Dallas game. We took her to a Dallas Cowboy game on December 12, 2004. She was so excited to be in Cowboy stadium, she loved being there, and was smiling from ear to ear. It was only a few days later that she began to feel badly.

She was a huge fan of Karl Malone of the Utah Jazz. He even sent her an autographed basketball. She was an avid Chicago Cub fan and watched nearly every game they played on TV. One of the last TV shows she ever watched was a Cub game.

At Texas Tech, she sat through football games in high winds, hot sun, and a game that turned into a blizzard. It snowed the whole game, and there couldn't have been more than a few hundred people left in the stands, but Cherry stayed to the very end.

She loved to travel, especially to the beach. It never got too hot for her, and of course, she tanned beautifully, and Todd and I just burned. We were in Tampa, Florida, on the night before Hurricane Andrew hit Florida. At sunset, the western side of Florida was amazingly calm, and the skies were fire red, which was an awesome experience. We left on the very last plane out of Tampa the next day.

Her love for this country was partially created and definitely expanded because of the places we traveled. She was determined to see as much of America as she could. So we went to the East to visit Philadelphia (Independence Hall); Washington, DC (the capitol and the museums); Boston (Lexington Green and the ship, The Constitution); Cooperstown, NY (The Baseball Hall of Fame); Hershey, Pennsylvania, and Florida (Miami, Disney World and St. Petersburg beaches – her favorite beach).

We went to Mid-America, to Louisville, KY, (Churchill Downs); Chicago (Wrigley Field, Sears Tower); St. Louis (the Gateway Arch); Memphis (Beale Street, Peabody Hotel, Graceland); and Indianapolis 'the Indy 500 racetrack). We experienced the West - the Grand Canyon, the Durango Silverton railroad, Albuquerque Hot Air Balloon ride, the Colorado River, Pikes Peak, a cabin in the Tetons, Yellowstone National Park, Yosemite National Park, San Francisco - Cable Cars, Los Angeles - a Dodger Dog at the ball park, Columbia River Gorge in Oregon,

She loved her puppies, Chicory and Sadie. Cherry had a special bond with her dog Sadie - a Shih Tzu. Sadie could hear her coming before Cherry got in the driveway. It was a love experience when she came in the house. Sadie ignored everybody else and headed straight for Cherry, and she had to drop everything and love her baby.

My favorite moments with Cherry were when

Todd was born. Second, was when we flew into Portland, Oregon, and the magnificent Mt. Hood was actually higher than the plane on the left, Mt. St. Helen's was on the right, and the beautiful Columbia River Gorge was beneath us. We then drove past the cleanest, neatest farms, and got into the mountains with deep gorges on the way to the Pacific Ocean.

We stayed on the edge of the Pacific Ocean, leaving the door open so we could hear the waves, while a fireplace burned all night. The next morning we drove 200 miles down the spectacular coast drive, then mostly alongside sparkling, churning rivers or streams. We ended the day at Crater Lake National Park, the most awesome, breathtaking view we had ever seen, bar none.

The next day we drove past apple groves, wheat fields, strawberry patches and commercial flower farms. To say the least, it was an unforgettable trip.

At supper that night, she innocently asks me what I had liked most about the trip so far. I told her the fact that she was with me was what I liked most about the trip. She had been a wonderful companion through the years. I will never forget that moment.

Todd remembered his favorite moments with his mom in writing. He recalled her recording his 8th grade band concert with a jam box bigger than should have been allowed in the auditorium, and her attending his sporting events, concerts and other activities, and the nightly "talks" before bed.

He recalled the snow and ice bound week in Birmingham, AL (making coffee over a fire in the fireplace), and hiding her "secret" brownie recipe from his friends. Most of all, he said he would never forget her constant concern for him as a student, teacher, and person, and that she was a great friend and mom and it was a real pleasure for him to be in her presence.

Cherry will always be remembered as a person

that everyone liked. We have never found anyone that didn't like Cherry. Her smile was contagious, and her love of life was a living example of her love for everybody she met. She was a teacher that never got in front of a classroom. Her living example was a lesson for others, and she made a difference in all that she met. We can be grateful for her gifts to us all.

Cherry passed away on Mother's Day, 2005. She had spent 4 1/2 months in Intensive Care, but never once complained, thus ending forty years of an eventful and successful marriage.

"GOOD LUCK, I HOPE THAT IS YOUR GRANDMOTHER"

I had known that the Payne side of the family had lived in and around the rural towns of Gibsland, Arcadia, and Ringgold, Louisiana. After the death of my father, the relationship between my mother and the Payne family is sketchy at best. I had wondered for years what had become of those family members.

As I drove out of my way through Ringgold, Louisiana, after my routine business calls that day, I decided I would do what I had been trying to encourage myself to do for a long time. I was going to try to find my grandmother, Willa Payne.

I stopped at the Ringgold Police Department and told them that I was looking for my grandmother. I had not seen her since the very earliest days of my life. I asked if they knew any Payne's. The officer stood up straight, with a sudden interest, and began to approach me with an excitement in his voice. He said, "Really, I know a Mrs. Payne. She's probably in her early 80's, and has lived around here for years."

The policeman was over-delighted, it seemed, to direct me to that Mrs. Payne's house on a nearby country road. His parting words were, "Good luck, and I hope that is your grandmother." He walked to the door of the police station with me, and we shook hands. He waved and watched me drive away. A tear began to well up from the anxiety of the close-at-hand possibility.

As I drove away from the police station, a surge of excitement came over me. A wonder of joy as if the rest of the story was about to fill a hole in my life. My palms were sweaty as my mind raced with speculation.

As I neared what I thought was the area her house was located, a white pickup truck turned into a nearby driveway. I followed them, and asked if they knew where Mrs. Payne lived. They looked concerned, and pointed to a green house across the road only a couple hundred yards down the way. Had my moment of destiny arrived?

I had a feeling of fear and euphoria as I turned back on the road and slowly drove the couple of hundred yards to the green house. With my hopes high, I remember saying silently to myself, "I feel good about this, and it has taken too long for this to happen."

The country house was a common wooden frame home, not uncommon in the red clay hills of North Louisiana. It was painted what was surely a dark green at one time, but had faded to a chalky light green. The house sat among a grove of trees in a wooded area. I had driven past thousands of country homes just like this one through my years of living in North Louisiana. This one suddenly took on a distinctive prominence of nobleness, and my imagination thought of it as a place where I could have played as a little boy if things had worked out differently.

At a snail's pace, I steered my car onto a dirt path driveway pulling to a stop in front of the green house sitting about 200 feet from the road. A shiver came over me with a feeling that this was too surreal. As I got out of the car, I briefly paused to gather myself and to soak in the surroundings and the moment. I took a deep breath, closed the car door, and approached cautiously what would surely be a dominant moment in my life. Every detail around me was magnified and imprinted clearly in my memory.

The wind was gently blowing through the mix of oak and pine trees, but all else was silent but for an occasional bird chirping. The day was warm and typically Louisiana muggy. I stepped up onto the solid wooden porch, and could hear the loud pounding of every footstep I took as I approached the screen door.

I started to knock, but I suddenly was struck with the fear of startling a lady of some considerable age with the sudden appearance of the grandson she had not seen in decades. I collected myself, went ahead and knocked, the screen door shook violently with a loud alarmingly unpleasant jarring sound. I stood and waited only briefly. I hardly had time to prepare what I was going to say to the grandmother I never remembered meeting.

A short stocky gray haired lady with an aging face shuffled to the door. Before I barely got out of my mouth the question, "Are you Mrs. Payne?" when, throwing her arms in the air as if to praise God, and with a huge smile coming over her, she called out, "Oh my God, Sonny, it's Jerry."

I was worried about startling her, but here she had shocked me. How did she know who I was, or what I looked like? I was the one surprised. I was the one shaking.

She pushed open the screen door, I stepped inside, and we embraced. Sonny, my uncle that I had never remembered meeting either, came running to the door and joined in the hugging. It was a long embrace that included a few tears of joy that I will never forget.

They told of keeping up with Ronnie and me through *The Shreveport Times* newspaper clippings of our sports and civic activities. They both recognized me immediately.

Inside the house, I could easily see they lived a typical a hard country lifestyle it was comfortable and homey, but certainly nothing extravagant. The furniture and fixtures were well worn, but adequate. I saw only one picture in the living room. The lamps provided only a low light in the otherwise dark room.

With amazement, we sat talking and holding hands. Only a few minutes into our excitement, and their recollections of a family history, which were none too familiar to me, the couple that I had asked for directions just across the road, came to check on Mrs. Payne. They were wondering what this strange man was doing inquiring about their mother and mother-in-law. They were my Aunt Betty, and her husband, Red Moore.

At last, I had talked to and held my grandmother. At last, that hole was filled in my life, and it felt like my heart was whole.

We talked for more than a couple of hours, sharing strong coffee and smiles. She kept saying over and over how she loved Ronnie and me, and how she was so glad to see me. A picture of my dad in his uniform sat on the mantle, and that was the only picture in the room. It was a moment never to be forgotten.

POLITICS - IT'S TIME FOR A WAKE UP CALL

Even though I had been dabbling in political races to some degree, writing ads, filming and editing television and radio ads, and always planning the strategy of various campaigns, it was time. In 1989, after nearly a year of trying, I decided to open an office in my home with my IBM PC Junior, and I never looked back. I formed Success Advertising and jumped into the fire. I worked with Tom Smith on a couple of local campaigns and quickly learned the two of us couldn't make enough money. At one point, I realized that people couldn't relate "Success Advertising," to me, so I incorporated and changed the name to Jerry Payne Advertising.

Almost immediately, I signed on to run the campaigns of Greg Barro and Ron Bean, Senatorial candidates, and Melissa Flournoy, a State Representative candidate. These were pretty big campaigns, all in all, spending in the neighborhood of $750,000.

These races were very contentious, and all would be big upsets. The biggest upset would be Melissa Flournoy, a liberal democratic woman, against 20-year incumbent Art Sour, an archconservative. This was the most conservative State Representative district in the state. I decided to attack his $28,000 pension as a result of serving in the Louisiana House for those 20 years. I pointed out that he only worked an average of 90 days a year to earn that pension. He claimed to have authored hundreds of bills on behalf of his constituents, only to find factually that he only authored three. For only three bills, he got a $28,000 a year pension.

A couple of ads directed at, and entitled, "Art, get your facts straight," and another depicting him in a lounge chair with a drink in his hand with one of those cute little umbrellas stirrers, and the radio by his chair playing scratchy and tinny music all the way from Hawaii, as he dreamed of his state retirement money.

That nailed him. Yet another cartoon television ad showed him with suspenders and a wad of cash stuffed in his back pocket patting his fellow political crony on the back, entitled, "Good Ole Boy Politics," which finished the job. Melissa won 58-42 percent, and that would not be the biggest surprise of the night.

The Greg Barro Senatorial district covered Bossier and Caddo Parishes. Television personality, Karin Adams, was married to Greg, and her job approval rating was higher than any of the candidates. Naturally, we used Karin in all print media since it was not ethical to use her on television. Even more convincing, I think, was Karin being pregnant and going door to door with Greg. The very likeable incumbent Senator, Sydney Nelson, publicly endorsed his Bossier law partner in this race, but Greg ended up winning more votes from Bossier than either of the other candidates. That became the second upset of the night, as Greg won handily.

Ron Bean, a candidate for the Senate seat made up of the southern part of Shreveport and all the way to Mansfield in Desoto Parish, was in the political fight of his life. His opponent, Tommy Armstrong, the incumbent State Representative in nearly that same area, was leading in the polls by 15 points with two weeks until Election Day.

Ron called and asked me to come by so we could talk about those poll results, and me producing his television ads. Winning didn't look possible. I asked him to show me everything written or said publicly by candidate Armstrong. Ron handed me a folder with some of Tommy's literature and other stuff. On top of the stack, and the very first thing I saw, was a copy of *The Shreveport Times* story about the nearly 300 lb. Rep. Armstrong falling asleep in his chair on the floor of the Louisiana House of Representatives.

I had been in Baton Rouge the day this event happened. The next morning I met several of my old Jaycee friends for breakfast, and as I walked in, they were laughing and howling about the story which also ran in the *Baton Rouge Morning Advocate.*

My first reaction to seeing this article in Ron's office was the absolute hilarity they had exhibited at that breakfast, and within one minute, I had a 30-second TV spot in my mind. Ron had turned and made a phone call, and when he finished I had already closed the folder and pitched it on his desk. He asked me what was wrong. I stated, with all the confidence I had, "This campaign is over, and you are going to win." In disbelief, he listened as I described my idea for a television ad, and asked him if he could get an old wooden rocking chair? He said yes, and we were on our way. He hired me on the spot.

The story in the ad went, as follows. It had been a very warm day, and Tommy had just finished lunch and returned to the floor of the Louisiana House Chamber. (This is a granite walled building with huge, very high ceilings, and every sound is amplified and has an echo). The chairs for the elected delegates were wooden, stationary, rocking chairs that swivels.

Tommy's desk and chair was beside the media area, separated with an ornate two-foot wrought-iron divider. He leaned back and dozed off, and the chair cracked loudly and broke, and the nearly 300 lb. Tommy went sprawling onto the floor with a loud thud.

The House Chamber rules did not allow anyone to cross the media divider, but fearing for his safety, the first person to get to the startled Armstrong was a reporter from *the Shreveport Times*. Kneeling over the fallen Armstrong, he asked, "Are you okay?"

Tommy Armstrong, the State Representative, gave the worst comment possible, "Oh, I'm okay. I have fallen asleep in that chair many times and it never broke before."

I called my high school and college friend, Jimmy Coleman. I told him, "I am going to make you a television star." Now Jimmy was heavyset with a slightly balding head, and even though he resembled Armstrong somewhat, that is not what made him come to my attention. I told him I needed him to be in a television ad, and he asked, "What he had to do." I told him, "Do what you used to do in class - fall asleep."

This was the best ad I ever conceived. It started with the Rob Smith voiceover whispering, "Psst, Psst, wake up Tommy. Tommy wake up, you're sleeping on the floor of the Louisiana House of Representatives"... (then with the sound of wood cracking and breaking and a loud thud) the voice continued, "You slept so hard you even broke the chair"...with that came a teletype sound of keys striking the paper typing his infamous words quoted on the screen about him sleeping in that chair many times before. The screen cuts to a shot of a huge alarm clock with two big bells on the top ringing as the voice says, "It's time for a wakeup call - Elect Ron Bean." The musical background was Rob Smith's little girl's wind-up toy playing, "Lullaby, and Good Night."

Ron Bean was elected by one percentage point, overcoming a 15-point deficit in the polls. That would be the biggest surprise of the night in the whole state. My political consulting career was catapulted to the top.

I was privileged to work with many talented media people, but two stands out as more talented than others do. Rob Smith has one of the most unique imaginations and creative minds of all. His sound track creations made the ads we fashioned memorable, to say the least, and award winning for sure.

Jason Stuart, just out of college, brought a totally new look to the political print world. He was amazing to work with and took our designs to a new level. He was responsible for voters comprehending our printed materials like never before. He made winning even more possible.

Most of the campaign ads and records have been lost because of computer hard drive crashes, but a partial list of the winning campaigns are, as follows: Shreveport Mayor Keith Hightower, helping him to win two terms that moved Shreveport forward and brought many improvements to Shreveport; Louisiana Senators - Ron Bean, Greg Barro, Sherri Cheek, Robert Adley, Rick Gallot; Louisiana Representatives - Wayne Waddell, Melissa Flournoy, Jane Smith, Rick Gallot, Beverly Bruce, Hoppy Hopkins, Richard Burford, Bob Barton; Louisiana Court of Appeal Judges Henry Brown, Jay Caraway; Louisiana District Court Judges - Mike Pitman, Francis Pitman, Woody Nesbitt, Michael Walker, Charles Adams; Bossier City Court Judge Mike Daniel; Bossier City Marshal Johnny Wyatt; Bossier-Webster District Attorney Jim Bullers; Caddo District Attorney Charles Scott; Bossier Parish Tax Assessor Bobby Edmiston; Bossier Councilmen - Bo McIlwain, David Jones, David Montgomery, Jr.; Shreveport Councilmen - Jeff Hogan, Mike Gibson, Monty Walford, Michael Corbin; Parish School Board Members - Randy Lefler, David Broussard, Mike Mosura, Allison Brigham, Bossier Parish Police Juror - Rick Avery; Greenwood Mayor, Jerry Melot.

I had managed 213 election campaigns on most levels of politics. In the 23 years that I had run political campaigns my clients won 192 elections, and lost only 21, winning 90%. Also, I had elected more women to the Louisiana legislature than any other consultant.

I have had many occasions to recall so many details of those campaigns, and as I have had the chance to visit with some of the characters who helped make these moments come alive, we help each other remember those details. It is no less interesting to hear what they think was memorable, compared to what I thought was epic. I truly have forgotten many of the great stories that made this part of my Life's Buffet of choices, decisions, and intriguing moments, which have been nothing less than amazing.

One of the more relaxing and satisfying moments

came when Elliott Stonechipher, Bobby Munson, and I had supper at Don's Restaurant in Shreveport. We met on an election eve in October 2008. We were all involved in a number of races, but none against each other.

That was a discussion of historical proportions in that we talked of many past elections, and the current state of Louisiana politics. During that dinner discussion the late Don Owen, the former Channel 12 - KSLA news anchor for decades, and the former Louisiana Public Service Commissioner, approached our table. He said, "I would love to be a fly on the wall during this conversation," knowing that a wealth of Louisiana political history had been made by these casual diners. We laughed, and laughed, and marveled at some of the stories, at least the ones we could recall.

I had worked for Buddy Roemer, a U.S. Congressman and Louisiana Governor, and Ross Perot at EDS. Both would eventually become candidates for President of the United States.

JACK BINION AND HORSESHOE CASINO "I GOTCHA"

The last thing any of my friends or their parents would have imagined was that some day full-blown Las Vegas style casinos would be operating in Bossier City. However, in 1994, Bossier City would become one of the top casino locations in America.

The only person I knew that had ever had any connection to the casino industry was our former neighbor, schoolmate, and family friend George Nattin, Jr.. George had gone to Las Vegas and had become one of the leaders in the casino business. He rose from being a shill on the gaming tables to the lofty position of President of Caesar's World.

Talk began to surface about gambling coming to Louisiana, but in New Orleans. According to George Nattin, the historic and tourist attractions in New Orleans made Louisiana a much more feared threat to Las Vegas than the Atlantic City, New Jersey, location. George an LSU star athlete, was thrilled at the economic boost and jobs casinos would bring to his home state.

Louisiana Riverboat legislation won approval while Governor Buddy Roemer was in office, but the implementation of Louisiana casinos occurred following the completion of his term in office. George Nattin was a former Bossier High School classmate, and childhood friend of the Governor Buddy Roemer. Edwin Edward's long Las Vegas tied friendship, also with George Nattin, would make Nattin the logical person to be the contact person with the Louisiana Governors.

It is apparent that George Nattin was the prime reason for Louisiana's sudden interest in Las Vegas style gambling. Caesar's Casino was one of the leading contenders to build a casino in New Orleans. However, when the final bet was made it wasn't Caesar's, but Harrah's, who won the rights to open in New Orleans.

That is as far as this book will go into how that happened. I will leave that story to a writer that doesn't mind putting his life on the line to tell it. George and I toyed with the idea of writing that book, and may still make that effort one day.

The turmoil around gambling in Louisiana did not stop with New Orleans. Suddenly, Shreveport, Baton Rouge, Lake Charles, and even Bossier City were all being considered for casino locations. The State legislature, under the ironed fisted control of Governor Edwards, contrived a way to create 15 licenses for casinos. Even with the political acumen of Fast Eddie, it took an agreement with legislators from the Louisiana Parishes that had shipbuilding yards to gain enough votes to finally pass the legalization of casino gaming, not gambling. The Louisiana State Constitution prohibits gambling.

Edwards would be in control of awarding the licenses to the various casino operators. These licenses would include Louisiana investors, at Edwards' insistence, as part of the casino ownership. Of course, those investor/owners were connected to Edwards, or his cronies, usually through business deals or campaign contributions.

Shreveport became one of the early competitors for a license; however, Hazel Beard, the first woman Mayor, was against gambling. It is amazing how she got twisted into cutting the ribbon for the grand opening of the soon-to-be Harrah's Casino –Shreveport.

Edwards had too many Shreveport friends to satisfy only one riverboat casino license. A second license was granted to the Casino Magic Company, and it would be located on the Bossier side of the Red River. There was stiff competition for the first Shreveport license, mainly between Harrah's and Jack Binion's Horseshoe Casino. Jack Binion lost, but won, also.

Enter George Nattin, Jr., the son of former Bossier City Mayor, George Nattin. Being the ultimate strategist,

Binion consulted with Nattin because he would have all the right contacts that would enable Binion to move forward. Nattin was a major player in the third Shreveport-Bossier riverboat casino license. Jack Binion was one of the most brilliant businessmen I would ever work for. He put together a team of local partners that had such power that, in the end, even Governor Edwards could not deny.

Edwards was determined that Shreveport-Bossier would not have a third casino license. Undeterred, Jack Binion proceeded to work through the process for a license on the faith that his riverboat casino would be the biggest and best of all the properties in Louisiana.

After lining up local partners Frank Pernici, and local attorney Robert Piper, and at Nattin's encouragement, Binion made his first hire, my brother, Ron Payne. Ronnie would be in charge of land acquisition, construction, and more importantly, keep Nattin apprised of local happenings.

With Nattin's encouragement, I would be the second person Binion hired because of my experience with the local political scene and my campaign association with nearly all of the local governing bodies.

The first time I met Jack Binion was in the back of the Bossier City Council chambers. He saw from my resume that I had lived in Amarillo, and he commented that he had a sister that lived there.

We were attending the Bossier Metropolitan Planning Commission meeting where he was expecting to be approved to build a casino in Bossier City. Several items for other building permits were also on the agenda that night. Everything was supposed to be handled by Pernici and Piper; however, the presentation ran into a major problem because the proposal contained no traffic plan that could handle the thousands of people coming to the casino site, and the road seemed blocked. The way the commission worked was all the proposals were presented, and at the end of the meeting, the commission would vote to approve or deny the projects.

Following our presentation, we all moved out of the Council Chambers into the foyer. Ronnie and I were on one side of the room, and Binion, with his lawyers, were with Pernici and Piper on the other side of the room. Binion was hot, to say the least.

After a short discussion, about what a possible solution might be, Ronnie and I approached Binion and suggested that we were going to try to get the Planning Commission to give us a temporary approval. That approval would be based on us presenting a traffic plan to the commission in a special meeting before the next regular scheduled commission meeting. Jack Binion was so frustrated he said, "Do what you can. I am leaving."

This was a long shot, at best. The meeting was well underway with other commission business. I thought, if I could first get David Broussard, my former candidate, friend, and a commission member, to come down off the podium. I could try to convince him to let us take this approach, and maybe we could save this proposal. Motioning for David, a Baptist, and graduate of Baylor University, to come down from the podium, we talked with him and he agreed, even though he was not in favor of gambling, he was in favor of economic prosperity. After an interesting conversation, he motioned for Dean Holt, the Director of the Commission, to join us. Dean liked the idea of approving our plan based on the Commission approving the traffic plan at a later date. We got each commission member to leave the podium while other business was in progress so we could talk to each one individually.

The commission voted unanimously in support of our proposal. The Horseshoe Casino was saved from within a hairs' breath of defeat. If the proposal had been defeated, it could not be re-proposed for six months, effectively killing the construction of the Horseshoe Casino forever.

Ronnie and I raced over to Ernest's Restaurant, where Jack Binion had gone, to tell him the casino had been saved. To say the least, he was a happy man.

Not long afterwards, George Nattin was named the General Manager of the new Horseshoe Casino. He had retired from Caesar's World in Las Vegas, and moved back home. Ron and I were both excited. This was going to be fun!

The *Shreveport Times* newspaper was against the Horseshoe Casino from the time of Harrah's Casino-Shreveport approval. The *Shreveport Times* has hardly ever written anything favorable about the across-the-river Bossier City. They have always been anti-Bossier, and this was probably *The Times'* high water mark for stifling anything good in Bossier. Their reporting was so unbalanced that I clipped every article written about the casinos and measured the column inches that were favorable or unfavorable about all three local riverboat casinos. It became so unbearable that I approached George Nattin and Mr. Binion about meeting with *the Times'* editorial board. They agreed, saying it can't hurt, but they were trying to kill us.

The editorial board allowed me an audience, and I met with the board to discuss the unfair reporting we had received. Attending with me was Natalie Linn, a cohort, just so I would have a witness. I proceeded to lay out the facts, with copies of the articles and the column inch history of their reporting. They had written 804 inches of negative or incorrect reporting about Horseshoe, while only 110 inches of negative about the other boats combined. On the other hand, they had written 919 inches of positive articles about Harrah's, and only 214 positive inches about Horseshoe.

I also pointed out strongly that *The Times* was supporting the Riverboat Gaming Commission, when in truth the Commission had broken the laws in enforcement and rulings against Horseshoe. All this done, in spite of the fact the Gaming Commission's own head enforcement officer had stated in writing and at public forums that Horseshoe had done no wrong.

For over an hour, I spoke, and they asked no questions. They did not dispute my facts; however, of course, drew the conclusion that the paper had fairly represented their case through its reporting. They did back off for a while.

In spite of all the negative publicity, the time came for the Louisiana Riverboat Gaming Commission to take up a vote approving or disapproving Horseshoe's gaming permit. The first showdown vote took place in the Bossier City Council chambers. It was a Saturday morning, and the scene was as intense as any meeting I have ever attended.

The meeting had its power players, all designed to affect the voting outcome. After the meeting was called to order, and right on cue and at a precise moment, the three local Senators, Ron Bean, Greg Barro, and Greg Tarver, made a grand entrance and sat at the front of the room. As they entered, we brought in executive chairs and placed them on a row directly in front of the commissioners, just to let the commissioners know that the Senate wanted this license granted. Ron Bean and Greg Barro were my clients, and Greg Tarver was a close friend with one of the local owners, Robert Piper. Horseshoe was approved for a conditional license right there in Bossier City Council chambers.

The problem was Jack Binion. He wasn't licensed to own a casino. He had been revoked in Las Vegas for financial reporting errors to the Nevada Gambling Commission. Even though those errors were immediately corrected those were the reasons used as the excuse to deny him a Louisiana license by the Louisiana State Police. The State Police leadership was appointed directly by the Governor, they were following his orders.

However, the real reason for the denial was that Edwin Edwards was not satisfied with the arrangement of the local ownership. If not for Horseshoe's association with Duke Robbins, a childhood friend of Louisiana Senate President Pro Tem, Sammy Nunez, and Nunez's friends on the Louisiana Riverboat Commission, the Binion Gaming License would have never happened.

The first vote was successful with a 3-2 margin. The Louisiana State Police Gaming Board, under the direction of the Governor, refused to give license approval to Jack Binion. They sued to have the license ruled invalid. The struggle continued all the way to the Louisiana Supreme Court, and the Supreme Court allowed the licensing process to continue.

A second hearing, and all-important vote, was scheduled in Baton Rouge. The hearing was contentious with Gaming Chairman Ken Pickering announcing from the podium just prior to gaveling the meeting to order, "I just received a phone call from the Governor, and he said he did not want Horseshoe approved for a license."

The Commission heard the Horseshoe presentation, and then heard comments from the audience. I will never forget or forgive Shreveport Mayor Hazel Beard, and the head of Shreveport's Economic Development Group, speaking against the approval of the Horseshoe Bossier Casino. I thought they were greedy SOB's.

The Commission had five voting members and the non-voting President, Ken Pickering. The President and I were longtime friends from our Jaycee days. Ken had served as Legal Counsel under my good friend Jaycee President, Jack Eversull. Parliamentary procedure was a way of life for some of us in that organization. Ken knew from our Jaycee experience that I was proficient in parliamentary procedure. An important point, one of the five voting members was absent when time came to vote. The vote came down as 2-2, a tie. Ken, as President, announced he was invoking his authority under Robert's Rules of Order to break the tie and vote no, thereby making the vote two for, and three against. Seeing we were in jeopardy, I immediately objected, stating that under Robert's Rules the Chairman could only vote to cause a tie or break a tie in favor of the issue. Now, I knew better.

The Chairman could actually vote any way he wanted. After my tirade, several other people objected, and there was much confusion in the room. I was bluffing, and Chairman Pickering bought the bluff. I sounded so sure in my arguments that Pickering called a 20-minute meeting recess to try to confirm the ruling.

Amazingly, the missing Commission member, a friend of Senator Nunez appeared at the meeting during the recess. When the meeting resumed it all became a moot point, because the missing latecomer voted yes, and the license passed by a 3-2 vote. Horseshoe had been granted a license.

As Ken Pickering passed out of the meeting room, he accidentally brushed against me in the crowded room. I turned towards him, and he looked at me and quietly grimaced, "You son-of-bitch." I smiled and replied, "I gotcha!" What a feeling of exhilaration and satisfaction.

On the drive back to Bossier City, on a long straight stretch of I-49, hardly a word was spoken between Ronnie and me. He broke the silence with, "That was more fun than beating Byrd High School in football!"

Byrd was our hated high school rival from Shreveport, the blue bloods of Shreveport. It was a moment of great pleasure and retribution for all those "we are better than you" insinuations by Shreveporters. So easily predictable, *The Shreveport Times* hardly commented on the story.

The real reason for Horseshoe's approval was because of George Nattins' friendship with Edwin Edwards. Edwards told George that if he came to Bossier City not to worry, that everything would be all right. George said, "Edwin Edwards never told me anything that he didn't do."

It had been over a hundred years since boats as large as these casino boats traveled up the Red River to Shreveport. The Harrah's and Casino Magic boats had already arrived a few months earlier. The turreted railroad bridge would have to be opened for the first time in over a hundred years. The railroad companies were not even sure they would open, but they did.

Those first two smaller boats moved through the bridge openings quite easily. Those two boats were much smaller than Horseshoe's "Queen of the Red." Our boat was hundreds of feet longer and many feet wider than the others were. Our boat had only 5 feet on either side to spare, and actually scraped the side of the railroad bridge support.

We had to wait for rain in Oklahoma in order to have enough water to come from the Gulf of Mexico all the way to Bossier City. I had hyped this historic occasion in the media, and thousands of people lined the riverbanks on both sides. The huge boat dwarfed the other casino boats, and was greeted with applause and cheers of excitement. Our boat would be the largest boat to ever dock in either Shreveport or Bossier City.

To this point, I was spending most of my time working and speaking to convince the local people that this was a great opportunity for everyone. I had done the marketing studies for the boats, and found that this would be a huge industry for our area in spite of the naysayers.

My brother was upset, and did not believe my figures concerning the projected attendance and income. Ron wasn't alone in not believing my numbers.

I had said publicly that more than 15,000 people per day would come to the three casinos. That is nearly 5.5 million casino patrons per year. Local businesses would be in line to do more than $1,000,000 per day. Motels, gas stations, food outlets, rent cars and other transportation operators would have to get prepared for the influx of new visitors.

New hotels and motels would need to be built to accommodate the influx out-of-towners. Retail stores would have to stock more goods for sale to handle the potential 500,000 new customers in their businesses. Traffic would necessitate improvements to our streets, adding more lanes for the additional 6,000 cars per day.

This would be a 24-hour-a-day opportunity for many local businesses. Over 11,000 casino employees would work three different shifts, and the employees would be shopping for groceries at all hours of the day and night.

I spoke to nearly every civic club, gave countless interviews via television, radio, magazines and newspapers from all over America. Every speech I gave started with, "Our future isn't what it use to be." We would be moving from an industrial-based economy to a tourism-based economy. To this day, nearly 20 years later, strangers will say I look familiar, but they can't place me.

Most of those figures have far exceeded my predictions. By 2013, over 27 new motels with 11,000 rooms have been built; roads have been improved to accommodate traffic; and the number of businesses and restaurants has increased, dramatically.

Jack Binion insisted that I come out to Las Vegas and work with him for a week or so. Even though I was fairly knowledgeable about marketing, I knew hardly anything about casino marketing.

Upon arriving at Jack's office around 10 am, I was

already gawking. He greeted me warmly, and as we were talking, he received a phone call. His words were exactly, "OK, I'll be there in a few minutes." He turned to me and said, "There is a guy on the craps table and he has won $4.5 million. I'll be right back."

I spent the day observing every detail he went through. He took me on a tour of the whole casino from the slot machine repair shop to the back of the enormous 30-foot neon sign. He was proud of the sign that went around an entire city block of the world famous Horseshoe Casino, a Glitter Gulch's centerpiece.

We met with the marketing director that was behind the whirlwind of the daily promotions, all designed to bring more and more gamblers into the casino. The goal was not to bring in non-gamblers, but people that would play the games.

Everything in that casino had a purpose, and I learned that Jack's key to it all was a friendly employee. They seemed to relish a chance to flash a smile at Jack, and he always had a smile for them. Finally, the non-stop day came to an abrupt pause when Jack suggested I go to the room and freshen up and meet him in the steak house on the 21st floor for supper. It was near 9 pm; the view high above Las Vegas glittered and flashed. I had already learned that glitter invites the gamblers. Jack called his casino a joint. If that was so, then this was a classy joint with classy people.

One of the first questions I asked that evening was, "How is the guy on the crap table doing?" Jack replied, "He was up about $6 million." The guy had been playing all day. We went on to enjoy a fabulous meal, and the conversation was scintillating. Jack seemed to enjoy my excitement about this new part of my life. It was like talking to an old friend, even though I hardly knew him. He is one of the best conversationalists I had ever talked with. I think he was a little excited about my excitement.

The next morning we resumed my lessons in casino life, and more especially casino/joint operations. I couldn't help but ask, "How is the guy on the crap table doing?" Jack said, "He played until around 3 am, then went to bed. He is up by about $8 million." He added, with a smile on his face, "Jerry, don't worry - this guy is a gambler. With him, it is all about winning. He will never take that money out of this casino. He will keep coming back and playing on that money. If he plays long enough I will win it all back." Now that is confidence; after all, it was $8,000,000.

For over a week, I followed this consummate businessman. He was totally immersed in this business and the people that worked for him. He was entirely different from Buddy Roemer and Ross Perot, both of which had personalities far different from most people in my life, but Jack Binion is in a world of his own.

A month later, the marketing head of the whole Horseshoe Casino Company came into my office in Bossier City and asked if I had ever done a national press release. I told him I had, and asked him why. He told me a guy had been playing craps at the Las Vegas Horseshoe Casino, and was up $27 million.

Jack wanted to let the world know you could win $27 million at his casino/joint. I leaned back in silence and said nothing for a few moments, and then I thought out loud that if we went public that might make the guy take the money and run. If the guy lost the money back to the casino, we would lose the argument that you could win that much money from our casino. I argued against the idea. After much discussion, we decided not to do the press release.

A couple of weeks later I was informed personally and face-to-face by a gleeful Jack Binion, that the guy had lost the whole $27 million back to the casino. Jack said, "Jerry, you see how this works?"

The excitement of seeing and being a part of this business growing from the first spade of dirt to thousands of people 24 hours-a-day was amazing.

We wanted to have the grand opening as fast as possible because every day not open was money lost. The State Police, the State Fire Marshal, and the Corp of Engineers - the list seemed endless, and each had to give their approval. We really did not know when the opening would occur.

We had planned to have a ribbon cutting and short speeches; Jack was to give Bossier City a check for one million dollars upon cutting the ribbon. Finally, on June 4, 1994, we received the final approval. We had no chance to make any huge announcements, but we hurriedly got everything together. We had to call in the new employees, over 2,000 of them, set up a ribbon to cut, arrange for the Mayor to be at the casino, all with about 3 hours notice.

At nearly 11 am, I had briefly notified the media that we may be opening about 2 pm, and that is about all the information I could give them. We quickly strung up a ribbon and found some scissors, got the dignitaries to the front door entrance, presented the check, and cut the ribbon. We literally communicated via walkie-talkies and hand signals to be sure that all the workers were in place.

All of a sudden, without any assurances that all employees were in place, Jack bolted for the front doors and slung them wide open. We almost got stampeded. Somehow, the word had spread, and more than a thousand people came rushing in and the casino was open, at last.

The new employees lined the various shops and restaurants along the long entryway leading to the brand spanking new casino, excitedly applauding the first customers as they streamed by. It was a fantasy moment. We had eight spotlights searching the night sky. There could be no doubt, where The Horseshoe Casino was located.

The summer travelers and locals quickly made this a tourist destination. Aided by over a million dollars of advertising, and word-of-mouth, Horseshoe would become the continuously highest grossing riverboat casino in Louisiana.

Fearing a downturn from the ending summer travelers, we turned the month of September, traditionally a slow month in the casino industry, into probably the most exciting and highest attendance month to date.

The promotion "A September to Remember" saw tens of thousands of gamblers per day pile into The Horseshoe for a chance to win a brand new car every day in September. It is a promotion people still remember twenty years later.

We had a huge turning basket placed on the back of the boat on the bottom floor of the casino, and to enter the contest you had to come into the casino, fill out an entry form, and walk down to the bottom floor and put the form into the basket personally. Each night we would bring the basket up to the main front entrance. Thousands of hopefuls would come back to see if they won. At 10 pm, we would draw the anticipated winning ticket. You did not have to be present to win, but I guess thousands of entrants didn't want anyone driving their new car.

We had an independent auditor oversee the entire month long contest. We had at least 50,000 entrants each day. I was there each night to announce the winners, and that caused some interesting personal stories. One winner lived only six houses from my parents' home. I had been to his home many times. He waved as he drove off in a brand new red Ford Mustang convertible. He wasn't present for the drawing. Thank goodness!

On another evening, Jack happened to be standing next to me as I announced the winner. We were both startled when the guy standing right beside Jack was the winner for that night. We did not know him, I swear!

One morning, during this promotion, I was walking though the casino corridor and noticed my former high school principal, Frank Lampkin, walking slowly towards me. I went over to say hello and ask, "What are you doing in here?" Now this was a real gentleman, and one of my heroes. He said, "I have as good a chance as anyone to win this car!" If I had been caught, gambling at high school I wonder what he would have said.

I was the personal tour guide for dignitaries including Governors, U.S. Senators, Legislators, and anyone else that needed to see how this place ran. Jack told me he wanted me to walk the floors of the boat a few times a day because he said, "You know so many people." Now, on top of doing all the advertising, speaking engagements, dealing with government entities, and the media, I had to also walk a few miles a day.

The casino's first tour bus was a group that appeared voluntarily at the front of the casino during the first week of operation. I received a phone call from security. There was a busload of people, and they wanted to know if we had anything to give them. I gathered some of our what-knots, and headed to the front of the casino. I almost fell out when I saw it was a group of elderly folks from a local Baptist Church. I immediately told the security personnel to keep those people there, and not to let them leave. I rushed back to my office and got my camera. I couldn't believe my eyes as I took a group picture of these Baptist brethren with the church name on the side of the bus prominently showing.

DEATH PENALTY AND THE LOUISIANA SUPREME COURT

This trial became one of the most interesting civic and gut-wrenching undertakings of my life. I was selected as a juror for the first-degree murder trial, and was further chosen as the jury's foreman. As if the sensationalism of the trial itself wasn't enough, I became the main reason for the appeal of the jury's verdict to the Louisiana Supreme Court.

It all began for me with my questioning during the jury selection phase of the trial. Having never been a part of this process personally, my answers were slow and carefully thought out before I spoke. That was an unsettling proposition for me.

On March 14, 2002, a Caddo Parish grand jury indicted the defendant, LaDerrick Campbell, for the February 11, 2002, first-degree murder of Kathy Parker. The trial commenced with jury selection on September 13, 2004. On September 22, 2004, the jury returned a unanimous verdict of guilty. After a penalty phase hearing the same jury found, as an aggravating circumstance, that the defendant was engaged in the perpetration of an armed robbery when he murdered Kathy Parker. The jury unanimously recommended the death penalty.

On February 25, 2005, after denying the appeal on the post-verdict motions, the trial court imposed the sentence of death in accordance with the jury's verdict.

THE TRIAL TRANSCRIPT

During the fifth day of jury selection the defendant requested that he be permitted to waive appointed counsel, and represent himself for the remainder of jury selection. At a closed hearing, the trial court granted the defendant's request and allowed him to represent himself. The following day the defendant conducted the remainder of the jury selection process himself. I had been selected to be on the jury prior to the defendant taking over his own trial. The trial began on September 20, 2004.

The state relied upon testimonial and physical evidence, including a video surveillance tape, to show that on the evening of February 11, 2002, shortly after 9:00 pm, the defendant and James Washington entered the Magnolia Liquor Club (hereinafter "Magnolia Club") in Rodessa, Louisiana. The defendant entered first, armed with a shotgun, his accomplice James Washington entered the Magnolia Club immediately behind the defendant. The defendant approached the store's counter, immediately to his right, and demanded that the victim, Kathy Parker, a Magnolia Club employee, "Give me all the money, the money out the other cash register, too."

The victim complied, and while giving him all of the money in the register, and cowering behind the counter, begged the defendant not to shoot her. The defendant reached over the counter, pointed the gun downward and shot the victim once in the chest. Both men immediately exited the Magnolia Club to a waiting vehicle, and then sped away.

Cardell Jackson, testified that he grew up in Rodessa, Louisiana, since he was a very small boy. He was present at the Magnolia Club on the evening of February 11, 2002, sitting at one of the video poker machines near the entrance that Campbell and Washington came through.

He recognized James Washington as he came through the Club door. As he entered the Magnolia Club after Washington looked him "straight in the face," he then recognized the defendant Campbell's voice after he heard the victim speak saying, "I'll give you anything you want-don't shoot me." He heard the defendant say, "Give me all the money, the money out the other cash register, too." He estimated that he was probably four feet from Washington and the defendant when Jackson heard the defendant ordering the victim to give him the money.

He heard the gunshot but did not see the shooting. Jackson did not recall seeing a weapon, but from his vantage point at a video poker machine, he saw someone make a motion as if he had a weapon and pointing at the victim. Jackson then explained that he was able to identify victim. He was also, able to identify both the defendant and Washington because they are both from Rodessa, he had known them both, since they were small children, and he was a friend with their families.

Also at the Magnolia Club on February 11, 2002, was Barbara Forte. She testified that she had been playing video poker and drinking that night and approached the victim at the counter to get change when two black men came into the store and also approached the counter.

Forte moved away to return to her seat, thinking the two men were customers and that she would wait until they were finished. One man was tall and one man was short. She recalled that the tall one was yelling, "Don't nobody move, this is a holdup." Forte remembered one of the men ordering the victim to open the cash register. She heard the victim say. "You can have anything I got, just don't shoot me." Forte did not hear a gunshot, but rather heard a sound she was unable to identify "somebody hit up against something real hard."

Detective Charles Bradford of the Caddo Parish Sheriff's Office was assigned to investigate the murder of Kathy Parker on February 11. He viewed the information when he arrived on the scene that evening including the club's surveillance videotape and concluded that "after I viewed the tape of both individuals going into the store and then as they exited the store he recognized both individuals. They had similar features to two subjects that I've known for a while." Detective Bradford identified the suspects as James Washington and LaDerrick Campbell.

After an investigation and obtaining an arrest warrant, Campbell the defendant and Washington were arrested at the same house in Cass County, Texas. After waiving extradition, the pair was returned to Louisiana and Detective Bradford conducted an interview of Washington.

Washington waived his constitutional rights, and admitted to taking part in the robbery of the Magnolia Club. He also stated that, "he knew where the shotgun used in the shooting was hidden and that he was willing to take police to it." He led police to the gun, which Detective Bradford identified in court.

Richard Beighley is a criminalist and an expert in firearms identification. Beighley testified the gun operated normally when Beighley conducted a test firing. The victim's clothes were also examined, and the holes in the victim's shirt. Beighley gave his opinion that the evidence was consistent with a shot being fired from that gun at a distance of two to five feet. The trigger pull on the shotgun was 7.68 pounds, meaning a person would have to apply that much force on the trigger to fire the weapon. Beighley's stated a "hair trigger" would only require less than three pounds of force to fire the trigger. The gun weighed less than 7.68 pounds.

Lakischa Holloway and Virginia Burkette, two of the twelve witnesses called by the prosecution, provided the jury with comprehensive details of the events. Burkette testified leading up to, and immediately following the shooting that, at the time of the shooting, she had been romantically involved with Washington, and through Washington, she met the defendant.

On the afternoon of February 11, 2002, Washington telephoned Burkette at her residence. Washington asked Burkette to give him a ride to his mother's house in Domino, Texas. Burkette agreed and drove from Domino to Atlanta, Texas, where she and Washington met the defendant at Lakischa Holloway's residence. However, by the time they reached Atlanta, Burkette's medication taken earlier that evening had begun to make her sleepy.

As a result, unwilling to continue driving her car, Washington suggested that Burkette stay at Holloway's apartment while he used her car. Burkette was unwilling to relinquish her car to Washington. The defendant then suggested that Holloway drive Washington, and the defendant with Burkette riding along. Burkette agreed, and Campbell and Washington were passengers in the rear seat. Burkette got into the passenger side front seat and immediately fell asleep.

Burkette testified that when she first awoke, the group had arrived at the home of a woman she did not know, later identified as Diane Cooper. According to Burkette, Cooper had "problems" with Holloway and the two women did not get along. Cooper followed the four at the house and attempted to start a fight with Holloway by beating on Burkette's car. The fight was subsequently broken up.

Burkette, Holloway, the defendant and Washington left Cooper's. Burkette explained that at some point they went to another house in Rodessa, and the defendant retrieved a long shotgun, and placed it in the car trunk.

Holloway recalled that she drove the group to the Magnolia Club. Washington was wearing a black sweater and the defendant was wearing a long camouflage coat. Holloway and Burkette waited in the car while the defendant and Washington entered the Magnolia Club. Holloway denied seeing either man with a gun when they entered the store.

The pair was not in the store for long before they exited and entered the car, instructing Holloway to drive off. Holloway testified the men instructed her to get on the back roads. After driving on back roads for a while, Holloway dropped off the defendant and Washington at the end of a road in Linden or Kildare, Texas, near the home of her brother's girlfriend. Holloway then drove back to Atlanta with Burkette, stopping briefly for gas.

After presenting this evidence, the state rested. The defendant also rested without calling any witnesses. Following closing arguments, the trial Judge read at length the legal instructions as to the specific charges.

JURY DELIBERATIONS

As foreman of the jury, you have the discretion to oversee the discussion of the twelve-jury members. I was astonished that no directions were given as to what the order of conversation or deliberations of the jury should be. I realized that it was up to me to organize the discussions that needed to take place.

The first thing I asked of each juror was to discuss the evidence as it was presented. In their judgment, what was the most important evidence? I was impressed with the recollections they exhibited as to the details. The discussion was thoughtful and complete, addressing the evidence from many different directions. After each spoke their mind, over a time frame of approximately 90 minutes, I suggested that we take 20 minutes of silent time to reflect on the decision before us of guilt or innocence.

Because of the ultimate challenge at hand, I observed the agony, pressure, and extreme seriousness on the faces of everyone in that room. None of us had ever faced a decision like this, and it was weighing heavily on us. For people that have never had this responsibility it is easy to say guilty or innocent. Saying you are for the death penalty, or are in favor of sending someone to prison for life, is different from actually having that burden. This group of jurors never wanted to make a more correct decision than this one.

Those 20 minutes were the quickest 20 minutes of my life. This whole trial, and nearly every word and emotion, all came rushing back at the speed of light. Now the question of the guilt or innocence of a young man was in our hands, and on the other hand, the life of the victim. The victim's memories of family, Christmas mornings, school days, birth of her children, her wedding day, are now gone forever. Those memories are silently left behind for her family and friends to recall without her.

The jury room was actually a medium sized room large enough to seat twelve people around a table. The jury deliberation space had a restroom, a utility room for supplies, and a room for refreshments, coffee, snacks, and cold drinks. As the twenty minutes were winding down, I began suggesting that we gather at the table. Ten of the jurors had taken their place; I went to find the missing juror. I found the juror in the utility room, and as I eased the door open, the juror was kneeling and looked up at me and asked, "What if the weight of the shotgun, pointed in a downward angle, could have caused the gun to fire accidentally?" I asked the juror to come and pose that question to the others.

After some discussion, some jurors suggested that the weight of the gun was not sufficient to cause the gun to fire without additional pressure on the trigger. To settle the issue, we summoned the bailiff for permission to bring the shotgun into the jury chambers. The Judge approved our request. I took the unloaded gun, cocked it, and held the gun by the trigger with the barrel straight down, leaving only the weight of the gun to cause the trigger action to engage. The trigger did not engage, and the curious juror said that satisfied her question.

At that point, I asked for any other comments and asked if they were ready to vote. All were ready. I passed out a sheet of paper to each juror and asked each to write their verdict, fold the paper one time, and pass them to me at the head of the table. I had another juror open and read the written verdicts aloud. All of the jurors had voted unanimously - guilty.

After deliberating for two hours, the jury returned, to the courtroom, and the court instructed the jury foreman to read the verdict. As foreman, I announced a unanimous verdict of guilty of first-degree murder. Each of the jury members were polled publicly as to their verdict vote and all affirmed.

THE PENALTY PHASE

The following day the defendant announced that he wanted to be appointed to represent himself for the remainder of the sentencing hearing. The state called four witnesses - the victim's husband, daughter, mother, and employer. The defense called eleven witnesses, including the defendant's mother, brother, three aunts, and school employees who knew the defendant. The defense presented evidence of the defendant's age, the circumstances of the divorce of defendant's parents, and the circumstances of the death of defendant's father.

Once again, the trial Judge read the instructions for deciding the penalty for the defendant's guilt, and once again, the deliberations among the jurors were left up to me to determine. The first thing I did was to ask each juror, one at a time, to state out loud the assurance of the oath each had sworn to during the jury selection phase of the trial. Each stated that they could fairly determine and apply either life in prison or the death penalty.

Each juror had input and comments. They were under tremendous stress, but made a conscientious effort to discuss the values of the life of the defendant. For some, it was easier than for others. However, after agonizing over the vote we were about to take, I suggested we take a time for silence to contemplate our task. After a lengthy time I asked if all were ready to vote, and all spoke or nodded that they were ready.

I again passed out a sheet of paper and asked each to indicate their selected penalty - life in prison, or death. The vote was tabulated as we had done before, and as each ballot was opened, the decision was announced aloud. All twelve ballots indicated a penalty of death. The process had taken just over one hour.

Following the penalty phase, the jury, having

found the defendant guilty of the sole aggravating circumstance urged by the state that the murder took place during an armed robbery, returned a recommendation of death.

TRANSCRIPT OF DEFENDANT'S APPEAL TO THE LOUISIANA SUPREME COURT

The defendant next complains of the trial court's denial of a cause challenge exercised against Jerry Payne, who subsequently served on the jury. Specifically, the defendant argues that Payne indicated that he would refuse to consider mitigating circumstances and would only consider a life sentence when the murder was "justified."

Payne responded: When asked his feelings about the death penalty, I think of the death penalty is as necessary to the degree that the murder was unnecessary considering the brutality, the savagery, and the unnecessity of the killing. Obviously, the mitigating factors with me have a bearing; some have no bearing on that list with me, but some could have a bearing with me.

When the prosecutor asked further questions about Payne's ability to consider the mitigating circumstances that might be presented, Payne replied:

I'm an opinionated person, but before I make an opinion I try to pull all the factors in. And just reading those seven things [mitigating circumstances], I understand there can be many other factors, but just reading some of those, for example, the first one up there - no significant prior criminal history, depending on the savagery of the murder, that may or may not have any significance with me.

The prosecutor continued, reiterating that Payne had just said that the mitigating factor "may or may not" have significance. Payne responded "absolutely" and indicated that he would still consider the information. Although he candidly admitted "it hasn't got much of a chance if it's a savage murder," he reiterated "but I will consider it." Payne stated

214

that he would require there to be strong evidence of a mitigating circumstance to prove to him that those considerations were a factor in the decision.

However, when asked point-blank whether he could consider imposing a life sentence, Payne responded, "Sure" and indicated he could consider either a life sentence or the death penalty. In addition, Payne told the prosecutor that he could vote for a death penalty, "but I won't do it because 11 other people felt that way. I believe twelve separate decisions would have to be made, individually. "

Defense counsel engaged in an extended colloquy with Payne. When defense counsel asked Payne to describe several aspects of his feelings about the death penalty, Payne responded:

Well, that's about an hour-long speech. I think it is necessary. I have to believe that when someone is intending to commit a murder, it has to be in his or her mind that there could be the death penalty involved. They probably never think that they're going to get caught or they're too angry or whatever the situation is. Are there downsides to it, sure, but I still think that it is a deterrent. If someone is convicted wrongly, then that's a horrible situation. But some of the savagery and some of the brutality that we see in murder, just the callousness I think make the death penalty extremely necessary. I don't have reservations about invoking the death penalty if the situation is warranted.

When defense counsel inquired further as to what type of situation would justify a death penalty, Payne responded, "if it's brutal" or "they meant to do it." He further explained, "If they have enough faculties about them and their thought process to know that they're intending to do it, and then I think the death penalty is appropriate."

When asked by defense counsel if he could be considered a person who was "middle of the road" as far as when the death penalty should be imposed, Payne replied, "I think that we've got to be reasonable." He reiterated, however, "Again, it's very hard to be reasonable when it's a brutal situation." Payne admitted to defense counsel that he would have "much difficulty" imposing a life sentence in a case where the murderer engaged in "overkill."

Defense counsel asked Payne if he leaned one way or the other as far as imposing the death penalty or a life sentence for an armed robbery and an intentional killing. Payne replied, "That's fully hard to answer that because I don't know the real facts of the case." Finally, as defense counsel began to ask yet another question on this issue, Payne answered:

"I'm open to anything, okay. But it's going to be very difficult. Again, I once said if you use mitigating circumstances with me, you're going to have to prove them beyond a really reasonable doubt. I mean, I hear a doctor come in and say the person is mentally ill, you're going to have to make me understand that really good for me to accept that."

When defense counsel asked whether Payne could consider mitigating circumstance if instructed to do so by the judge, even if the mitigating evidence was far less than beyond a reasonable doubt, he answered, "Yes, I would consider it."

Defense counsel then pressed Payne further, asking, "Now, in terms of considering it, could you use a mitigating circumstance that has not been proven beyond a reasonable doubt as an actual reason for imposing a life sentence?" Payne responded, "I'd just have to see the situation, I don't know that I could do that." Defense counsel followed up with: "So the answer is it would depend?" Payne answered, "It sure would." Payne described to defense counsel that he would expect a beyond a reasonable doubt level of proof of mitigating circumstances before the circumstances "would make certain that I would give them life rather than death."

When asked to describe his feelings about a life sentence, Payne indicated: "I think that's a tough sentence assuming they don't get out of prison. I have to consider the victim in that, also, and I think that the death penalty is going to put an end to it for that person, for the two people, the victim and the accused, but that doesn't end it for the other folks.

I don't like this term closure because I don't think there is closure. On the other hand, a life term sentence, I think the reason we should send people to prison is so we can redeem them. And if you're sending them for life with no parole, redemption is not necessary because they're not ever going to get out anyway."

Defense counsel then asked if a life sentence was nevertheless an extremely severe punishment. Payne replied "most definitely, particularly if there's no parole," and "that's a real punishment," although acknowledging a life sentence was "not quite as tough as death, the death penalty, of course." In determining whether someone who had committed first-degree murder should receive the death penalty or life imprisonment, Payne indicated that "he would want to know whether the person intended to commit the crime through callousness or meanness."

When asked later whether religious ideas about redemption were valid considerations for a life sentence, Payne replied: "They're all considerations, but I too am a religious person, but you know, you can be forgiven just before you are executed, too. So I don't have a problem with life imprisonment, but it has to be a pretty good standard for me to get out of the death penalty, assuming the kinds of crime that I have discussed previously about the brutality, the savagery, the callousness, the intent, the meanness. Mitigating circumstances are going to have to prove to me that life imprisonment may be deserving."

Finally, Payne indicated that "anger was not an excuse for a first-degree murder."

Defense counsel challenged Payne for cause arguing that he would require the defense to prove mitigating circumstances beyond a reasonable doubt; thus, holding the defense to a higher burden than was required by law. The trial court after listening to the argument of counsel denied the objection.

The Supreme Court stated in its writings in affirming this denial of the defense counsel challenge. Considering the whole of Payne's voir dire testimony, we do not find any abuse of the trial court's discretion in denying the challenge for cause. Payne's willingness to follow the court's instructions combined with his willingness to impose life imprisonment or the death penalty, depending on the circumstances, negated the defense's inference that Payne was biased, prejudiced, or unable to render a judgment according to law. Thus, the trial court properly denied the defense challenge for cause.

JUDGE C.J. CALOGERO - THE SUPREME COURT'S DISSENTING VOTE

I respectfully dissent from the majority decision affirming the conviction and sentence of death. I disagree with the majority's resolution of the defendant's claim that the trial court abused its discretion in denying a challenge for cause against juror Jerry Payne, who was empanelled on the petit jury, on the basis that Payne would place upon the defense the improper burden of proving the existence of mitigating circumstances beyond a reasonable doubt.

The record of the voir dire examination does not expose any rational basis for a finding that this juror could, under any particular circumstances, set aside his acknowledged presumption in favor of the death penalty and fairly consider imposing a sentence of life imprisonment. The majority thus errs in finding that this juror was not substantially impaired in the performance of his duties.

Although the majority opinion does not cite it in the discussion regarding juror Payne, the only Louisiana case that might arguably support the majority's rather facile conclusion that Payne's answers "negated the defense's inference that Payne was biased, prejudiced, or unable to render a judgment according to law," is State v. Lucky.

In Lucky, the prospective juror would have required "some pretty heavy evidence" in mitigation to merit consideration of a sentence other than death. The Lucky court found no error in the denial of the challenge for cause because, the court opined, the trial judge there had "perceived [the juror's] responses to mean that his predisposition toward the death penalty, balanced with his willingness to consider mitigating circumstances and to credit those that he deemed 'pretty heavy,' did not significantly impair [the juror's] performance of his duties as a juror in accordance with his instructions and his oath."

I believe Lucky was wrongly decided, as I explained in my dissent to the denial of the rehearing in that case Lucky, 96-1687, 755 So.2d at 861, Calogero, C.J., dissenting from the denial of rehearing. Because the legislature did not provide any presumptions or fixed standards for a capital sentencing jury to use in considering aggravating and mitigating circumstances, that body intended that a qualified juror not enter the penalty phase of trial with a presumption that death is the appropriate penalty, a presumption the defendant would necessarily bear the burden of overcoming.

In Lucky, I stated that any juror who would begin the penalty phase with a presumption of death, unless "heavy" evidence in mitigation were presented, is unfit to serve on a capital jury, just as would a juror who would begin the penalty phase of the trial with a presumption that life is the appropriate penalty.

In my view, the instant case presents a juror even less willing to consider mitigating circumstances than was found in Lucky. Here, when Payne was first asked about his willingness to consider mitigating circumstances, he stated: "I'll say this, if there are any mitigating factors that affect me, they're going to really have some strong evidence to prove to me that those things are a factor." Although Payne did respond affirmatively when asked if he could consider a life sentence, his actual statements otherwise demonstrate that he would hold the defendant to a burden of proof not required by our laws.

Counsel explained that when the jury reached the penalty phase, the defendant would have already been found guilty of armed robbery and intentional murder: "So, if we reach the penalty phase it's because that [the defendant meant to do the killing] is a foregone conclusion." Juror Payne explained at length the need for death as a possible punishment, especially when the killing was intended: "They meant to do it, then I think, if they have enough faculties about them the death penalty is appropriate. If their thought process is to know that they're intending to do it, then I think the death penalty is appropriate."

When told again that guilt of armed robbery and an intentional killing will be a foregone conclusion when the penalty phase is reached and then asked if he would consider himself "in the middle" with regard to the sentences of death or life, the following exchange occurred:

A: That's fully hard to answer that because I don't know the real facts of the case.

Q: And I don't want to put you on the spot but I'm just trying to understand.

A: But it's going to be very difficult I'm open to anything, okay. Again, I once said during the mitigating phase, if you use mitigating circumstances with me, you're going to have to prove them beyond a really reasonable doubt. I mean, I hear a doctor come in and say the person is mentally ill; you're going to have to make me understand that really good for me to accept that.

Q: If the judge were to tell you that you must consider any evidence that proves a mitigating circumstance, even if it's far less than beyond a reasonable doubt, could you consider it?

A: The judge would ask me to do what with that evidence?

Q: Consider any mitigating circumstance evidence?

A: Yes, I would consider it.

Q: Now, in terms of considering it, could you use a mitigating circumstance that has not been proven beyond a reasonable doubt as an actual reason for imposing a life sentence?

A: I'd just have to see the situation. I don't know that I could do that.

Q: So the answer is it would depend?

A: It sure would.

Q: If I understood your answer before that, you would want to see them prove beyond a reasonable doubt before it would have any impact on you?

A: Before it would make certain that I would give them life rather than death.

Q: Okay. You would expect that level of proof?

A: Absolutely.

Mr. Payne was never rehabilitated after this exchange on the burden of proof that he would impose on the defendant before he would consider a life sentence, nor was he even questioned about the burden of proof. Indeed, in response to general questions about a life sentence, Payne later reiterated that, though he acknowledged being able to consider life imprisonment, "it has to be a pretty good standard for me to get out of the death penalty, assuming the kinds of crime that I have discussed previously about the brutality, the savagery, the callousness, the intent, the meanness.

Mitigating circumstances are going to have to prove to me that life imprisonment is deserving." While that statement in and of itself life imprisonment is deserving, may not warrant removal, it is clear from reading the record on voir dire as a whole that this juror, before he would consider returning a life sentence, would place upon the defendant an improperly onerous burden of proof with regard to mitigating circumstances to overcome the juror's presumption in favor of the death sentence.

Furthermore, while the juror could easily describe the situations in which he would impose the death penalty, he could not state with any particularity under what circumstances he might consider a life sentence. He indicated that, where there was intent to kill, it would be "hard" to overcome the death penalty. He also indicated that if the killing were "brutal," he would have "no reservations" in imposing the death penalty, stating "it's very hard to be reasonable when it's a brutal situation."

Payne referred with approval to the statement of another prospective juror, Leland McNabb, who was eventually removed for cause, who had described as brutal every murder he had seen in his 25 years as a paramedic. Payne agreed with McNabb, stating: "Well, every murder is brutal, he said that and that's exactly right." Finally, Mr. Payne explained that a life sentence without benefit of parole serves no useful purpose, because the only reason for sending someone to prison "is so we can redeem him or her." If you're sending them for life with no parole redemption is not necessary, because they're not ever going to get out anyway."

Defense counsel challenged Mr. Payne for cause on the basis that he would require the defense to prove mitigating circumstances beyond a reasonable doubt, a burden of proof not provided by law. The State argued that Payne did not say he would have to be strongly convinced by mitigating factors only that such evidence would have to be proven beyond a doubt.

The trials judge on this record, I believe denied the challenge without reasons and could not have reasonably found that this juror's clear admitted presumption in favor of the death penalty. This was a presumption that was not tempered by any demonstrated willingness to consider mitigating circumstances as directed by our law substantially impairing his ability to sit as a fair-minded and impartial juror during the penalty phase.

Moreover, I believe there should be a level playing field for the accused and the state in jury selection in capital cases. In this case, the majority found that the trial judge had properly excused on the state's challenge for cause prospective juror Rosie Lee. The majority reasons, "Lee's admission that she would consider the death penalty under certain extreme circumstances is outweighed by her consistent statements during the majority of voir dire that she would not impose the death penalty under any treatment of the defendant's circumstance."

That same rationale should have applied to the majority's challenge for cause of juror Payne. Payne repeatedly expressed his presumption in favor of the death penalty and his unwillingness to even consider a life sentence unless the defendant proved the existence of mitigating circumstances "beyond a really reasonable doubt." Therefore, this juror's mere acknowledgment that he could consider a life sentence was surely "outweighed" by his consistently strong statements during the majority of voir dire that the death penalty was the "appropriate" sentence for this crime and that he would hold the defendant to an improperly onerous burden of proof to overcome that presumption. Thus, had the trial judge and the majority today applied the law even-handedly, in my view, both would have found that juror Payne was no more qualified to sit on the jury than was prospective juror Lee.

For these reasons, I believe the trial court abused its admittedly broad discretion in denying the defendant's challenge for cause against juror Payne, resulting in reversible error. Accordingly, I would order a new trial.

> Footnote: I ultimately served on the jury, and the defendant accepted me at a time when he still had virtually a full complement of peremptory challenges to exercise. The record shows that I appeared in the first twelve jurors submitted for final selection, sandwiched in between the defendant's first and second peremptory strike. The defense had the opportunity to chose a peremptory strike and eliminate me from the jury.

THE LOUISIANA SUPREME COURT RULES AGAINST THE APPEAL 2-1

THE DECREE

For the reasons assigned herein, the defendant's conviction and sentence are affirmed. In the event this judgment becomes final on direct review when either: (1) the defendant fails to petition timely the United States Supreme Court for certiorari; or (2) that Court denies his petition for certiorari; and either (a) the defendant, having filed for and been denied certiorari, fails to petition the United States Supreme Court timely, under their prevailing rules, for rehearing of denial of certiorari; or (b) that Court denies his petition for rehearing, the trial judge shall, upon receiving notice from this court under La.C.Cr.P. Art. 923 of finality of direct appeal, and before signing the warrant of execution, as provided by La. R.S. 15:567(B), immediately notify the Louisiana Indigent Defense Assistance Board and provide the Board with reasonable time in which: (1) to enroll counsel to represent defendant in any state post-conviction proceedings, if appropriate, pursuant to its authority under La. R.S. 15:149.1; and (2) to litigate expeditiously the claims raised in that original application, if filed, in the state courts.

AFFIRMED - TRAYLOR, Chief Justice. JOHNSON, Justice, CALOGERO - Justice, dissents and assigns reasons.

THE CONCLUSION

Thus ended a trial of over a week of sequestration with my fellow jury members. This assemblage of jurors were from all walks of life. I will never again question a jury's decision, especially in a trial that is labeled as this sensational by the media.

An irate person on the street discussing the media hype in the Casey Anthony murder trial in 2011, commented indignantly that the jury must not have heard all we were hearing in the media about this trial. Exactly! A jury only hears what is admissible by law. A jury shouldn't have to wade through unproven assumptions or the story lines that media personalities use to increase TV ratings. The media builds ratings with the word 'sensational'.

I believe that the jury system is as fair as it gets. This was a very humbling and extraordinary fate to be part of one of life's ghastly tragedies. The emotions for so many people are strained beyond imagination, and nothing can prepare humans for this realism. While the human mind cannot explain this senseless action, each juror is thrust into the inner thoughts and actions of this horror for all involved - the victim, the victim's family, the defendant, and the defendant's family. Every jury member is burdened with the agony of a life or death decision.

This was the one decision that required everyone's best. America's legal system required we get it right! This jury exhibited an unusual sense of dedication, seriousness, and attention to detail while applying common sense to the decision before them. Nobody asked for this jury duty, but in my opinion, each juror accepted this responsibility with a conscientious effort to be totally fair and impartial.

The judge struggles with the complexity of the law and to apply the law fairly. The judge, jury, attorneys, and families, struggle to reach the ultimate conclusion of guilt or innocence, life or death.

The inner workings and mechanics of participating on a jury require a precise operational machine. The bailiffs go to extreme measures to protect the jurors from the public, news accounts of the trial, and even contact with family. We were allowed to talk to spouses, occasionally, but with a bailiff sitting by your side.

It became obvious that the jurors were to be kept comfortable and provided with all the comforts of home. The jurors became like a family drawn together in a time of crises. Every effort was made to keep outside concerns from interfering with the duties at hand.

This jury experience drew total strangers together in a way much different from retreats or summer camps from the past times of my life. We were being harbored in total seclusion but with a purpose of determining the value of human life.

MY LIFE BEGINS TO CHANGE

With the excitement that was happening with my casino work, and my political involvement, the fruits of my labors were making a difference to my hometown. However, the bedrock of my very being was beginning to change. My life's buffet was giving me more serious choices, and I found out God is in control of those buffet of choices.

There are times in life that things are just not in our control. Even with my successes that seemed to be a regular thing, I began to realize that I had not taken advantage of the really important things in my life. Since the loss of my friend in the seventh grade, my first experience with the death of a real friend, and the terrible loss of my dear sweet grandmother, I had to face the death of my stepfather on June 11, 1995.

Paul Cedric Thie had been there for us, and I now realized the impact he had on our family. There is no question that in these times your life races before you. Oh, the choices we make that we would like to take back, or just relive. If I only had another chance, I would have done some things differently. Even if it would have been one more simple thank you, or one last hug.

Here was a man that tried so hard to be a good Dad. I didn't know until later in our relationship the range of caring he had for us. Nevertheless, my relationship with him had a very good last several years. I loved his humor and his good will. As I think back, oh, how I would love to be able to get up at 4:30 am, go sit on cold log squirrel hunting with him, all the while looking forward to that baloney sandwich lunch.

My beloved mother passed away on November 1, 2001. Always the caretaker, provider, and supporter, Ora Laverne Parnell Payne Thie made sure this family stayed together and celebrated life with exuberance. If one word has to be used to describe her, and one word cannot describe her, I would choose - kind. She had the ability to make everyone feel a love that left you with a true and lasting relationship.

Now Ron and I had to make some big decisions about the family estate, and that landed us right in the middle of a lot of work, of which we had no experience. Nevertheless, we both had the opportunity, piece by piece, to go back through our lives, and our parent's lives, through the pictures, letters, documents, and the keepsakes of our mom and dad. What a wonderful way to recall some of the blessed memories of our family at a time when we both needed something uplifting.

We discovered some things we had never seen or known. Paul had written a detailed diary of his time in World War II. It covered a complete description of his tour in India, and military life during the war. The diary also included his troop ship ride home with singer, Tony Bennett on board. He had beautiful penmanship ability. His handwritings, even in the throes of war times, were perfect. There was not one scratch out, misspelling or grammatical error.

I discovered a sign-in booklet used at the memorial service for our biological father in 1942. We uncovered scores of family photos taken in the 1930's through the 1950's.

My life began to return to some normalcy for a while. Now it seemed that every day had more order and my career was busier than ever. Several major political campaigns challenged me to bring in more winners. I went though a stretch of victories that were very important to the local area and state.

Then, in the middle of the 2004 state elections, Cherry began to have medical problems. Her eyesight began to worsen, and we discovered she had a seriously high blood pressure problem. The high blood pressure had damaged her kidneys. Following many doctor visits and several different diagnoses that went on and on, she became seriously ill in late December 2004. She was finally diagnosed with cervical cancer. After nearly five months in intensive care my wife, and partner, Cheryl Holt Payne, passed away on Mother's Day, May 8, 2005. We had married in January 1965, forty years earlier. Mother's Day will never be a completely happy day for our son, Todd. Cherry was a doting mother that loved her son, and to hear their conversations was a celebration of life for both of them.

Now each day and night became long. I no longer had my mamaw, mom, dad, or wife. It seemed I had no direction or desire. Alone, I was just counting June bugs and watching spiders weave their webs.

The Midyett Sunday School class at the First United Methodist Church in Bossier had been the glue that held me together during this time. Their support and love led me through those floundering days.

I began to feel satisfied that what I had done was about as well as I was going to do in life. My standing in the community was sealed, and in my mind, I had accomplished about all I could, and began patting myself on the back. However, it wasn't for me to make that decision. God knew more was in store because His plan for me was not finished. There wasn't any more time for self-pity. I had to get busy.

I threw myself energetically into more involvement with my work with the local Independence Bowl football game, even into occasionally teaching Sunday school. I was managing five major campaigns, and those campaigns benefitted from my recommitment to purpose. I now had no idle time.

For the first time in over 25 years, I got the urge to listen to my record collection in depth. I began pulling out all the old songs; I use to play my drums along with in the 50's and 60's. All at once, I felt the compulsion to buy the set of drums I always wanted, but could not afford. Todd, connected me to his music instrument dealer in

Texas and I ordered a special set of Pearl drums complete with seven and a half feet of Zildjian cymbals. I soundproofed my music room and began reliving my music days.

I never intended to play professionally again, only to entertain myself. Well, playing the drums isn't like riding a bicycle. I had forgotten almost everything. It was harder teaching myself to play the drums the second time than it was when I was a teenager. I couldn't get my hands or feet to do what they used to do. I could still recall being able to do almost anything, I wanted on a set of drums. No sound or rhythm was too difficult - back then.

In April/May of 2006, I began noticing I had very little physical endurance. I happened to go to my nephew, Dr. Daniel Payne, for a blood pressure medicine refill. Danny did not even say hello. After looking at me, he told his nurse to get blood tests done on me, immediately. He never asked any other questions of me in his office that day. It was about 4 pm, and he said he would call me as soon as he got the blood tests back. I was thinking I would hear from him the following day.

Leaving his office, I headed back to my office and worked until 9 pm. I arrived home, and Danny had left me a phone message to immediately get to the emergency room. He said, "You are already checked in; just get there as soon as possible."

My caring and concerned neighbor, Barbara Winkler, drove me to the hospital. My brother Ronnie met us at the emergency room. As Ronnie and I were walking to the emergency room assigned to me, we passed a young girl with her father. I told Ronnie, "Did you see how pale that girl was?" He told me, "Have you seen how pale you are?" It seems that I was very anemic.

It turned out that I had a large cancerous basal cell carcinoma growth on my left arm. Following surgery to remove the tumor on my arm, I was hospitalized for six nights, and after receiving six units of blood and an iron infusion, I was in pretty good shape. Danny had more medical specialists come see me than I knew existed.

Friends that I known for years that had become nurses came to check on me. Either I was an extraordinary medical case, or, as I came to realize, I had crossed paths with a lot of people in my life. During my hospitalization, I had an untold number of visitors. It seemed like everyone I knew came to visit and comfort me. I don't know how they found out so quickly, but they came to pray with me, and let me know they were there for me. I felt so humbled by all of the caring cards, flowers, and especially the friends that came by to visit.

This was the first time I had been hospitalized since my tonsils were taken out at the age of six. The fear of knowing I had cancer was enough to scare even the strongest of people. However, I was in the best of hands, and big surprise - the food at the hospital was really good!

From out of nowhere, friends came to see about me and check on me. People I hadn't seen in years and friends from school and church came by in droves. I believe even some of my enemies came to be sure I was sick. Oh my, even Jay Murrell, a Republican through and through called to wish me well. I thought I must really be sick.

My friend, Larry Little, and our Associate Pastor, John Robert Black, were visiting with me just minutes before a follow-up surgery procedure. Larry had to step out of the room for a business phone call, John Robert approached the bed, and the tears started flowing from my eyes. He said, "I know you are scared, but this surgery will go fine." I finally composed myself and told him, "I'm not worried about the surgery. God will take care of that. I'm crying because I am so overwhelmed by the love of my friends, and so thankful for them and their nurturing affection."

My friends, and especially the Midyett Sunday School class, had shown such an outpouring of love, caring and grace during the ordeal Cherry had gone through, and now they were at my side, again.

I had been blessed with a wonderful gift, and I just couldn't hold back the gratitude I felt in my heart. I had to let it out. I was overcome by their kindness, and I was experiencing a speechless moment.

I had gotten myself in this mess, and I believe the doctors, with God's guiding hands, took over and graced me with a whole new beginning. His plans for me were being put in motion. I certainly could not have imagined in a million years the direction my life was about to take. The black clouds were about to turn to gloriously sunny days.

MY RECORD COLLECTION - JUST ME AND SCATMAN!"

My lifelong collection of music record albums has given me thousands of hours of pleasure. Collecting record albums became a passionate desire to find the obscure, unheard of, artists, their rare music, and the actual life stories told in music. This is bona fide American history.

The power is in the message as told by a hardly-melodic, unknown artists/messengers from decades ago when the recording equipment was unrefined and raw. Yet, this music told the daily account of human struggles on hot sweaty sunshiny days, to the menace of rainy cold dreary days. It is a way of life long since passed into the folklore of America's past and struggles of hard times and love lost.

The excitement was to find that piece of music history that would make me feel as though I had at last heard a song, or a sound, that only that recording artist and I had heard before. The discovery of those rarely ever-heard bits of musical history made the effort of collecting a compensation of satisfaction.

Listening for hours in order to find that little gem of a life gone wrong or right provided unique stories in extraordinary verses of an unrefined form of poetry. It could be in love or tragedy, in a cotton field or a roadhouse bar, happiness or sadness, a teardrop, or wistfully longing for a lost woman through a rain-splattered windowpane.

I only had one rule, and made myself a promise. I would keep collecting only if I would listen to every record I bought. I did not need to hear the whole record, but enough to know sufficiently about the artist and the mission of his music. If the record looked interesting, or had a song that I did not have, I would buy it. The excitement of the expectation of the musical sounds I would hear from an artist's song that I have never heard before, more often than not, also made the hunt worth the effort.

The first record I ever owned was bought from a Five and Dime Store in downtown Shreveport. My grandmother bought it for me, because I kept begging for a record. She didn't know anything about records, but we had a little RCA Victrola record player, and I needed to have a record. I was seven or eight years old.

I never forgot that record; it had a red label (don't remember the label company). The song was "The Birmingham Jail," by an artist I don't remember, either. Don't know why I picked that record. It was a bluesy song that would be the beginning of my interest in the blues. I really didn't like the melody, but the guttural, sad story struck me as different from any music I had ever heard.

I always had a love of music, and my first recollection was of country music, because country music was huge in Shreveport. The Louisiana Hayride was the incubator for most of the country musicians in America. Hank Williams, Ernest Tubbs, Kitty Wells, Faron Young, George Jones, Bob Wills, Johnny Cash, Jim Reeves, and so many more.

When I was six years old, I was in the operating waiting room at the Schumpert Hospital about to get my tonsils taken out. I will never forget they had a little radio sitting in the window. The window was open, because there was no air conditioning. The nurse asked what kind of music I liked, and she tuned to Shreveport's KWKH, one of the most powerful radio stations in America, or the world, for that matter. The station's slogan was, "From the Yukon to the Yucatan", because their radio signal reached that far. The songs I vividly remember from that morning were, "I'll Walk the Floor over You," and "San Antonio Rose." It is funny how some things never leave your memory.

The radio was always a major part of our lives. The music we heard in the mornings getting ready for school to every other minute we turned on the radio was a music that was in transition. I remember the songs, "Slow Boat to China," "Shrimp Boats are Coming," and "Boogie Woogie." The music ranged from Tommy Dorsey to Rosemary Clooney, and the new music, "Rock and Roll." Music was an all-consuming part of our lives.

As I became enthralled with the beat of the songs, I began to tap on the furniture with pencils. After damaging some pieces of furniture, my parents made a life-changing decision. They bought me a set of Bongo drums. That saved the furniture, but not their eardrums or their sanity.

My dad bought me a Scatman Crothers album, "Rock n' Roll," that I credit with doing more to help me learn to play the drums than any other record I ever owned. I could sit down on my drums and play for hours - just me and Scatman! The album had some great rudiments and different rhythms that were elementary in playing the drums.

My brother had some Lenny Dee records that were perfect for practicing different drumming fundamentals. I had a various artist album,"Jazz Confidential." Those albums had some amazing rhythms, and they were the beginning of a basic drumming career.

My parents recognized my incessant interest in drumming, a passion I learned during my homeroom class period, thanks to the high school band director, Kenneth Green. He encouraged me to play the school's set of drums during homeroom.

During my sophomore year, I got a set of rag tag drums for Christmas. This created the need for different records and genres of music so I could learn to play all forms of music. From Big Band, to Blues, to Boogie Woogie, to Rock and Roll, my logical source for all this music was records - more and more records.

Shreveport's Stan the Record Man had one of America's largest record mail order stores. They carried all kinds of music, but it was the blues records that interested me. Little Walter, a blues harmonica-playing creative giant recorded on the Chess label, made an album titled, "Little Walter," and it was very first record I ever purchased.

I bought a few more albums at Stan's when I could. I remember trying to organize my small, but about to be important collection. I took pieces of adhesive tape and numbered each album, and I recall there being 101 albums. Those 1950's records were a great array of that era's music.

The albums' future values never entered my mind. Today they are some of the most valuable and priceless in my collection, minus the tape damage to the covers.

As the collection grew, friends would come over and I would challenge them to name a song I didn't have. Occasionally they would name a song I did not have, or could not find. Those songs became my 'to get' list. The collection has grown to over 5,000 33-rpm albums and 45rpm records. The value of each individual record varies from expensive to not so expensive. The collected works consists of artists of every genre of music. More than 1,300 blues albums and many more 45-rpm blues records.

Unusual and significant albums in my collection include: Elvis Presley- pink vinyl, and Elvis's first album; Buddy Holly, "That'll be the Day"; The Midnighters with "Annie had a Baby"; Pete Fountain and Brenda Lee "Together"; a various artist album "Rock'n Roll" on the Aladdin label; Brother Dave Gardner; Lightnin Hopkins, "Lightnin and the Blues"; Little Walter, "Little Walter"; and The Complete Works of Tex Ritter, The Mills Brothers, Elvis Presley, The Beatles Anthology, Big Joe Turner, The Legendary Sun Sessions, Nat King Cole, Coleman Hawkins, Earl Hines, Glenn Miller, Hank Williams, Sr., Bob Wills, Muddy Waters and Robert Johnson, and others.

As a result of my interest in collecting musical albums, I have met some of the initial icons of rock n' roll music. I met Arthur Alexander, the writer and singer of, "You Better Move On," a huge blues hit, and the only song also recorded by The Rolling Stones, The Beatles, and Elvis Presley.

The Birmingham, Alabama, Record Collector's Association, which I helped start, sponsored a Record Collector's Convention in Birmingham, complete with a concert featuring Arthur Alexander, who at the time was driving a city bus in Cleveland. We paid his way back to Birmingham to perform in front of thousands of people at the Boutwell Auditorium. He did not have the money to even ride a bus from Cleveland to Birmingham. Other performers at that concert were Sammy Salvo of "Oh, Julie," and The Mysterians, "96 Tears."

Rob Smith, my sound engineer and the voice for my radio and television ads through the years was re-mastering some recorded songs for local record producer, Wes Attaway. The story goes that Wes had purchased the rights to several Lighting Hopkins songs from Stan Lewis of Stan the Record Man. Wes had been told the songs had never been published before.

We had invited Rob and his wife over for supper, and began to listen to some of my more rare records. I already had in my possession the recordings of the Lighting Hopkins songs Rob was working on. I had remembered the songs that Rob was working with in his studio, and unbeknownst to Rob, I began playing the same songs he was re-mastering. I waited and waited until he suddenly realized I already had the recordings of the same, supposedly unpublished, songs he was working on. Wes Attaway used my record album in court to sue Stan Lewis.

My record list is computerized and alphabetized by categories. The record list contains the artist name, album title, and date of the album, album identification number, the record label name, the value of the album, the rated album condition, and any distinguishing information about that particular record issue.

The album covers are historical documents of not only pictures, but also the liner notes tell important stories about the artist and their music. I have spent hours reading album covers about these obscure artists and the music most people have never heard.

My special favorite artists are Jimmy Reed, Slim Harpo, Chuck Berry, Bo Diddley, Fats Domino, Buddy Holly, Duane Eddy, Ray Charles, James Brown, The Everly Brothers, Jerry Lee Lewis, Ricky Nelson, Little Richard, Bobby "Blue" Bland, John Lee Hooker, Mississippi John Hurt, and literally hundreds of powerful and inspirational story tellers and instrumentalists. I have most of the recordings of these artists, and certainly all of the most important recordings of these artists.

THE BEST BUFFET, YET

A few weeks prior to my medical episode, I had gone online to the Classmate.com website, and had an unanticipated message from a former friend from Bossier High School, the beautiful Madonna Bigelow. Madonna had left me a surprising message asking that I contact her, I answered immediately. We traded a few messages, and then we exchanged phone numbers, only to futilely miss each other a couple of times.

Finally, one night around 8 pm, the phone rang and it was Madonna. It was like talking to an angel. She was so pleasant and easy to talk with. Her voice was as soft and caring as I had recalled. We talked with the greatest of ease even though it had been over forty long years, and so much of our lives had passed through those years. We talked about our lives, our jobs, and our families. It was hard to describe each of our lifetimes in just over an hour's discussion. That phone call was one of the highlights of my life. I hadn't felt that good about life for a long time. I was so excited I couldn't sleep that night. I could not believe I had actually talked with Madonna. How incredible, I thought, when we figured it had been 42 years. I remembered vividly the last time I had seen her in Bossier City. The more I thought, the more I realized how special she had been to me, and how easy our conversation had gone as we reconnected during that magical phone call. We also talked of seeing each other at her upcoming BHS Class of 1961 reunion in October 2006. That April 2006 phone call was about to change my life.

Nearly a month after that phone call I had my surgery. Todd and I had planned a June trip, featuring baseball in Memphis, Louisville, Cincinnati, Cooperstown Baseball Hall of Fame, New York City and Yankee Stadium, Washington, DC, with side trips to Niagara Falls, Atlantic City, Asheville, and Atlanta.

I was getting stronger, but Todd still had to change my bandages everyday during that trip. I returned home to finish the campaigns I had going on at the time.

The excitement about talking to an possibly seeing Madonna had not receded. We continued to exchange some emails prior to her high school class reunion which began on Friday, October 6, 2006. I was nervous and very excited that morning about seeing her for the first time in so long. I knocked on the door to room #402 at the Boomtown Casino Hotel, and as she opened it, and she was a picture, I will never forget. Her smile and graciousness were simply everything I could have imagined. She was as lovely and cordial as ever.

She had not been back to Bossier in a long time, so I proceeded to show her the new Bossier. It was perfect weather, blue clear skies, 72 degrees, so I put the convertible top down. We went riding all over Bossier City remembering places from years ago, and to places new to Bossier City. Heading back from North Bossier on the Benton Road near the Brownlee Road, I turned to look at her. Her movie-star-like sunglasses sat on her head protecting her waving hair from the breeze. Madonna was as beautiful and stunning as ever. This was an unforgettable moment, and there was no way I was going to let this mesmerizing electric moment end!

I suggested we have lunch at the Saltgrass Restaurant at the new Louisiana Boardwalk Complex. We proceeded to order an appetizer, another appetizer, then yet, another one. The conversation had flowed so effortlessly all day. We ordered a salad, and then the entrees. No way could we have eaten all of that food. I was stalling so this dream would last forever! We strolled around the Boardwalk, enjoying every moment. That Friday night, after a BHS football game, everybody gathered for a reunion party. I couldn't be in her company enough that night.

Following that exhilarating reunion on Friday, I could not wait for Saturday. The next morning opened with a buffet breakfast, followed by the graduate's tour of the high school, but the most amazing moment happened the first thing that morning. I arrived at the group's breakfast buffet, and saw Madonna standing in line with several of her former high school girlfriends. My life was about to change forever. I approached her, putting my hands on her shoulders, gave her a gentle kiss, and said, "Good morning, Madonna." That became a life-changing, thunderous, moment. I felt like I was turning back flips without touching the ground. If ever I have had a 'wow' moment that was it. That is a moment I try to recreate every morning I am with her. All of our kisses are good, but I just can't seem to recreate that magical kiss. I'll just keep trying.

Surely, she would be with me all day on Saturday! I was anxious to sit with her that morning, but no, Madonna was already surrounded by fellow graduates that had missed her too. I looked, but there were no seats near her. I had to sit with Richard Auchard, a CPA, and cowboy, Jim Coleman. Now that was a lively conversation. I hardly spoke for watching Madonna across the room. After breakfast, suddenly she skipped the school tour and went off somewhere with her girlfriends. I couldn't find her anywhere, and I was a little distraught. I had been asked to do some work on a reunion photograph which required me to call my graphic artist to the office. After completing the task, and stewing until 2 pm, I went home. I was crushed, and I had decided I wasn't going to the reunion that night. I was watching some football games on TV, and still bothered by the turn of events. Then Madonna called about 4:30 pm and asked where I was. It only took hearing her voice again to decide to go to the reunion that night.

That night, before the banquet began, I walked to the area where all the graduates had gathered waiting to be seated. As I turned the corner, there standing among the crowd - it was as Madonna was in Technicolor, and all the rest were in black and white. We spent the whole night together enjoying, laughing and growing closer every minute. I watched with hilarity as the sixty-something-year-old-girls giggled and rolled Cathy Lowe's house. We ended the evening by closing down the bar that I called my bar from my days of working at Horseshoe. It is a quiet, very intimate place, and we reflected on our long overdue reunion. This had been so enchanting for each of us. This was not a plan we had expected, wanted, or even knew was possible. Only God could have arranged this weekend and what was to follow.

Being at that same buffet line many times since, I look at the spot where that happened, and still feel the enormity of that moment. That was the best buffet, yet.

We had experienced an amazing weekend at the first high school class reunion she had ever attended. She left that Sunday morning for Atlanta to visit her Aunt Betty, but came back through Shreveport on her way home to Houston. I was ready with roses and all. We had the first of our many romantic dinners at Jack Binion's Steakhouse.

With each conversation, a new and powerful relationship grew stronger. After months of telling her I was going to come to Houston, it only took four days to get down there. It was a four-hour drive to her house, barely enough time to prepare myself and keep from shaking with excitement. I clearly remember every turn I made approaching her house. The closer I got to her home my heart raced even faster than the last turn, and finally a left turn into her driveway. I will never forget that thrilling moment she opened the door to her home to greet me. The twinkle in her eyes, and the excitement in her big smile, were feelings I knew I never wanted to be without ever again. I don't think I have ever been that overjoyed. I was actually trembling. That night she made the first meal she ever prepared for me - cornbread, turnip greens, and black-eyed peas. This lady was perfect, and had captured my heart!

That weekend was like a dream. We thrilled with each glance, and the enchantment grew to a new height of pleasantness. We just enjoyed being together, and we constantly smiled. Joy was now no stranger to me. Never have I hated to leave something as much as leaving her that weekend. This had grown to a fever pitch, and we couldn't stand the thought of being apart. Phone calls became constant (a $389 phone bill), and visits became regular with each moment more meaningful. The next weekend she came back to Shreveport for Ronnie and Mary's Surprise 50th Wedding Anniversary Party.

On December 18th, we celebrated her birthday with a special breakfast I prepared for her. It included the works, with hot biscuits and the only candle I could find in her house, (a blue candle). The only place I could find to stand it up was in the hot biscuit. She was giddy as she ate around the blue wax drippings.

The sounds of Christmas filled a Houston mall with the spirit of the holidays. Over the mall sound system, "I'm Dreaming of a White Christmas" began playing, and I turned to Madonna and we began to dance as the crowds watched. I never felt more in love.

Each of our meals took on their own nostalgia. The lunch at Katz Deli, and the dinner at Perry's Steakhouse with three lemon-drop martini's (each), and the light shinning on her beautiful face was magical.

I was so in love with this magnificent lady. During 'that dinner a waiter, not even our waiter, came to tell us how much in love we looked, and how we treated each other with such affection. He was moved by our love for each other. I was absolutely spellbound by the devotion Madonna was showering on me. I had never felt warmth and love like that. It seemed everything we did was memorable, lasting, and so special.

After each visit, my return trips back to Shreveport became harder and harder. Instead of leaving Sundays, it was delayed until Mondays, then Tuesdays. She always made me lunch to take back with me, and she would call to check on me several times just to be sure I was okay and awake.

Our friendship had been strong during, and just after high school. She was always concerned about me, and was always delicate with me. This had developed into so much more. God had given me the love of a lifetime. I would just have to make up for those 42 lost years.

On one return trip, I asked to borrow her 1960 high school yearbook, saying I could not find mine and needed to look up some things. I was going to ask her to marry me, and I wanted this to be a special proposal. I wanted this proposal to be reflective of our longtime relationship. The proposal came via her borrowed yearbook. I wrote in her yearbook in all the places where I had so unassumingly signed her yearbook 46 years before. On the next to last page where I had written a half page all those years ago, I added new words in gold ink, "Continued 46 years later, God opens doors for us to go through. I love you, will you marry me?" Then I gave her the ring and she said, "Yes!"

THE WEDDING PLANNING

Our decision to get married set off a chain reaction of events and memories. The planning gave us a great reason to relive and recount so many of our younger days, and was an enormously happy and fun experience. Those days had left a recollection of friends and events that had an indelible imprint on our life's path. We wanted to include as many friends as possible, as these were the friends that were so easily remembered and cherished.

We both grew closer and needed each other. Through these days, I came to know a mature lady, but not so different from the sweet and beautiful girl I first met and knew in high school. Madonna is a real lady, first class, thoughtful, pleasant, kind, tender, just as beautiful as ever, and she radiates with real elegance. The word amazing is the only way to describe our experience.

This wedding was going to be a gloriously unforgettable occasion. The written words, music, flowers, candles, self-designed invitations and programs, the participants, a designed logo, favors for reception guests, decorations, dresses, tuxedos and even the wedding night in room #402 at Boomtown, the same room she had stayed in for her Class Reunion. Absolutely, every detail was covered the planning the dinners, luncheons, and the rehearsal dinner, writing a toast to my love, arranging for our family members to stay at the same motel. It was a beautiful time in our lives.

The invitation list became the glue that bound it all together as we discussed each name, why they should be at our wedding, and how these people had been a part of our lives.

Two parties were given by our friends to honor us, and as I met her friends and she met mine, we realized this was a wonderful way to begin a new life - sharing with our friends.

THE REPUBLICAN AND THE DEMOCRAT

It all started with that first phone call, "What have you been doing for the last forty-two years?" Then the inevitable question, "What kind of work do you do?" I told her that I was a political consultant and managed campaigns. Madonna did not ask, but I immediately told her how sorry President George Bush was, hated Dick Cheney, and Governor Rick Perry was stupid, and that all Republicans were not very bright. She never said a word. For the next several months, I never held back my disregard for the Republican Party. She seemed so interested in my political views, and the distain I had for the actions and views of President Bush and republicans in general. All the while Madonna patiently and quietly listened and smiled.

Early one beautiful Sunday morning, before attending church in Houston, I was sitting, all so unsuspectingly, in her living room drinking a cup of coffee and reading the Sunday paper. She came into the room and announced with some certainty that there was something she thought I should read. She then retrieved a Houston magazine publication from the bookshelves across the living room, and turned it to the exact page I was to read. As she approached me, her tone left me little choice that I should stop and read the article.

It was a full-page, very in depth story about her bail bond business, the James Bond Bail Bonds. Madonna, after many years in the legal profession, had opened a successful bail bond business in Houston. This story was accompanied by a picture of four of her bounty hunters, the toughest and meanest looking men I have ever seen, carrying weapons fit for a small war against crime. I will always reflect on that morning and wonder if she was sending me a subliminal message. Was this a chilling message about don't mess with her, treat her right, or else?

I began reading as instructed, and as I read down a few paragraphs, I found, "Madonna Raines was named the Texas Republican Business Woman of the Year by the National Republican Party," and further stated she was the Chairwoman for President George Bush's Business Advisory Committee. I sat in stunned silence, wondering what all I had said over the past few months. Make no mistake, this was no subliminal message; it was a hydrogen bomb aimed directly at my political beliefs. I sat my cup of coffee on the table, and placed my head in my hands and said aloud, "Holy Crap."

She was standing just around the corner waiting for the shockwaves to hit me upside the head. As I groaned aloud, she stepped up behind me, put her hand on my shoulder, and with little to no compassion, asked, "What's the matter, honey?" Before I could utter a word, she rather staunchly informed me, "We are having lunch after church with several of my friends; they are all Republicans, and you better not embarrass me."

Sure enough, after church Madonna's closest personal friends joined us for lunch. Make no mistake; I was being interviewed to see if I met with the seal of approval. I don't remember what the sermon was about that Sunday morning, because I had concentrated on preparing for the lunch to follow, and the necessity of acting appropriately as I had been so sternly instructed.

Shortly after the prayer of thanksgiving and blessing of the food we were about to partake, the rapid-fire interrogation began. Typical questions about my heritage, my family history, did I have any communists in my background; you know the questions you might find on the highest secret service clearance form. Then came the question I was prepared for, "What line of work are you in?" I responded with all of the political acumen I had drilled into my candidates over the years. Getting past that question easily, next came, "What party are you in?" I looked them all in the eye and said, "I am a Democrat," but quickly added, "I have worked for both parties, and probably elected more Republicans than Democrats.

I think the person and their abilities are the most important thing in selecting a candidate to work for." That was good enough for most of the questioners. I had gotten by this test with only some remaining consternation among the group.

Thinking I had slid past this huge hurdle in our relationship, I brilliantly kept my mouth shut for the most part over the months to come. I was about to learn of Madonna's non-failing, long-term memory. Time heals all wounds - well, not exactly. During the preparation for the wedding, we were picking out the wedding cakes, which included the groom's cake. I had meticulously chosen a German chocolate cake with strawberries on top. All settled, I thought.

Without my knowledge, Madonna, not quite even with my political views, and me had my groom's cake changed. She had an employee that wrote children's books, and he had an illustrator that helped him. She had the illustrator draw an image of a donkey with his rear facing the viewer of the picture. The donkey's head was turned looking 180 degrees toward his rear, and he was dressed with a top hat on his head and a bow tie with an incredulous look on his face. On top of the donkey, was an elephant sitting backwards facing to the rear of the donkey holding her hand high in the air, as if riding a rodeo bucking horse, a veil on her head, earrings, a huge ring on her finger, and wearing a little tutu. Instead of pinning a tail on the donkey there was a "Just Married" sign stuck on the donkey's tail. Needless to say, all the reception guests were delighted, and, of course, Madonna had the last word.

MY TOAST TO MADONNA

(Given at the Rehearsal Dinner)

You have given all my moments, breaths and heartbeats a renewed vitality. You are the essence of love, and your sheer beauty, both inside and out, makes me tremble. I am enthralled by your sharing ways; your Christian beliefs; your kind hands; your sweet kisses; your lasting embraces; and your gentle smiles.

My love for you is so complete and lasting. Your warmth is so enduring and stays with me all of my days and nights. No words can describe the flutters in my heart when I am with you, or the enchantment I feel when you look at me with your sparkling eyes. I miss you when you aren't with me; I get excited when I am with you.

Now, as we begin a marriage we feel was made in Heaven and blessed by God, may all of our moments be filled with loving memories and happiness - May all our days ahead be full of treasured thoughts, sweet love stories, tender moments at home, lingering dances and loving glances.

May our wine be warm and tasty, our meals be filling, and our desserts be as sweet as our love.

OUR STORY PRESENTED IN THE WEDDING PROGRAM

Our Story!

We believe, with all our heart that God opened this door for us, and we have chosen this day to go through that door together. Only He could have positioned us at the precise time, circumstance, and place to fall in love. We realize that the series of events that occurred could have taken so many different paths, leading us in another direction. We marvel that we have reached this point, and for the wonderful event, that is taking place.

Although we were very good friends in high school, as it often happens, we lost track and allowed over forty years to pass without us seeing or even talking to each other. However, our friendship was suddenly recaptured by a simple phone call. It was as if we had been apart only a few days. Then, while attending a class reunion, driving around town, sharing a special lunch, and having the time to catch up, our admiration and respect for one another was quickly rekindled. After many hours of visiting, sharing our thoughts, dreams and experiences, being together was as natural as breathing. It was as if God handed us this precious gift to be treasured and nourished. At this stage of our life, we appreciate this love and each other so much more than we ever could have before.

Now, as we begin a marriage we feel is blessed by God, we are truly excited about our future together. It is our hope and prayer that our gift of love can be shared with you, our family and friends. We thank you for being a part of this celebration and sharing this special day with us.

THE WEDDING - ROSES, CHAMPAGNE AND A MARRIAGE LICENSE

Busy probably describes our wedding better than anything else. However, it was busy in a phenomenal way - friends, family, food and fun. After all, we had the world's greatest event planner, Madonna. Every detail was considered, and every feature was executed under the scrutiny of her talented and watchful eye.

Whom would we invite to this wedding? I don't know exactly what kind of wedding Madonna initially thought we were going to have, but I wanted a celebratory event. I wanted everyone to know I was going to marry Madonna.

Who were the people that had been a part of our lives? That would be way too many invitees. So the many years of friendships required thorough research in order to recall those friends. We literally went back through our lives remembering those former high school, work, church, even our neighbor friends. This became a really fun exercise putting this list together and recalling those friends.

She had her list, and I had my list. The lists grew way out of hand. I had resorted to the telephone book to help me remember my friends. Madonna exercised her right of refusal.

This was turning out to be much more than a wedding event. Besides being a huge social event, it was also becoming a high school reunion of sorts. This all started in high school, and after all, was rekindled at a high school reunion. This had every feeling of young love.

In the old country - weddings lasted for days well -we could do that. People came from all over the country to share our very special day - Florida, Oklahoma, Texas, Alabama, Georgia, Tennessee, Maryland, Arizona, Oregon, Arkansas, Mississippi, and all over Louisiana.

The dresses and tuxedos were ready, the flowers were chosen, and in selecting the music, each song had a personal meaning. The distinctively designed invitations were mailed, the favors prepared, the wedding cakes ordered, the programs printed, the band hired, the decorations carefully placed, the reception arranged, the honeymoon (which was going to be unbelievable), and the photographer and videographer were in place.

In the end, we had 27 hotel rooms booked for mostly family, and some out-of-town guests. Now, it had turned into a family reunion also. On Wednesday of the wedding week, we drove over to the Dallas airport to pick up the children, Dennis, Monica and Mark, and their spouses and the grandchildren. The fun began from that very moment.

Friends and family were taken care of, now for the food and fun. Both carloads stopped and met my son, Todd, for a late lunch at Posados Mexican Restaurant. Everybody was in a great mood, and the Posados people were probably glad when we left. After arriving in Bossier and settling in at the hotel, pizzas were delivered and the party started.

It was really nice having just the kids together for that evening. We spent the night having a few drinks, munching Southern Maid Donuts, and lounging at the hotel. It was a late night and everybody was ready for bed, except for the grandchildren. I thought what the hell, let'em play. They didn't get the chance to be together that much since it is a long way from their homes in Arizona and Oregon. Besides, Madonna and I weren't spending the night there anyway.

After a decent night's rest, Thursday morning started with the grandchildren ready to check out the town. We took them to the Sci-port Science Center for all kinds of energy-burning activities, and the IMAX Theater.

As we arrived, back at the hotel in early afternoon the big event was beginning to take shape. The Mississippi, Maryland, and Alabama side of Madonna's family had arrived; it was full-fledged southern hospitality and fun from that point on. The hotel was packed with family, including several close friends from Houston. The hotel party that was escalating wasn't one of the planned events, but make no mistake the party was on.

It's a good thing the hotel owners were very good friends. No, they were the best of friends. I didn't know until everybody checked out that all 27 rooms were going to be free gratis. That is not the way we had agreed some months earlier. The hotel was open to our guests, and the workers at the hotel were treating our family, as they were part of their family. We will never be able to thank the owners, Frank and Diane Campisi, his mother, Mrs. Rose Campisi, and Buck and Bobbie Rose Wharton, enough for that gracious act of kindness.

That night over forty family and friends gathered at Monjuni's Italian Restaurant in Shreveport, and the celebration began in earnest. What better way to start than with an Italian touch, and what a gathering of exceptional people. There was a festive special feeling of love and laughter all over that room. The family all returned to the hotel for more of the family gathering. I was seeing a new family come together, as the excitement was building.

Friday was more than just the day before the wedding, it was full of even more events centering on food, hugs and laughter. Madonna held a luncheon at The Glenwood Tea Room for the ladies in the wedding party and friends, and was a dainty happening with classy ladies from our lives.

Across town, the men in the wedding party gathered at The Country Tavern for barbeque. I taught my new Grandson, Ethan, how to clean the meat off of a barbeque rib bone, and the food did not disappoint.

Thankfully, Madonna's dad, John Bigelow, was

there, and was determined not to miss anything. It would have been exciting to watch John and my deceased stepdad, Paul, sitting and talking. Both being very frugal, they both would have been shaking their heads in disbelief at the all the happenings and goings on.

The anticipation of the wedding day was building to frenzy as family and friends were arriving in town for tomorrow's anticipated event. The wedding rehearsal was being coordinated by Jane Cooper, and the realization of our wedding day was collectively becoming a celebration of true joy.

The only thing missing from this whole romance was our mothers and my stepfather, all deceased. What elegance, charm, and humor they would have added. I can see them smiling pleasingly as their son and daughter were obviously in love. They never had a chance to meet each other, and neither had a chance to meet their new daughter-in-law or son-in-law. We missed them.

The rehearsal dinner was held at the Horseshoe Casino in a private dinning room across the hall from the G. Ron Payne Executive Board Room. Here, the wedding party enjoyed an opulent dining experience complete with wine and champagne. Several toasts were lifted, and I delivered my toast to Madonna. It was a very fashionable event.

The day of the wedding, as I waited for the appointed time to arrive, my dear friend and guitarist, Jerry Beach, came to tell me he would not be able to play the classical 'Ava Maria' as planned. He had just broken a string on his classical guitar as he rehearsed with the organist. He was crushed, and I felt so sorry for him, but he made up for it during the reception. The organist covered for Jerry, and played 'Ava Maria' beautifully. All the while, the photographer and videographer were busy documenting every detail.

Finally, the Big Event - The Wedding Day arrived

April 14, 2007, Saturday, 2 pm. As I waited to enter the church with the best man, Todd, groomsmen, Dennis and Mark, Madonna's sons, and preachers, we saw that a large crowd had been seated. The music started and the guests' murmur dwindled to a reverent silence.

Being a musician, we didn't have any slouch musicians. The organist had played for years at Shreveport's First Methodist Church. Todd's former college roommates, and special musicians, Dave Sterling, pianist and Eric Smith, vocalist, provided some of the most moving music. Dave has recorded several of his own compositions, and Eric had sung with the Fort Worth Opera.

The bride's attendants, Madonna's daughter Monica, and daughters-in-law, Manda and Jody, looked vibrant. The wedding participants included all of the children and grandchildren, except for Madonna's grandson, little Jace. This event was too long for him to be that good. He still dazzled in his tuxedo just like the rest of the guys. Madonna's granddaughters, Katrina and Selah, served as the flower girls, while her grandsons, Ethan and Dylan, were the ring bearers.

Conducting the ceremony was our pastor of the First United Methodist Church of Bossier City, David Dietzel, assisted by Madonna's uncle, retired Baptist minister, Charles Barnes. Now those are two powerhouse preachers.

Everyone was in his or her places, the Wedding March began, and Madonna, in all her radiant beauty, was standing there as the doors opened. She was beaming with her eyes sparkling, and her smile as warm as ever. I was overcome with joy, and my heart was pounding. The sanctuary was full of a lifetime of friends, along with our families. Her dad, John Bigelow, 89 years old, was walking her down the aisle. That was as special as anything about this wedding.

Madonna's uncle, Charles Barnes, a stalwart and shining star in the Barnes family, delivered the homily at our wedding. He had made that family prouder than even their hopes had held. Sure, he had become not only a preacher, but had risen to the top echelons of the Southern Baptist Convention. This day he spoke so eloquently, and so profoundly, saying, "So today in this house of worship we witness the commitment of Madonna and Jerry to each other in the presence of loving families and faithful friends. Now you will feel no rain, for each of you will be shelter to the other. Now you will feel no cold, for each of you will be warmth to the other. Now there is no more loneliness, for each of you will be companion to the other."

The service was full of blessings, humor, and spectacular music. Eric Smith sang the Lord's Prayer with such power it would undoubtedly be one of that church's most memorable moments.

Then we were pronounced "Man and Wife." Almost instantly, the Handel's Hallelujah Chorus rang out, and we stepped into our next life together. WOW!

Then came the merriment and cheerfulness of the reception, all meticulously planned for the enjoyment of all three occasions - a wedding, a high school reunion, and a family reunion. Decorated lavishly, the aura was perfect for our remarkable day. The music was tasteful, and the food was elaborately displayed. The buffet, once again, had many choices. The room was filled and everybody was in a gala mood, and there was a sense of gratification among the attendees.

As we entered the reception, I will never forget the look on Madonna's face. It was a look of surprise and happiness. I felt a fulfillment also. I had the satisfaction that she had come back home and was loved by everyone. It had been a long time since high school, but the years had not diminished the respect and admiration these friends had for her. I could not be more pleased.

Her life had been interrupted by tragedy, yet she was determined to be a loving Christian mother, and a support parent for her children, providing for them financially through her hard work, and being the solid rock on which they could rely. I had learned in only a short while that her motivation was driven by her continued focus on making her children's lives happy and better than the heartaches she had endured. She could hold her head high with dignity. It was a moment of magnificence to witness her being held in such high esteem. I had fallen in love with Madonna, but I also admired her.

Especially humorous amid the large group of my political clients, and in particular for the mostly Republicans in attendance, was the groom's cake which represented a huge victory for Republicans over a Democrat. Madonna's political acumen was supreme for the moment.

My longtime friend, and Louisiana Music Hall of Famer, Bill Bush's combo, played at the reception. Always one to push to the edge, I had decided to sing this day for Madonna. I knew when I had tried to sing in the shower the hot water would turn cold.

This was once in a lifetime, and I was not going to let anything keep me from conveying my love to the loveliest lady in the world with my adulation. Bill had given me a CD of his band's recordings. One of my favorites on the CD was Bill Bush singing "The Way You Look, Tonight." I thought, I can do that, and the words were certainly perfect for the occasion.

Even though I had never sung publicly, I was determined to try anyway. The last time I had tried to perform musically for the first time, it had worked out pretty good, but that was on the drums.

Just to recall the moment, here are the words that meant so much to me, and this is exactly how I felt that day, and will continue to feel, for Madonna.

> *Some day, when I'm awfully low,*
> *when the world is cold, I will feel a glow just*
> *thinking of you...*
> *And the way you look tonight.*
>
> *Yes, you're lovely, with your smile so warm*
> *and your cheeks so soft,*
> *there is nothing for me but to love you,*
> *and the way you look tonight.*
>
> *With each word, your tenderness grows,*
> *tearing my fear apart...*
> *And that laugh that wrinkles your nose,*
> *it touches my foolish heart.*
>
> *Lovely ... Never, ever change.*
> *Keep that breathless charm.*
> *Won't you please arrange it?*
> *Cause I love you ... Just the way you look tonight.*

Madonna looked stunning that day, as always. But this special day I gazed at her as she was standing nearby with friends, I froze in a moment of wonderment. Now, I was married to Madonna. How sweet was that?

As an added attraction, the original "Classcutters" joined me, and the Bill Bush Combo, to play for the first time together in over 40 years. Jerry Beach, George and Jerry Horton, and I were taken back in time.

Among all this happiness we still had empty feelings as we were missing guitarist, Van Weaver, who had passed away a few years back, and maraca player/out-front dancer, Butch "Bones" Toland, now living somewhere in Idaho. In spite of that lonesomeness, it was Chuck Berry, Bo Diddley, Fats Domino, and Dale Hawkins all over again. We hadn't lost our touch.

Our former high school classmates had not forgotten the sounds of The Classcutters. The rest of the guests, having never experienced this 1950's and 60's phenomena, had no idea that I played the drums. There were very surprised looks on the faces all across the room. Even my own son had never heard me play the drums. He had only heard that his daddy was a rock n' roller. The feelings of exhilaration were still there. We didn't just smile we broke into laughter. This was a great day, and life was good!

The over two-hour wedding reception/reunion had been everything we hoped it would be. We left the reception in an all-white 1932 Buick Roadmaster, with a horn that blew, "Here Comes the Bride".

After arriving at the hotel room, we had a glass of champagne to top off this day of memorable events. We changed clothes, and went quickly to the *the '1800 Degree'* Steakhouse restaurant in the hotel to finally eat something in private. We were starving. We had not had time to eat anything at the reception; just too many people to visit with. We were still too excited to really enjoy the meal, but the company was delightful.

It wasn't over yet - later that night we met a group of family and friends in the lounge, and partied and danced long into the night. The main subject of discussion that night was of the spectacular day, but mainly of the way this story had come about, and how this love affair had come so far, and in such a miraculous way.

For the final event, we met our family for a breakfast buffet at 8 am on Sunday morning. This was the exact same buffet place that I had met my fate and fell in love with a simple breathless kiss, and a "Good morning, Madonna."

The amazement of God's plan for us, the momentum of the events, and priceless moments Madonna and I had shared together, had passed by at warp speed. However, the everlasting memories were being written with smiles, laughs, and sweetness. We had been surrounded by family and friends that had created a genuine foundation for this new life together.

This was only the beginning of many action-packed days of sharing our love and admiration.

This was a dream unfolding right before our eyes. Every event, every word, every moment of that day held a memory of love. We gained so much pleasure from the exhilaration of our friends' blessings, and the happiness expressed through the smiles of our families. What a blissful way to start our new life together.

It had been 49 years since our lives had crossed paths in 1958, and 42 years since we had seen each other. We had come from childhood through adulthood to our early golden years, and we would not have reunited so effortlessly but for our sweet recollections of each other.

We spent our wedding night at the Boomtown Hotel in Bossier City. The same hotel, and the very same room where Madonna stayed for that momentous high school reunion. Nearly fifty years after we first met, and only a few months after that high school reunion, room 402, was now filled with roses, champagne, and a marriage license.

THE HONEYMOON "LOOK OVER THERE"

At last, just the two of us. Our love had grown to a crescendo, and we were off to see the world, experience each other, and create our own memories. The exhilarating events had left us with a desire to live life to the fullest, and our future had to make up for lost time.

Without a doubt, the best trip of my lifetime was just ahead of us. Our month-long honeymoon trip to Europe would be a trip of dreams. Madonna may have been the great event planner, but I was the trip planner. My sweet Madonna and I had shared many things that had made our life together so extraordinary, but this trip would be even more.

As we glided out of Galveston Bay on Royal Caribbean's cruise ship, Splendor of the Sea, a breeze was gently blowing, and my heart was racing with excitement. This would be our home for the next 13 nights cruising together on the Atlantic Ocean.

There would never be an idle moment, and our honeymoon would provide some of the most lasting moments of our life. A lot of firsts, such as the thrill of being alone with my love in the Crown Viking Lounge, the romantic carriage ride through Seville, Spain, the exceptional dining in Nice, France, and seeing the beautiful Sistine Chapel.

Perhaps the most astonishing may have been as we walked outside the walled city of Cortona, Italy, and experienced the most beautiful scene of all. We gasped at the sight of the painted rays of golden sunlight cast over the valley below as the sunset across the distant, painstakingly terraced and manicured crops.

Without a doubt, my favorite romantic moment was walking along the Seine River in misty Paris with my love on my arm. The beauty and significance of that scene seemed like it was right out of an old black and white movie. These moments were only the beginning, because when you are sharing all this with the angel God had sent to you, everything to come would forever have a place in your heart.

The 14-day cruise had so many activities. While in Key West we stopped to have a drink in the Hog's Breath Saloon as the chickens walked freely around the place. Just as we walked out of the bar, we walked directly into the Wyland Art Gallery. Madonna found a painting she had admired in Hawaii a few years before. It was a Gicleé, meaning the artist would actually add paint to the numbered print, and then sign it. She was so taken with this piece of art that I bought it for her.

While in Key West, we ran into Farris and Carolyn Baughman, our fellow Bossier High grads, and we were surprised they were on the same cruise.

My favorite of the cruise highlights were the formal nights, and what a stunningly gorgeous lady I had at my side. At last, following months of nonstop activities, we finally had a chance for resting; the relaxation of the spa, eating, and eating some more, as food was everywhere. The ocean was calming, and our card games, and watching the sunsets from the cruise ship, made for peacefulness.

I entered the "Best Legs Contest" poolside, and while I did not win that, I did win a first place medal for the "Best Booty", all to the hilarious delight of Madonna. I proudly wore my medal at dinner that night.

We stayed up until 2:30 am to see the Rock of Gibraltar. There was total darkness, but I believe I made out a huge dark object on shore that I am claiming was absolutely the "rock".

Boarding a tour bus in Ponta Delgada, Portugal, we thought we were headed for an actual pineapple plantation, but pulled up to some greenhouses in town that grew the pineapple from seed to harvest.

Well, at least we got to see a pineapple! Then we headed to the top of the mountain supposedly to see the beautiful landscapes and water below, and found ourselves above the clouds, and therefore could not see anything. Didn't matter, we were in love, so everything was enchanting.

We stopped at the port city of Cadiz, Spain the oldest port in the world. Founded in 1104 B.C., history was all around. It is the oldest continuously inhabited city in Spain, and the oldest in Western Europe.

We travelled north to Seville, founded in 712 A.D., and experienced a different culture of charm, color, and old world romance. Seville is a pleasant city, with important monuments and an illustrious history. It is essentially famous for Carmen, Don Juan and Figaro, and the Andalucian architecture. We spent our time in Seville's old city along the east bank of the Guadalquivir River. We made our first purchase there an eight-pound clock which we lugged all over Europe. We took a pleasurable and delightful carriage ride all through Seville's important sights.

Disembarking from the ship and picking up our luggage in Barcelona, Spain, there was a loud thud behind me, and as I turned to see, Madonna had disappeared, having fallen flat on the floor. Trying to find ice for her knee was nearly impossible. Then the trouper she was, she walked nearly 5 miles around Barcelona that afternoon. While in Barcelona we never did figure out exactly when the restaurants were open, only to find out after we left that Barcelona supper begins very late in the evening.

Barcelona is a spectacular and beautiful city. We spent three days there and could have been there a year and never seen it all. The Les Rambles, "a street for everybody" - sights, including live artists, shops, crafts, picturesque outdoor cafes, a huge food market with everything eatable and uneatable, is a must experience. A wonderful place to "people watch". The Barcelona Cathedral brought of both us to tears, and the Sagrada

Familia, Gaudi's famous cathedral that has been under construction for 100 years, and will not be finished for 50 more years, are absolutely must-sees.

We traveled on to Nice, France, via train along the Mediterranean Sea coast. What spectacular scenery, and the beginning of our, "Look over there's." The most romantic night of the whole trip for me was in Nice, France, walking along the streets full of fashionable people, and then eating outside at Milo's Restaurant. The meal lasted at least three hours. The people watching was the best ever. It was a perfectly cool night, the food was tasty, the wine outstanding, and the dessert was as sweet as our love. The Albert 1er Hotel was a perfect location, as our room overlooked a colorful floral park and the gleaming Mediterranean Sea was shimmering in the moonlight from our hotel window. What a night!!!!

Next, on to Florence, Italy via train, we arrived after dark, heading to The Villa Ambrosina Hotel in Impruneta, a 16-mile ride via taxi. We had no idea where we were going, and began to wonder if our slightly English-speaking taxi driver did either. We went through a small village, and then out of town again, when he suddenly turned left onto a gravel road. It was very dark, and we didn't know if this was going to have a happy ending or what? We wound around tight curves climbing at a very steep rate. Suddenly a palace with beautiful lighting was right in front of us.

We had no idea where we were, or what this place looked like outside except for the lighted area. After checking into a very spacious and exquisitely decorated room, we went straight to bed. It had been a long day.

I awoke just as the sun was barely rising, and peeked out of one of our three huge windows. I saw a breathtaking landscape of purple and orange hues with farms, family mansions and three cathedrals, all seemingly painted across miles of hillsides. I gently woke Madonna so she could see this sight. We marveled at

God's work. What a special way to be introduced to the allure of Italy.

That morning we discovered we were on the top of a 1,000-foot high peak, and the little village of Impruneta lay almost straight down below us. We had a great breakfast, and asked how to get back into Florence. The desk attendant was incredulous that we did not have a car; suggested we walk down to the village below where we could catch a bus into Florence. We took a leisurely, but very, very steep stroll down into Impruneta, gazing at serene homes, churches, and flowers everywhere. This is how Italian villagers live. The weather was ideal for a walk. This was picture perfect Italy.

Upon arrival in Florence, we thought we would first get our bearings, look around, and ride the bus back to Impruneta. Madonna was positive we could catch a taxi back up the 1,000-foot hill to the hotel. We planned to rent a car the second day in Florence. I'll get back to Florence later. Upon riding the bus back to Impruneta, I'll make a long story short; there are no taxis in Impruneta. Now we are looking straight up a 1,000-foot hill to climb, not walk, to our hotel. Looking up at the hotel, we started trudging along the steep narrow street. It had already been a tiring day, and Madonna, breathing heavily, suddenly stopped, and said, "You are on you own. I'm going to do whatever it takes to flag down a car and get a ride up this mountain!"

Only two cars had passed us on the same street we had strolled down that morning, and the only thing looking up was us. We were getting desperate. At last, a young Italian girl came along and saw me, and stopped to offer us a ride.

We had supper at the hotel that night, and it could not have been a more impressive Italian meal and experience. It was complete with fine wine, and a musician with a voice like Dean Martin singing, Volare'. There we were, a table for two, with a view overlooking the valley around us, and real Italian music. Isn't this what love is suppose to be like?

We spent six nights in Florence (Impruneta). It is not possible to describe this artistic center of all of Italy. The day trips included the walled city of San Gimignano, built in the 10th century, and one of Madonna's favorites; a place where you expected to see Jesus walking down the cobbled street. Then on to Monteriggioni, built in 1203, a medieval walled city with 14 still-standing towers. On to the Chianti Trail wine-growing region, with its spectacular rolling hills, huge family homes lived in by the same families for centuries, and pristine grape vineyards and olive groves that are so picturesque. Every small village had an impressive cathedral filled with aged art and frescos.

Pisa, the town famous for the leaning tower, not far from the sea coastal town of Livorno, is much more than a tourist trap, as some had warned us. We loved it, and feel that Pisa is not to be missed. It not only has the leaning tower, but a wonderful cathedral and baptistery. We visited Arezzo, the home of the Church of San Francesco, dedicated to St. Francis of Assisi, Madonna's favorite saint.

Cortona, Italy, definitely was a defining event of all the travels I have ever taken. It is a walled city built in the 11th century and considered to have the most beautiful view of all the Tuscan ancient walled cities.

It was here that we had a moment when you know you are in the presence of God. We had gone through one of the old city gates, and walked to the opposite outer wall overlooking the valley. We stepped out onto a terraced overlook, and Madonna, a few steps ahead of me, suddenly stopped and gasped aloud. Then I saw what she saw. The Godly painted rays of golden sunlight spread across the distant, painstakingly terraced and manicured crops. The expanse of the huge valley view below was an explosion of orange and gold hues as the sun began to set on the vastness of greens below. A sky of heavenly blue sheltered the scene. Madonna started crying, and I was taken aback. I looked at her, and I felt the presence of God. I felt He was there with us to make this a divinely spiritual moment.

We held each other close, and realized that God had truly blessed us. It was as if He was saying, "Let me show you what I have made for you!" What a powerful moment!

One night we asked our hotel desk attendant for a suggestion for supper in the area. This was the best tip we ever received. He guided us to a place about 5 miles away, the village where Albergaccio Machiavelli, the philosopher famous for the Machiavellian principal, had lived. He was expelled from Florence because of his controversial writings, and he came to this Italian rural community. A restaurant, a church, a winery, and a few residences, with not more than 50 inhabitants, were the total makeup of that village.

The sun was setting quickly over this quaint idyllic place. As we parked we noticed a vineyard and olive grove in a valley just below. Our eyes followed the crop rows to the top of the hill above that valley in the nearby distance. On the hilltop was a magnificent picturesque villa silhouetted in the setting sun. It looked just like the numerous paintings seen depicting Italy and its best. This scene set the ambiance for the evening. After being seated, I briefly went out before total darkness set in to take pictures of this old fascinating place, a model for Old Italian communities.

Madonna was trying to decide what to order and having a hard time since the menu was all Italian. The waiter brought out a huge cut of Chianti beef to show to the table behind us. When I got back to our table she exclaimed, "I know what we are going to order." It was one of those, "I'll have what they are having," moments. When that huge steak for two arrived, my eyes must have been as wide as saucers, and Madonna started laughing. That meal, and the atmosphere in that place, was unforgettable. Mind you, we never had a bad glass of wine in Italy, Spain, or France, but the wine with that meal, a bottle of Machiavelli Salatio Del Tani Chianti Classico 2004, was the best wine we had ever tasted.

An even more amazing story about this little village of the old world occurred when we returned home. Within a few days, Madonna picked up a book at the house. It had been lying on the end table for months, and she began to read. Amazingly, it was a story set in this very village of Machiavelli, and the little church next to the very restaurant where we had spent that very special evening.

Our last evening in Tuscany we had intended to return to the same restaurant; however, we found it closed for the night. Disappointed, we began looking for a winery in the area in lieu of a place to eat. What better way to substitute a meal than a few glasses of wine?

We drove for several miles, gave up, and were returning in the direction we came from. We came to a wine tasting sign, turned in, and hoping they would still be open. We had little hope, as it was getting late. I parked, and saw no directions to a wine tasting room, but went through a courtyard with an iron gate leading to a metal door. I pushed the door open and was greeted by a gentleman in a tuxedo. Turned out he was the Maître de, and I could see it was a dining place.

I ask if they were serving meals, and he replied, "It is only for the guests at this resort." I told him this was our last night in Tuscany, we were looking for a place for dinner, and we were running out of options. He graciously invited us in, and I went back to the car to get Madonna. This was too good to be true.

Unbeknownst to us, this was a very exclusive resort with only the finest foods and wines. We had come in the back door, just as southerners do. It was decorated with huge wine vats, the finest table linens, crystal and silver. The art on the walls were huge black and white photographs of nude women taken by a famous photographer. They were tastefully done, and exquisite.

Even more staggering to us, this was the same spectacular picturesque villa silhouetted in the setting sun from a few nights ago. Our meal consisted of rabbit and veal. Absolutely one of the finest meal experiences we have had, and what a way to end our time in Tuscany.

The next day we were at the train station waiting to depart for Rome. I went into the restroom, and inside the stall written on the wall, *Madonna*, with phone number scribbled underneath. I came out and told Madonna, "Damn, you haven't been here six days and some man is letting the world know that for a good time to call Madonna." I happened to have my camera with me and had taken a picture to prove it.

We took the train to Rome, and by the time we arrived Madonna was suffering from a kidney infection and felt terrible. Fortunately, she had medication, but her first night and day in Rome she was not having a good time. We stayed at the Eursotars Domus Aurea Hotel.

She improved enough so that the next day we could get out and check out Rome via the hop-on, hop-off Gray Line tour bus to all the sights. There was so much to see, and the Vatican was the top choice. We lucked into a church sponsored guided tour, and we didn't have to wait in the regular line with the hundreds of tourists waiting to go into Vatican City.

The tour included at least four hours of seeing all of the history and art in St. Peter's Basilica, the Sistine Chapel, and the Vatican Museum of Art. The tour guides were excellent.

After the tour, we went back inside St. Peter's Basilica. I caused quite a stir among the crowded church as Madonna and I were separated among the people by about 20 feet. Searching across crowd, I saw her, and spoke her name aloud, "Madonna." Everyone in hearing distance turned toward me as if I had blasphemed; some may have thought I had seen a vision, and some even made the sign of the cross. See, I really am blessed with a heavenly angel.

Beyond seeing the usual sights of Rome, and eating the wonderful cannoli, we weren't that impressed. After seeing Barcelona, with its beautiful architecture, flower filled balconies, and clean streets, we found Rome ugly and dirty. We had watched two robberies from atop the tour bus, and as we were leaving for the airport, we were robbed in a slick bag pick up as the driver was loading our bags into the car. We didn't know we had been robbed until we arrived at the airport.

We believe the driver and the hotel clerk were in on the scheme together. We lost some travel stuff, but more importantly, we lost all of the jewelry Madonna had carried for the cruise, including her new wedding ring, which she kept hidden because of the thievery we had encountered.

Trying to put that horrible experience behind us and after four days in Rome, we caught a plane to Paris. We arrived in early afternoon. Nearly as soon as we checked into the Saint Dominique Hotel, on Saint Dominique Ave. a converted convent, it started a misting rain. I thought, isn't this how Paris is in the movies - a misting rain?

The hotel rooms had thin and not so soundproofed walls. The elevator (lift) only held one person and a suitcase. The first room we checked into just wasn't right for us as we heard a person sneeze from the thin walled adjoining room, and we said, "God bless you." The window view was overlooking the courtyard in the back of the hotel. We requested, and received permission, to move to a room on the street side of the hotel.

As you looked out our fourth floor window, to the right was the Eiffel Tower standing regally above the Parisian street only a couple of blocks away. After getting settled, we immediately headed for the Seine River, also only couple of blocks away. Here I am with the love of my life strolling down the historic Seine River in Paris arm in arm in the misty rain.

The moment touched me. How did I ever get to this point in life? Here we are, 42 years later, in the heart of Paris. My heart was swooning. This had to be one of life's most romantic moments. We saw the buildings and the bridges reflecting in the river. It is a place where lovers kiss, children frolic, everybody smiles, and this is how life should be all the time. I know God smiled, and said, "This is only a little bit of heaven." On this day, we had nearly the whole place all to ourselves. It is as if Paris said, "We have reserved the whole Seine River for you two lovers." We took a riverboat cruise up and down the Seine River with our hearts racing as we tried to take it all in.

Our hotel was on a typical Parisian street, narrow, busy with a tolerable amount of foot traffic. Even from the fourth floor window at night, some lady in loud clicking high heels kept walking up and down the street, and we could hear every step she took. We decided - a busy streetwalker.

We had heard Paris was a dirty city. Not so. They picked up trash twice a day. I remember that, because we slept with the windows open, as no air conditioning was needed. The bar across the street below us must have sold a thousand bottles of beer a night, because every time they dumped the trash into the garbage truck it sounded like a thousand bottles of beer crashing. On either side of our hotel entrance on our side of the street were Parisian pastry shops. Two of them - how handy. These people weren't just bakers, they were artists!

Paris is a great city, and the people were friendly; just the opposite of what we had heard. We never had a bad interface with a single French person. Now we had to try to do as much, and as fast as we could - the Eiffel Tower, the Louvre, fresh flower stands, sidewalk eateries, Notre Dame Cathedral, the Arc de Triumph and much more.

Our day at the Louvre Museum was about as much culture as anybody can take in one day. We saw everything from the Mona Lisa to seemingly miles of paintings and sculptures. We stood in line to see the Mona Lisa, perhaps the most famous canvas painting in history. It was a little disappointing, because of its size in comparison to the huge and detailed paintings we had seen in every country up to that moment. The Mona Lisa is 21" wide x 30" high.

To say the Louvre is big is misleading at best. It is huge, and we only viewed some from the 12th through the 16th centuries of the world's greatest art, skipping the newer works. We got completely lost, and after asking the same caretaking worker for the third time, "How do we get out of here?" she put her bucket and mop down and led us out of the history of the past, and back into today's world. We toured the Notre Dame Cathedral, and it is a grand bit of architecture, but never saw the hunchback.

One of my goals was to buy a baguette and walk down the streets of Paris like a real Frenchman. I did. French food, especially the pastries, was better and more appetizing than we ever knew existed. Those pastries are even better than the pictures you see in magazines. However, to our surprise, we had possibly the best Thai food in Paris.

We visited French artist, Claude Monet's home on the outskirts of Paris, and viewed his famous gardens and the pond where he painted his lily pads, perhaps the most famous and most valuable of all of his paintings.

Our final night in Paris we ate at a local neighborhood French restaurant that seated about thirty people. The owner and chef was a short plump lady with rosy cheeks, and so personable. The meal was complete with appetizers (two), wine, salad, entree', tasty breads, and desserts (two).

This meal was much like the first lunch we had on the first day we saw each other again, after 42 years. The meal when I kept ordering items so the moment would never end. This was the last night of our honeymoon, and we did not want it to end. As we finished this night, a dining experience par excellence, we had the jolly little chef stand between the two us for a picture commemorating that special night. That was my favorite photo of the trip.

My life's dreams came to fruition in so many ways on this trip of a lifetime. We sailed across the Atlantic Ocean at peace with life. We walked hand in hand the streets of Key West, Ponta Delgado, Portugal, Seville, Barcelona, Nice, Florence, San Gimignano, Pisa, Cortona, Rome, and finally, Paris. Each offered a special closeness to God in the divine, ancient cathedrals, and a real appreciation of art from Florence to the Vatican to the Louvre.

The unforgettable memories of dinner at our hotel near Florence overlooking the Italian countryside, and listening to the music of Italy, the romance of that special and dreamy night at Machiavelli's, then eating at the bakeries in Paris, was equally matched by the carriage ride in Seville. We were euphoric as we strolled along the Seine River in Paris, sauntering through Monet's gardens, experiencing the stirring cathedrals of Spain, Italy, and France. The unquestionably treasured evening in Nice, all shared with a lady of impeccable elegance, class, beauty, the warmest of smiles, always the twinkling eyes, and holding her hand every chance I could. The breathtaking moments just kept coming true, and the memories will last forever.

Our most frequent comments were, "Look over there," "Com'on Madonna," "Look where we are now," and "I love you." All of Europe was so exciting. For eight months our life had become a whirlwind of non-stop activities, and the best part of the trip is hard to say, but the cruise, and the time we got to rest and spend alone, relaxing and giving our complete devotion to each other certainly comes close to the top.

Sharing my life with Madonna has shown me just how love is intended to be. I cannot sufficiently put in words the depth of our love for each other. Nor could I ever put all the amazing moments we have shared into written words. Our honeymoon put an indelible impression of the possibility of how deep our love can grow. I can't wait for another day to get here to share more memories.

FAVORITES - RECALLING THE BEST

West – Road Trip

Madonna and I took a three and a half week road trip out west. I was proud to introduce her to my Amarillo friends Jerry and Karen Irwin, Richard Hadley and DL Malicoat and his new wife. The trip included the Petrified Forest, Painted Dessert, Phoenix, and Monument Valley, Durango to Silverton Railroad, Bar D Chuckwagon, Mesa Verde NP, Moab, Ut, and Canyonlands by Night boat ride, Arches and Canyonlands NP, Flaming Gorge NP, Jackson Hole, Wy. Grand Tetons and Yellowstone NP, White water rafting, Cody, Wy, Cheyenne, Wy, Wichita, Ks, Parsons, Ks, Rowlett, Tx, This was the first time Madonna had returned to her home in Parsons, Ks, since her teenage days.

Trips to Phoenix

Very Large Array VLA, New Mexico, Sedona, Az., Barrett Jackson Car show, a rare snow in Scottsdale, Grandchildren.

East – Baseball Road Trip with Todd

Memphis, Graceland, Sun Records, The Rendezvous BBQ, Louisville Slugger Bat plant, Churchill Downs, Cincinnati Reds game, Niagara Falls, Buffalo, Ny, Anchor Bar and the original Buffalo Wings. Cooperstown Baseball Hall of Fame, New York City, Yankee Stadium, Yanks lost, Empire State Bldg., Battery Park, Broadway, Hop on-Hop off tour, Atlantic City Casinos and Boardwalk, Washington DC, Nationals baseball game, Yanks lost, again, Smithsonian Museums, Asheville, Nc, Atlanta, Ga. Coca Cola World, Birmingham, Al, our old eat places.

Oregon

Bend - Snow on Christmas day, our walk in the snow, a Christmas tree put up the old fashioned way, Columbia River Gorge, Multnomah Falls, Alpacas, Timberline Lodge, Camp 18, Canon Beach, Rick and Monica's home, Pok Pok, Pine State Biscuits, Ferry boat to Victoria, BC, eating with Dennis, Mark and Monica at Taverna Greek Restaurant, Victoria, BC., Butchart Gardens.

Alaska

Seattle, Wa, Pike Place Market, 3 a.m. Hotel fire drill, Gay Pride parade, Branzino's Italian Rest. with Italian music, Inside passage, Juneau, Skagway, (White Pass Scenic Railway), Original streetcar, Glacier Bay, Ketchikan, (Duck boat tour/eagles), Victoria, BC, Canada.

Cozumel

Condo, snorkeling, swimming with the dolphins, jeep rides, beachside massages, sunsets with drinks and card games, Sorrissi's restaurant, shopping in Cozumel.

Most Tranquil Places

The camp Raton, Nm, with Western Data people, Plain Dealing Bollinger's camp, Yellowstone –Lamar and Hayden Valley, Tuscany, Chianti Trail, Columbia River Gorge, Cruising across the Atlantic Ocean, Cozumel, Mexico, Butchart Gardens, Victoria BC, Canada, Rocky Mountain NP, Glacier Bay, Alaska; Glacier NP, Montana.

Favorite Baseball Parks

Rickwood Field, Birmingham; Wrigley Field, Chicago; Comiskey Park, Chicago, Cardinal Stadium, St. Louis; Braves Field, Atlanta, Astro Stadium, Houston, Minute Maid Park, Houston; Cincinnati Field, Cincinnati; Yankee Stadium, New York; Washington Stadium, Washington DC; Dodger Stadium, Los Angeles; Candlestick Park, San Francisco; Albuquerque Stadium, Albuquerque; Royals Park, Kansas City; Rangers Park, Dallas: Sports Park, Shreveport, La; Fort Smith Park, Bossier City, La.

My Favorite Sounds

Birds, waterfalls, babbling brooks, wind, rustling leaves, jazz, blues, harmonica, floor tom-toms, orchestra and symphonic, Todd's Texas All-Region symphony performance (Battle of Dresden), Texas Tech marching band's (America the Beautiful), good ole rock and roll, gospel. Best Melody-The Easter Parade.

The Most Sacred Places - Outdoors

Arches NP, Grand Canyon, National Monument Valley, Crater Lake NP, Columbia River Gorge, Oregon, Glacier NP, The valley below Cortona, Italy, Our back yard with the water fountain, flowers, with the birds.

The Most Sacred Places - Indoors

Santa Eulalia Cathedral, (Barcelona) Spain; Church of San Francesca, (with the Cross St. Francis of Assisi), Arezzo, Italy; St. Peters Basilica, Rome, Italy; First United Methodist Church, Bossier City.

Favorite Large Cities

Chicago, New Orleans, Paris, France; Barcelona, Spain; New York City. San Francisco, Portland, Or. Florence, Italy; Miami, Washington DC; Boston, Dallas, Seattle, San Antonio, Houston, Baltimore,

Favorite Small Towns

Jackson, Wy; Moab, Ut; San Gimignano, Italy; Santa Fe, Nm; Durango, Co.; Taos, Nm; Manitou Springs, Co; Sedona, Az; Natchitoches, La; Leadville, Co; Cody, Wy; Estes Park, Co; Cannon Beach, Or; Key West, Fl; Parsons, Ks; Hot Springs, Ar; Jefferson, Tx; Rockport, Ma. , Blowing Rock, Nc.

Favorite Museums

Cooperstown, Ny; Smithsonian, Washington Dc; Museum of Natural History, Chicago, Il; Dealy Plaza, Dallas, Tx; Hearst Castle, San Simeon, Ca; The Louvre, Paris, France; Vatican Art Gallery, Rome, Italy.

Special Occasion Meals

All with Madonna, Saltgrass Steakhouse, Bossier City. Perry's Houston, Tx; Katz, Houston, Tx; Bella Fresca, Shreveport, La; Jack Binion's Steakhouse, Bossier City. La; Ernest's, Shreveport, La; Milo's, Nice, France; Machiavelli's, Machiavelli, Italy; Sorrisi, Cozumel, Mx; and along with Todd, Del Frisco's, Dallas, Tx., Texas State Fair,

Strangest Town

Jerome, Arizona.

I Like Different Places

Jackson, Wy; Bend, Or; Sedona, Az; Durango, Co; Moab, Ut; Vernal, Ut; Santa Fe, Nm; Pecos, Tx; Roswell, Nm; Cozumel, Mx; Barcelona, Sp; Nice, Fr; Florence, It; Impruneta, It; Cortona, It; Rome, It; Paris, Fr., Machiavelli, It., Albuquerque, Nm., Lincoln, Nm., Eureka Springs, Ar., Seville, Sp.,

Favorite Sports Teams

Baseball, Shreveport Sports, Chicago Cubs. Brooklyn Dodgers; Football, Texas Tech, The old Chicago Cardinals, Dallas Cowboys; Basketball, Dallas Mavericks.

Favorite Meals

Black-eyed peas, Turnip greens and cornbread, by Madonna and Mamaw; Chicken and Dumplings with Fried Apricot Pies, by Mamaw; Spaghetti with homemade rolls, by my mother. First Thanksgiving dinner at Aunt Ann's in Stonewall, MS.

Water Places

Pacific Ocean; Atlantic Ocean; Gulf of Mexico- Deep Sea fishing caught a 32 and a 29 lb., Red fish; Columbia River Gorge, Or; Multnomah Falls, Or; Snake River, Wy; Jenny Lake, Wy; Colorado River; Missouri River, Crater Lake, Or.

Favorite Sayings

"The future isn't what it use to be." - "It doesn't matter how wealthy you are, or what your stature in life is, or how many friends you have, the size of your funeral depends on the weather." - "It doesn't matter what decision you make, work hard to make it the right decision."

Best Foods

Hot chocolate: Timberline Lodge, Mt. Hood, Or; **Steak:** Frankie and Johnnie's, New York, Bern's Steak House, Tampa, Fl, Del Frisco's, Dallas, Perry's, Houston, Tx; **Italian:** Lil'Italiano, Bossier City, La; Brocato's, Shreveport, La; **Spaghetti:** my Moms, Bossier City, La.; **Sandwiches:** Muffeletta, Central Grocery, New Orleans, La, Shrimp Po-boy, Sam's, Shreveport, La, BBBLT and Vienna Sausage, my own, Shreveport, La, Hot Link, Cobb's BBQ, Bossier City, La; **Appetizer:** Mary Payne's Marinated Shrimp; Benton, La.; **Salad**: Salad bar, Brocato's, Shreveport, La; **Fried Catfish:** Jan's River Restaurant, Shreveport, La; **Apple Pie and Fried Pies:** Mamaw, Bossier City. La.; **Chocolate Pie:** Nell Carpenter, Bossier City, La: **Chocolate Cake:** Betty Smith, Bossier City, La; **Cornbread:** Dorothy Ward's, Bossier City, La; **Barbeque:** Country Tavern, Shreveport, La, Cobb's Barbeque, Bossier City, La; Stubbs Barbecue, Austin, Tx, The Rendezvous Memphis, Tn; and my own; **Donuts:** Southern Maid, Shreveport, La. Voodoo Donuts, Portland, Or; **Asian:** Pok Pok, Portland, Or.; **Fried Chicken:** Chicken Shack in the 1950's, Shreveport, La.; **Breakfast:** Camp 18, Hwy. 26, Or.

My Favorite Recipe

Grilled Pork Tenderloin. 4 pork tenderloins 1lb each, salt and coarse pepper to your desire, place on hot grill, baste with soy sauce continuously until a reddish color. Turn meat regularly until charred, cook about 40 minutes. Slice at an angle and serve with your favorite side sauce. Sweet and sour, or orange marmalade my choice.

My Most Romantic Moments

Seeing Madonna at her high school reunion in the buffet line, and kissing her so gently, and telling her "Good Morning, Madonna"; Madonna greeting me at her front door for the first time; Holding Madonna's hand. Our dinner at Perry's Restaurant in Houston having Lemon Drop Martinis with the light shining on her face. Her eyes were sparkling, her smile so sweet, and she had never looked more beautiful; Strolling in the misty rain along the Seine River in Paris; Walking in the new snow on Christmas day in Bend, Oregon; Experiencing deer strolling around our cabin, and the silent reverence of snowfall at the Grand Canyon; Dinner at Milo's in Nice, France. Our sunset experience at Cortona, Italy.

50TH HIGH SCHOOL REUNION – IT FELT GOOD!

For some this event was a dreadful, but necessary event. There were those that felt compelled to attend simply to fulfill the need to at least go to their 50th class reunion. Others felt it was an occasion not to be missed. We had 250 graduates in the 1960 Bossier High School Class, and we located 231. That was amazing, and it included thirty-three graduates that we confirmed were deceased.

Jeanette Bryant Edmiston and me have always been the facilitator of these reunions. Nobody had more fun putting these events together than we did. This was going to be more special than all the others. You can't have a 50th high school reunion if you can't find the graduates. We were the ones that always had all the fun of zeroing in and finding the lost graduates, but this time it was all about getting as much involvement from everyone as possible.

All graduates were given a list of the other graduates, and we ask them to, "Talk to someone you haven't talked to in 50 years." We coaxed and really encouraged our graduates to call and talk to former classmates. That caught on, and I believe was responsible for the large turnout. Those calls were responsible for building a lot of the excitement.

Fifty years. Did I say fifty years? Wow! What a special group of friends. There was a large group of friends that had stayed in touch for most of those years that began in the first grade.

Nobody quite knew what to expect. It had been a long time for many of our classmates, but the jitters quickly passed once we made the initial contact with our smiling faces. For some, we had not seen each other since the day we graduated, and it was a genuinely warm and pleasant experience.

With the help of nametags with our high school pictures on them, the hugs, the laughs, and the memories began to gush out of the past. Our grads had passed the test of time, and I thought they looked pretty darned good.

Here was a group of people that you could call real lifelong friends. If you hadn't known a person from such an early age, you really couldn't call them lifelong friends.

After planning, cajoling and twisting some arms - here we were! The hugs were more sincere, and the, "I think of you oftens," had real meaning this weekend. Friday night was memorabilia night, and all events were casual. Egos were left at home. It was just real good to see everyone.

Saturday morning at the High School Cafeteria, we featured our own Southern Maid Donuts followed by the bus tour, themed "Fifty Years! How Bossier Has Kicked Shreveport's Ass," highlighting the changes of Bossier City over the last fifty years.

The fun was watching the faces of those 32 grads that had not been back to Bossier since we graduated. They had never seen the high-rise casinos, the Bossier Parkway, the CenturyTel Arena, the Bossier Parish Community College, the Cyber Innovation Center, and we ended at the spectacular Louisiana Boardwalk. Those that had stayed here for most of those fifty years, and watched our little town grow, seemed to be especially proud to show off Bossier's progress.

Saturday night included the five teachers that were still living, a proclamation from the Bossier City Mayor, making it the "Bossier High School Class of 1960 Day," honorariums for the deceased classmates, a reading by Carolyn Lee of "The Keepers," and a short personal talk by our classmate and former Louisiana Governor, Buddy Roemer.

It is worth mentioning that the centerpiece for each table was a beautiful grouping of three Metamucil bottles with colors, also our school colors, green, white and gold, and were topped with large green bows – PERFECT.

For me, it was special to see the following for the first time since we graduated Tim Crawford, now living in the state of Washington; John Lenard, Loree Johnson, Duane Martin, and Pat Vaughn of Texas; Tommie Cook, of Tennessee; James Harrist, of Monroe; and Freddie Watters, of West Monroe. These were among those I had not seen in many years.

I talked on the telephone for the first time since we graduated with Susan Allen, Bobbie Bennett, Bill Caldwell, Bill Carter, Larry Cordell, Linda Fisher, Kay Goss, Betty Graham, Inge Padgug, Robbie Pardue, Gary Ricketts, Carol Parks, Fern Owens, and Edith Seyburn...

Much like the High School Reunion that rekindled my life, our 50th reunion produced an almost identical love story. My very good friends since the first grade, Betty Jean Carter and Donnie Lewis, had nearly an exact experience. They also went through the same feelings and shared a new beginning. They were married only one week shy of our fifth wedding anniversary. Don't miss your high school reunions; they can change your life!

For some, a 50th class reunion is a milestone, a time to remember good and bad, laughs and tears, a time to relive our youthful days. For me it was a time to learn how my rehearsal of life - that being my schoolhouse education - worked for me. I found you choose to remember what you want to remember. I chose to remember the friends more than the events, to remember the choices from so many of my life's buffet of acquaintances. I don't know or remember all of those things that we had lived on a day-to-day buffet platter, but I do know I had absolutely no remorse about the people or the friendships earned during those years.

While this event was certainly a reminder of some of my life's buffet of choices, it was these very friends, my lifelong friends, which had skipped down my life's path with me.

I had already learned what my greatest buffet surprise was. Besides that, I had the most beautiful girl from school with me.

Sadly, as we ended the weekend, it was as if, some of my life was ending. I knew full well that I would never see some of these special people ever again. However, I am left with a catalog of hugs, kisses, handshakes, smiles, laughs, warm wishes and especially a satisfaction that God had put these people in my life for a reason, and for that, I am eternally appreciative.

CANCER - *"Jerry, There is Nothing I Can Do for You."*

BE STILL!

So many of my friends have personally experienced the dreaded cancer disease. Many have had relatives that have fought too often with no success. This horror is like facing the dark abysmal unknown. Out of nowhere, I was suddenly faced with a doctor telling me I had lung cancer.

At 69 years of age, I had been playing tennis 2-3 hours, 2-3 times a week, and never noticed any concerns with my breathing. The only thing hurting was my right shoulder. I knew it was my rotator cuff; I had put off surgery until I just couldn't play tennis without pain.

I visited the orthopedic surgeon in preparation to finally get my right shoulder fixed. Upon arriving at home following the doctor's visit scheduling my right shoulder surgery, and as I was getting out of the car, I lifted a box on the rear seat and tore my left shoulder rotator cuff so badly that the doctor hurriedly scheduled an unplanned surgery on that shoulder. In preparation for the surgery, a routine chest x-ray was taken.

I went through the surgery in January 2012, and had begun rehabilitation exercises. In early March, I was informed that my chest x-ray showed a few spots on my lungs. I had never smoked except to try maybe one or two. I never had the urge to smoke, but I had been around many people that had smoked. The doctors began a whirlwind of scans, MRI's, biopsies, and many other probes and pokes. It was if there was not a minute to spare. The last thing on my mind was lung cancer.

On the morning of our pulmonary doctor's appointment we were all too unsuspectingly told that it was in fact cancer of the lungs, and that it was squamous cell carcinoma. How could that be? I felt great!

Here I was enjoying the happiest days of my life with the love of my life, and suddenly everything changes. We went from the doctor's office straight to the preacher's office, because we both knew that is where our faith needed to be directed. The thought that God, through his miraculous and meticulous planning, had shown Madonna and me what wonderful love we could share. Was this going to be taken from us?

Life is about choices, and here I was with a buffet full of decisions. With Madonna's inspiration, faith and guidance, I gained the strength to face my greatest fears. I could be angry and question what God had done to us. I could feel sorry for myself. Through our prayers and faith, I believed that we were to use this time in our lives to recommit and strengthen our love. More importantly, to show God that we would put our trust and love in Him. I have said many times, "God is eager to share his love with us. God longs for us to love Him, and God puts people in our lives to teach us about love." Was this our time to be the teacher?

There were too many unanswered questions. Originally, the cancer was diagnosed as squamous cell, but as we began, more testing the doctors seemed to have some disagreement on the diagnosis and the course of action. Finally, we had two doctors' appointments on the same day, one with the radiologist and head of the Shreveport Willis-Knighton Cancer Center, Dr. Lane Rosen. The second appointment two hours later was with oncologist, Dr. Anil Veluvolu.

Dr. Rosen's nurse came in the room first and started asking routine questions, and made a statement about me being treated for basal cell. We quickly told her we had been told it was squamous cell. We were puzzled but didn't know enough to push the conversation.

Dr. Rosen came in and talked about his prior radiation treatment on my arm. He had remembered treating me on my left arm six years prior, and explained to Madonna that he had given speeches on the tumor I had because of its enormous size. In fact, he said it was the largest he had ever seen. Then he got right to the point and explained that this was basal cell carcinoma that had metastasized to my lungs. He said, "This is a very rare form of cancer only found in 1 in 50,000 cases, and I have never heard of basal cells (a skin cancer normally) ever getting into the lungs." Furthermore he said, "My partner, who has been doing cancer treatment for 14 years longer than I have hasn't heard of it either, and he was trained at the M. D. Anderson Hospital."

He said, "It can't be treated with surgery, chemotherapy or radiation." Then came the worst words we could have heard, "Jerry, there is nothing I can do for you." He said, "I would give you 6 months to three and a half years to live." I can tell you we were stunned, but you will never know just how stunned.

Reflecting on that moment, I am reminded of the biblical passage when Jesus said, "Be still." Believe me, in that moment everything was still. In the somberness and silence of the next moment, it was as if God spoke through Dr. Rosen. It seemed as if Dr. Rosen was only relaying angelic words that changed our lives saying, "I have to tell you what happened on the way home a two nights ago. Keep in mind I read maybe 20 articles on cancer every day." Continuing, he said, "I looked over on the seat of the car where my closed briefcase lay, and a paper was lying on top of my case. I should have never picked it up because I was driving, but I did. It was about a half page notice from the Federal Drug Administration announcing the approval of a new drug. This new drug was a pill to be taken daily, specifically for patients with basal cell carcinoma that has metastasized in the lungs." This drug had been approved only two of weeks before I was told by Dr. Rosen that he could not do anything for me.

Do you believe in God? How did that paper appear outside that closed briefcase in that particular moment addressing my particular situation?

Now we were really stunned and dazed, but realizing quickly, we weren't in this alone. God was showing us how eager he was to share his love with us, and that we should believe in him. God was in complete control. We went to meet Dr. Veluvolu, and the first thing he said was, "I knew something was wrong with the early diagnosis." He said he was aware of the new drug "Everidge", and he would immediately start the process to get the drug for me.

He showed us the PET scan of my lungs, and he didn't have to point out the black spots all over both lungs. There were at least 25-30 lesions. I told him I had never felt bad or weak, and that the only reason I wasn't still playing tennis was because of my shoulder surgery. He told us to live life, and I could do whatever I wanted.

We had avoided mentioning my health condition publicly until we knew the diagnosis. Madonna sent the following message to friends and prayer warriors explaining my condition, and asking for prayers:

"It's going to be hard making a long story short, but leave it to Jerry Payne to have something so rare that he will undoubtedly be written up in the medical journals. We found out today that the type of cancer in his lungs were misdiagnosed as squamous cell when in fact it is basal cell carcinoma that has spread from his skin to his lungs. This is so rare that none of the local doctors had heard of this before (Even a doctor that trained at MD Anderson).

The biopsy was sent to the Mayo Clinic to have it confirmed, and only 1 in 50,000 has ever had basal cell to metastasize to another part of the body. (Jerry had a large basal cell cyst removed from his upper left arm in 2006). It is slow growing, but apparently, he has had it for some time in his lungs. He is not a candidate for surgery, radiation, and the conventional chemo will not work.

This was not good news, but would you believe that the FDA had just approved a new drug "vismodegib" (Erivedge) especially for patients that had prior episodes of basal cell carcinoma that had metastasized in internal organs such as the lungs.

They gave us an article regarding this drug. It's a pill that is taken once a day, and is approved for the treatment of patients whose basal cell carcinoma has spread from where it started into internal organs, and for patients who can't be treated with surgery, chemo, or radiation. The oncologist has to order the drug, and hopefully when we see him again on 4/23 he will have it, and Jerry can begin taking it. They will then do further tests in 3-6 months to see how Jerry is doing. Now that we know, we can get very specific in our prayers by asking that this new drug will be the miracle that we need. Thank you all so much for your uplifting calls, emails, cards, and especially your prayers. You mean the world to both of us. - Madonna"

I took my first pill on May 8, 2012. The side effects I experienced were violent muscle cramping and some loss of hair and taste. The response from people all over America, resulting from my friends and family members asking for prayers, was overwhelming. The cards, calls and visits made us realize how amazing God's love abounds among His believers.

I visited Dr. Veluvolu every two weeks with blood tests on each visit. My tests results were normal. I was feeling great and my spirits were high. The encouragement and mostly the prayers on my behalf from nearly everyone was helping me continue with a regular routine. I never felt more loved than through this time of my life.

At last, the first three months of taking the pill was finished, and the doctor ordered a CT/PET scan. I will let the message from both of us telling of results of the test speak for itself:

"Jerry had a Pet scan last Friday to determine if the 'miracle drug' is working. This morning we went to the doctor to find out the results. We were shocked, stunned, and amazed at the two x-rays we were looking at. The cancer is almost all gone from his lungs! Where there were large, black spots all over his lungs before, there are now just a few pale gray spots remaining.

He is to keep taking the drug, and they will do another scan in three months. The doctor said that whatever he was doing to keep doing it, and for us to go out and celebrate. Jerry told him about all the prayers that were going out for him, and the doc said, 'Well, they are working, and tell everyone to keep them up.' So, folks, thank you from the bottom of our hearts for your prayers and concerns, and keep them coming.

I've told you before that I am a strong believer in prayer, miracles, healing, etc., but today I got a very clear reminder of my lack of faith. I had prayed BIG this morning, asking for a clean x-ray, but expecting and believing that it would only be slightly better.

Once again, I had underestimated God's power and His amazing love and grace for us. He now has my attention, and I am proud to give Him all the praise and glory!   Love and appreciation, Madonna"

And I added: "Let me just add that I actually went into the doctor's office feeling God's presence. Yes, I was apprehensive, but there was calmness about me, knowing that God was very attentive to our needs, and I felt a complete trust. I wasn't surprised at the news, nor would I have been surprised if the news hadn't been this good. This was in God's control.

With all the prayers from so many being lifted up on my behalf, it has been easier to meet the challenges placed before us. I am moved by your prayers and concern. I ask that you please continue praying. This is much better, but not a victory yet. I am feeling great and smiling BIG. Thank you all,   Jerry"

This doctor's visit was another "Be Still" moment.

God will answer prayers sometimes even on our time schedule. To say that we were excited doesn't really put into words how we felt. We were grateful that is what we were. The comparison of the before and after scan pictures of my lungs were so different, and was as stark as day and night. The more recent picture showed almost all of the lungs clear with only two or three small light gray spots versus totally black spots all over both lungs previously.

We both realize that every moment is a gift from God, and even understanding that the very scenes of this earth are created for reasons more important than something to simply admire. We are also so appreciative and grateful for the people God puts in our lives, and we now strive to share our love with each other and God.

Decisions, decisions, decisions, all from this enormous buffet of life. This challenge in my life made life much simpler, when before I usually made life difficult. Trust in God. No, I mean really trust in God.

Ruth Ann and C.L. Madden, two of my friends from the very earliest days of my life, upon learning about my illness, sent us a book, "Jesus is Calling", written by Sarah Young. This book is a daily devotional, teaching and reminding us on a daily basis how to enjoy peace in God's presence. I will be eternally grateful for this gift.

On August 13, 2012, the day of our doctors visit to see the PET scan results to find out if I was going to live or die, this was the amazing devotional for that day:

"LEARN TO ENJOY LIFE MORE, Relax, remembering that I am God with you. I crafted you with enormous capacity to know Me, and enjoy My Presence. When My people wear sour faces and walk through their lives with resigned rigidity, I am displeased. When you walk through a day with childlike delight, savoring every blessing, you proclaim your trust in Me, your ever-present Shepherd. The more you focus on My Presence with you, the more fully you can enjoy life. Glorify Me through your pleasure in Me. Thus you proclaim My Presence to the watching world."

I could have been resigned to the worst, but I had that childlike delight about me, and without doubt, I was savoring every blessing, and my blessings have been many. Proclaiming my trust in Him was something I delighted in telling the world about.

The very next day after being told to, "learn to enjoy life more", from the day before, the August 14 devotional explained that even modern science can't match His relationship with me:

"I AM YOURS FOR ALL ETERNITY. I am the Alpha and the Omega: the One who is, was, and is to come. The world you inhabit is a place of constant changes - more than your mind can absorb without going into shock. Even the body you inhabit is changing relentlessly, in spite of modern science's attempts to prolong youth and life indefinitely. I, however, am the same yesterday and today and forever.

Because I never change, your relationship with Me provides a rock-solid foundation for your life. I will never leave your side. When you move on from this life to the next, My Presence beside you will shine brighter with each step. You have nothing to fear, because I am with you for all time and throughout eternity."

You can see how God was speaking directly to us about the specific events we were encountering through those two devotionals. Jesus is calling, "Be still, and listen."

AMAZING CREATIONS AND PRECIOUS PEOPLE - GOD IS SMILING WITH US

All my years have brought into my life an experience and appreciation of truly inspirational creations. I have been blessed and guided through life by my family, many friends, sights, sounds, scenes, beauty, spiritual moments, all sorts of people, and even a new family.

I have longed to see or experience something new each day, and I always will. The amazement of the places, sights and people in my life are not just passing memories. Those things that are burned into my past are so powerful, and the awe is so undeniable.

"Millions of years our wondering eyes, Shall o'er our Savior's beauties rove; and myriad ages we'll adore, the wonders of His love." (Author, unknown)

We all have shared the amazing creations made possible only by God. He leads us to the very places that touch our heart and soul. He leads us to the precious people that are more valuable than gold. No one should have to live alone as we grow old, and not have someone there to share the grandeur of life. Being able to catch our breaths and exclaim, "Look over there!" God is smiling with us.

God's beautiful creations are all around us, even though we share His inspirations every day in our usual habitat. I believe we appreciate it more when we are out of our everyday surroundings gazing at the mountains, plains, rivers, waterfalls, wild animals, the beautiful vistas, and the gentle people.

We can only marvel at places like Monument Valley with the Navajo Indian chants; the quaint towns with a rugged history - Silverton and Durango, CO.; the harsh conditions of Mesa Verde; the pure contrast of the Flaming Gorge; the breathtaking splendor of Crater Lake, Oregon; the stunning sunset majesty at the Cortona Valley, Italy; the simple beauty of the flower-lined streets of Vernal, Utah; the sheer cleanliness of the sweet taste of the next breath you take in Glacier National Park, or Jackson, Wyoming; and the places that only God could have imagined and shaped - Arches National Park, Yellowstone NP, Columbia River Gorge, the Grand Teton NP, the huge vastness and panoramic views of Montana, and the Louisiana lakes filled with moss strewn cypress trees.

Ambling through thousands of years of history in America, Italy, France, Portugal, Mexico, and Spain, I realize that what we experience today is but a simple sharing of the trials and tribulations of centuries of souls that have embraced God's creations in their everyday life.

One of the great treasures of my life was having the gift of a new family. Never to replace the family that I had lived my life with, but to additionally experience a remarkable love and companionship with young children that provided me with new warmth only a child can offer.

Madonna's three children, Dennis, Monica, and Mark, are as dear to me as Todd is. Each has given me a special love bounty to share. Each one of them has accepted me with a genuine respect that has touched me with a lasting softness.

My new family came complete with sons, a daughter and daughters and son-in-laws, aunts, uncles, cousins, and especially grandchildren, even great grandchildren. What a glorious addition to my life.

Our grandchildren, Ethan, Selah, Dylan, Katrina, and Jace, each share a special relationship with me that is like a renewable energy. Each is different, and offers another new perspective to life. They are not different when it comes to being so easy to love.

Amber and Chris, the older grandchildren, are finding their way through life, and it is my prayer they find the happiness they seek.

Amber and her husband, Frank Smith has provided us the new experience of great grandchildren.

Lexi and Laci are two beautiful little girls full of energy and love.

This new life has been full of laughter, good food, kissing grandchildren good night, and hugging and holding each other. One of my great blessings has always been being part of a family that sincerely says, "I love you."

My family has grown, as my nephew Dr. Daniel Payne and his wife Ann, have raised three of the most talented and beautiful children. Chelsea and Sofia are two of the greatest ballet dancers ever to come out of Shreveport, and Alex is an independent thinker like his dad, and turning out to be an extraordinary moviemaker. Danny has a very successful family practice and many of my Bossier City friends speak very highly of his abilities, and the warm friendly patient care he provides. No one has ever said anything bad about him, and they better not.

My nephew, Scot and his wife, Donna Payne reside in California. He is a very successful mechanical engineer for a company that does industrial heating, ventilation, and air conditioning work at large industrialized sites i.e., hospitals, manufacturing plants, and large office buildings. His projects are multi-million dollar jobs.

My favorite part of life has been being with the people and family I love. Nothing has been better than having family and friends to share belly laughs with, or to comfort each other when needed. Even less dramatic is a simple smile, or just holding hands that makes this life so special.

If only I have shared some special moments with all of my friends in places or times that seem so far away in distance and years. Yet, I am thankful for the days and hours, and even minutes, we had together. Know that those short moments, smiles, and embraces have never been that far away from my everyday life.

Life is a glorious buffet, and over the years, God has offered me a lavish spread of choices. No, we do not set or prepare the Buffet of Life; that is God's hands at work. However, the role the people of my life have played has given me a grateful opportunity to love to live life. From the Spread of Life come the choices we make which determines our friends, our attitudes, our legacy on earth, and our eternal salvation.

From the choices that life gives us, we find that doors are sometimes obstacles, but sometimes they open to the newness of life. Most of the obstacles along my life's path were not really that big. Recognize the doors God holds open. Those doors that do not have doorknobs on our side of the door; the doors that can only be opened by God.

God always provides us with what we need, usually when we least expect it, and not necessarily what we want. Accept God's gifts and grace from Life's Buffet. Perhaps, through God's grace we will someday all be inside heaven's gate and experience God's eternal buffet.

WHO KNEW?
THE PAYNE ANCESTORY AND GENEALOGY FROM 1350 A.D.

To tell the complete story of my life it is necessary that my family's history be told. Where had I come from? What connections did I have with my long ago past?

I had related my search for my paternal grandmother to a Bossier City friend, Frank Pierce. He heard me tell of driving through Ringgold, Louisiana, in search of my grandmother, and the connection that was made. He was struck by the touching story.

He had several years of experience in genealogy and began to work on the history of our family. All unbeknownst to me, with the help of Madonna, Ron and Mary Payne, he completed the following study of the ancestry and genealogy of the Payne family.

In grateful appreciation for the outstanding and very diligent hours and weeks of work by Frank Pierce, I am proud to include his research, and the story of the ancestors of Guy Ronald and Jerry Parnell Payne as part of our story and this autobiography.

The Summation of the Genealogy of Ron and Jerry Payne

All your ancestors came to this country very early on, mainly in the 1600 and 1700's. The Payne's came from the English Isles, as were most of the related families. They were primarily farmers. Analyzing the migration pattern, most started out in Maryland and Virginia, migrated south through the Carolinas to Tennessee, Georgia, Alabama, Mississippi and finally Louisiana. In Louisiana, they settled in and around Claiborne and Bienville Parish. The one big exception to being farmers was Dr. Everett Payne, who became a doctor and traveled throughout the area, from Homer, to Gibsland, to Montgomery in Grant Parish.

Your grandmother, Willia's side of the family, was most interesting. She was French and German. Her French ancestors came to this country in the early 1700's to Mobile, Alabama. They came to the Saint Landry Parish just before the Revolutionary War. The Fontenot's and related families intermarried so that they were each other's cousins. Willia's father was of German decent.

The Parnell's and their related families are of English and Scottish decent. They lived for many years in the three corners area of Alabama, Mississippi and Tennessee. That would be Lauderdale County, Alabama, Tishomingo County, Mississippi, and Hardin and Wayne Counties in Tennessee.

The Payne, Robinson, Shuff, Fontenot and Related Families

Your Payne ancestors date back to at least 1350 in Leicestershire County, England. Thomas Payne was born in Bedfordshire County in 1612. Thomas was your immigrant Payne, having come to America before about 1630. His son, Isaac Payne, was born in St. Mary's County, Maryland, in 1651. The Payne family stayed in Maryland until they migrated to Virginia and John Payne was born in Maryland County, Virginia in 1755.

From there the family moved from Virginia to Georgia in the early 1800s. John's grandson, Alston Haynes Payne, was born in 1823 in Georgia. Sometime before 1843, Alston moved to Alabama where he met Martha Webb, born in 1826 in Alabama. They married about 1842, most likely in Alabama, in that their first child, Amanda, was born there in 1843, as was her sister, Susan, who was born in 1847. Martha is the daughter of Benjamin Berry Webb and Margary Harper. An interesting thing is that Margary's mother is a Payne from Virginia, whose Payne ancestors are from Maryland, although from different counties. No relationship was revealed between the two Payne families.

Alston and Martha had at least four children, one of which was your great-grandfather, Everett Henry Payne. E. H., as he was known, was born in Mississippi in 1854, as was his older brother, Rufus, who was born in 1852. The family appears in the 1850 census living in

Panola County, Mississippi, so it would appear that the family migrated from Alabama to Mississippi around 1848-1849.

Sometime around 1860, Alston is in Claiborne Parish, Louisiana, and on June 1, 1863, is mustered in to the Confederate Army as a Private in Co. A, Claiborne Regt. La. By 1870, Alston Payne and family have moved to Homer, Louisiana. Alston is a widower, as Martha has passed away sometime before 1870, as she does not appear in that census. There is no record of the family in the 1860 census, which could mean they were on the move and were missed by the census taker. Living within the 1870 census are his sons, Rufus and Everett.

By 1880, the family is still in Claiborne Parish, and Everett is married to Sallie Robinson, born 1862 in Tennessee. She is the daughter of William Robinson and Elizabeth Mumm. The Robinson's came from North Carolina via Alabama. The Mumm family came from North Carolina via Tennessee. At this time both Alston and Everett are farmers. In 1881, Alston took another wife, Mattie Knight. Little is known about her, and Alston died before 1900. There is no 1890 census to track the Payne's; it was destroyed in a 1924 U.S. Archives fire.

Everett and Sallie are in the 1900 census with their two children, your grandfather, Joseph A. Payne, born in November 18, 1879, and Mattie, born May 1886.

Everett, Sallie, and Joe appear in the 1910 census living in the town of Montgomery, Grant Parish. Everett is a doctor and Joe is a house painter. By the 1920 census, Everett and Sallie have moved to Gibsland, Bienville Parish.

Very soon after the 1910 census, Joe moves to Jennings, Louisiana. Everett died Feb 3, 1930, and Sallie died May 29, 1927, in Bienville Parish.

Because Everett died early in 1930, he does not appear in the 1930 census; however, Joe is back with his wife, Willa and their children, Guy Cullen, Clayton, Florence, Robert, Laverne and Sallie. At this point in the research, Willa's maiden name was not known. Your father, Guy Cullen Payne, was born in 1913 in Jennings, Louisiana. He met your mother, Ora Laverne Parnell, born October 8 1917, in Bienville Parish, Louisiana. They had two children, Guy Ronald Payne, born October 31, 1936, and Jerry Parnell Payne, born April 21, 1942.

The History of Jerry and Ron's Grandmother

Willa is a most interesting tale. After an exhaustive search and many false leads in the Bienville and Claiborne Parish areas, nothing could be found on a Willa, born in 1893. Finally, the marriage record of Joseph A. Payne and Willa Shuff popped up. Joe and Willa were married on September 11, 1911, in Calcasieu Parish. It is not known what Joe was doing in Calcasieu Parish, but he probably was working as a house painter, since that appears to have been his profession.

Once it was known that he was in Calcasieu Parish in 1911, a search of the 1900 census found Willia, born March 1895 in St. Landry Parish, living with what appeared to be her mother, Evelia Fontenot, born 1871 in St. Landry Parish, Louisiana, and stepfather, Frank Leger. According to a descendant of Frank Leger, Donna Varman, Evelia was first married to a L. Walter Collier on March 8, 1890. Walter and Evelia had one child, Claude, born in 1891. Virtually nothing, more is known about Walter, as he seems to disappear from the scene.

Several years later, Evelia meets a man named Shuff. No record of a marriage can be found, but Evelia has twins by this man, which she names Willa and Willie, born March 11, 1895. Willie dies at about age two months. A year or so later, Evelia meets Frank Leger and appears to live with him, as again, no marriage record can be found. Frank and Evelia have four children over a period of eight years. By 1906, the liaison between the two of it is over and Frank marries a Marie Magnon, and has another child by her.

Evelia disappears until 1920, where she is living in Jennings, Louisiana, with her Leger children; Joe Payne, Willa and their children; Guy, Clayton, and Florence. Donna Varman, who is descended from Eldrige Leger, has done an extensive research on the Fontenot family including Evelia. This excerpt of Donna's narrative in the Payne Birth, Death and Marriage source reference pages explains her research on Evelia.

As to Willa's biological father, he is most likely William Alfred Shuff. William is descended from the first Shuff (Schoff), Eli Theodore Schoff, who came to St. Landry Parish before 1820. William is the only unmarried man of the right age; he was born in 1864, to have been available to have an affair with Evelia. All the other male descendants of Eli are either too old or married with children. Evelia continues to be unlucky in love. William marries Cora Soileau on September 18, 1895, and went on to have five children with her. That left Evelia with six living children and no husband or man in the house.

As Donna Varman stated in her coverage of Evelia; "EVELIA WAS A WOMAN OF THE 1990s BACK IN THE 1890s!

Evelia was the daughter of Francois Jules Jacques Fontenot, born in 1841, and Eledanie Saucier, born in 1848, both in St. Landry Parish, Louisiana. The Fontenot family dates back to the 1770s in St. Landry Parish. Prior to that, they resided in Mobile, Alabama. Jean Louis 'dit Colin' Fontenot, born in France in 1686, was your immigrant, coming to Alabama in 1720. According to

Donna Varman, "Our first Fontenot ancestor to appear in America is Jean Louis Fontenot." Jean Louis was a Sergeant in the French Colonial Marines. His job was to protect the French interest in the area. He left his home in Poitiers, France, in 1720, on the ship Drommadaire for duty in the French-controlled territory of Alabama. He first came to Mobile, Alabama, the French

Military headquarters and the seat of government for the Louisiana Territory. He was assigned to Fort Conde near Mobile. About 1730, he was assigned to Fort Toulouse, about 300 miles away, and remained there until his death in 1755. He raised his twelve children at Fort Conde. His wife and children remained at the fort until 1763, when it was surrendered to the English.

From there the family resettled on land grants in Spanish-controlled Louisiana. One son, Francoise, died much earlier in Mobile. The remaining sons and their families, including the widow, Marie Louise, settled around Opelousas, Chataignier, Ville Platte, and Church Point. It is from Jean Louis Fontenot that all of the Fontenot families descended. Jean Louis is the only Sergeant listed among forty soldiers. When his children became of age, the boys joined the marines and married daughters of other marines. The daughters married sons of other marines at the fort. Some of the family names the children married into are Doucet, Brignac, LaGrange, Lobell and Berthelot.

Jean Louis is buried in an unmarked grave at Fort Toulouse. In 1998, a monument was dedicated to honor the memory of Jean Louis at Fort Toulouse. The Fontenot name was spelled Fonteneau and was probably changed to its current spelling by the Spanish when the family settled in Louisiana. Source: Official Fontenot Family Home page on the World Wide Web.

The Parnells, Simmons, Webbs, Robertsons, and Related Families

The Parnell family can be traced back as far as Bartlett Minus Parnell, born in 1810, in Tennessee. In 1830, he married Nancy Tacker, born in 1810, in Tennessee. The family moved to Lauderdale County, Alabama, sometime before 1850, in that Bartlett and Nancy appear in the 1850 census.

Bartlett, an educated man, as he could read and write. Not many people in the rural parts of the USA could do that. According to the various census records, he was an assistant teacher, a mechanic, and a farmer. Nancy died in May of 1865 in Tennessee, and six months later, Bartlett married Elizabeth Martin, twenty-four years his junior. Bartlett died in 1896, and is buried in the Garrett Cemetery outside Pickwick, Hardin County, Tennessee.

Bartlett and Nancy had ten children, one of which was your great grandfather, Jacob T. Parnell, born in 1831 in Wayne County, Tennessee. Jacob married Sarah Ann Black in 1853, in Alabama. Sarah was the daughter of Cyrus Black and Sabra, a full-blooded Cherokee Indian. Jacob and Sarah had at least three children, one of which was your great grandfather, William W. Parnell.

Jacob lived for a relative short time, as he died in 1859. Following Jacob's death, Sarah returned to her parent's farm with her three children. In 1863, she married George Shaw, a widower and brought her children into his household. Sarah had at least four children with George. She died in 1903 in Lauderdale County. William, born in 1854, married Louisa Webb, born in 1852, in 1872. William was a farmer, as were most of the people in and around the Waterloo area of Lauderdale County. Louisa was the daughter of William Jackson Webb and Lucinda Catherine Beckham.

William Parnell and Louisa Webb had eight children, one of which was your grandfather Benjamin B. Parnell. He was born in 1880 in Waterloo. He married your grandmother, Verdellah E. Simmons, in 1901. She was born in 1879 in Hardin County; Tenn. Verdellah was the daughter of William M. Simmons and Sabra Jane Robertson.

By 1910, Benjamin and Verdellah are living in Jonesboro, Craighead County, Arkansas, farming the land. Benjamin and Verdellah stayed in Jonesboro until after 1920, and then they moved south to Columbia County, Arkansas. Benjamin died in 1924 in Columbia County. Benjamin and Verdellah had four children, one of which was your mother, Ora Laverne Parnell, born October 8, 1917, in Brookland, Craighead County, Arkansas.

By 1930, Verdellah, Ora, and two of her brothers, Elmer and Henry, are living with Verdellah's daughter, Elzora Hatcher and her husband, Leon, in Minden, Louisiana. Five years later, Ora meets Guy Cullen Payne, and they are married in early 1936.

Guy was in the Army Air Force during WWII and was killed on July 13, 1942, when his plane was shot down over the Gulf of Mexico. In 1946 or 1947, Ora marries Paul Thie from Ft. Dodge, Iowa, and she and Paul raise Ron and Jerry. Ora died November 1, 2001, and Paul died June 11, 1995, both in Bossier City, La.

The Background on Joe and Willa Payne

In 1920, Joe and Willa were living on Gallup Street in Jennings according to the 1920 census. Living in the house with Joe and Willa was Evelia, his mother-in-law, three of her children from Frank Leger, Guy and his siblings, Clayton and Florence. Your father, Guy, was the second child of Joe and Willa. Their first child, Everett Austin, died eight days after he was born on October 12, 1912. Joe's occupation is listed as a decorator and is the only employed member of the household.

On September 12, 1918, Joe registered for the draft during WWI. There is no evidence that he was ever drafted. Joe and family probably stayed in Jennings until 1927, when Joe's mother, Sallie, died on May 29, 1927, leaving E. H. alone. Anyway, by 1930, they are living in Gibsland, on 3rd Street. By that time, Joe and Willa have had three more children, Robert, Laverne, and Sallie. The 1930 census was taken on April 7; E. H. died February 3, 1930. Very possibly, they were living in his parent's house.

Joe is still a professional house painter during this time. Sometime during the 1950's, Joe and Willa moved to Ringgold. A long period of time passes before there is any contact with Joe or Willa. Contact was made a few times with Willa until her death. Eventually, a relationship was reignited on a limited basis as Ron and Jerry visited with most of the remaining Payne family at a family reunion in late 1980s.

Ron Payne tells the poignant story about his baseball team, Bossier High School playing against Ringgold High School; an older man approached him on a bicycle behind the visiting team dugout. The man told him he was Ron's grandfather. Having never met the man before, Ron was completely surprised. The conversation was very brief, and then the man said, "Play good," got on his bicycle and rode off. Ron never saw him again.

Jerry Payne recounts his touching reunion with his grandmother Willa in a previous chapter of this book. Joe, the grandfather, died in 1967. Willa stayed in Ringgold, and died there in 1986. She was 93 years old.